Feeding the Healthy Vegetarian Family

Ken Haedrich

Bantam Books

New York   Toronto   London   Sydney   Auckland

FEEDING THE HEALTHY VEGETARIAN FAMILY
A Bantam Book / April 1998

Library of Congress Cataloging-in-Publication Data
Haedrich, Ken, 1954–   .
Feeding the healthy vegetarian family / by Ken Haedrich.
           p.   cm.
     1. Vegetarian cookery.   I. Title.
        TX837.H22   1998
   641.5′636—DC21   97-35149
                                                  CIP

ISBN: 0-553-37936-4

Published simultaneously in the United States and Canada

Bantam Books are published by Bantam Books, a division of Bantam
Doubleday Dell Publishing Group, Inc. Its trademark, consisting
of the words "Bantam Books" and the portrayal of a rooster,
is Registered in U.S. Patent and Trademark Office and in other countries.
Marca Registrada. Bantam Books, 1540 Broadway,
New York, New York 10036.

PRINTED IN THE UNITED STATES OF AMERICA
FFG   10 9 8 7 6 5 4 3 2 1

This book is dedicated to my family:

Sam, mega-maker of mashed potatoes, and ace salad dressing dude;

Alison, baker of marvelous muffins, fearless in the kitchen;

Tess, connoisseur of cookies, the queen of organization;

Ben, doer of dishes, and all around fine cook;

Karen, for all of the above, and the many good meals we've shared.

Acknowledgments

This is my fifth cookbook for Bantam, so if my thank yous sound like a broken record, forgive me.

At Bantam, Katie Hall has done a great job seeing this book through its paces; her assistant, Ryan Stellabotte, has been more than patient and never yelled at me once when I lost his faxes or detailed notes.

Thanks also to Nita Taublib, and to the rest of the Bantam team I've had the pleasure of working with.

And to Fran McCullough for getting this project off the ground with me.

My agent, Mega-Meg Ruley, is still the best there is in Agentdom.

And of course, this book wouldn't have been without Sam, Alison, Tess, Ben, and Karen, with whom I've shared the best meals of my life.

Contents

Introduction

If you've come this far, then chances are you're wondering if it is actually possible today to raise a happy, healthy, well-fed family on a vegetarian diet. Well, you've come to the right place because that's precisely what my partner Karen and I have been doing now for the last sixteen years. We have four children—Ben, Tess, Alison, and Sam, ranging in age from sixteen to eight—and none of them has ever had a taste of meat, save for the time Ben got into the cat food and one incident in 1984 when Uncle Harvey tried to slip then-two-year-old Tess a taste of pork and beans with the explanation that a little meat wouldn't kill her. Indeed it didn't, though it probably won't surprise you that we haven't swapped very many recipes with Uncle Harvey in the years since.

So, yes, a family, your family, can get along quite nicely on a vegetarian diet, even if you've followed a traditional meat-based diet for years. Understandably, you might have concerns that *your* child and *your* spouse won't be led gently into this new way of eating. Change is more difficult for some than for others. But where diet is concerned, the bottom line for most children and adults is: Does it taste good?

Seventeen years ago I pulled up my New Jersey roots and moved to New Hampshire. I was looking for a change, and the opportunity came when I was offered a job as the chief cook and bottle washer at a group home for children here in the White Mountains. The hours were long, the staff dedicated and caring, and the scenery out of this world. My salary was $75 a week plus room and board.

My new home took what you'd call a holistic approach to the children in its care, most of whom came from troubled situations. Part of this approach was feeding both kids and staff a wholesome vegetarian diet: We ate no meat, fish, or fowl, though we did use dairy products.

Under the circumstances, you might think that these kids—all of whom had eaten meat their entire lives—would fight a meatless diet to the grave. But it didn't happen. Sometimes, of course, a rebellious adolescent would come on board and let everyone know that he wasn't going to eat any of this crap, that not eating meat was about the stupidest thing he ever heard. Which way, he would demand, is the McDonald's?! (Twenty miles straight through the woods and have a nice walk.) But without fail, within days after a new child would arrive, the issue of no meat almost never surfaced again. As the kids occasionally put it, they were blown away that a plant-based diet could taste so incredibly good. There was always plenty of good-tasting food around and that's all that mattered to them.

That's what this book is all about: plenty of good-tasting vegetarian food for you and your family. Whether you're planning a gradual switch to a totally vegetarian diet or just looking for an occasional meatless entrée, you will find it here.

One of the key words in the title of this book is *family*. There are a lot of vegetarian cookbooks floating around out there—my own shelves are full of them—but it is surprising how few seem to be grounded in the reality of family life. Much of it seems overly complicated and precious. There's a tendency, I've noticed, in many books and magazines to try and raise the credibility of vegetarian cuisine by making it look as stunning and sophisticated as "regular" cooking. These recipes, however, often look like something you'd pay $50 for at an uptown restaurant—then go home hungry.

So here is vegetarian fare that worries less about how it looks and more about questions like: Does it taste really good? Will my family eat it? Can I prepare it in a reasonable amount of time? Are the ingredients easy to find? (We assume you have a supermarket in your neighborhood, but not an Asian market.) Is it wholesome and balanced? A diet that says *Yes!* to all those questions has plenty of credibility on its own.

I think it is safe to assume that most people are drawn to a vegetarian diet by some combination of health, environmental, and ethical concerns. The degree to which each one of those factors affects you will largely dictate the style of vegetarianism you choose—occasional, practically full time, lacto-ovo (dairy included), vegan (no dairy), whatever. Even under this one roof we have different styles. When I first became a vegetarian twenty years ago, I ate no meat, fish, or fowl. After a while because of my career as a food writer I gradually added a bit of each. But now I've eliminated them again. Karen, on the other hand, has eaten no more than a handful of shrimp and scallops in the past twenty years, but that's it from the animal world. She seldom eats dairy products anymore. I use them sometimes, depending on my current projects, but we use them much more sparingly than we once did. Frankly, Karen is such an adept dairyless cook that we seldom miss it when it isn't there. And the kids, by the way, are free to eat meat if they choose. They simply don't.

It has been an ongoing challenge to accommodate a variety of vegetarian diets in a single household. These recipes represent the fruit of that labor, as they reflect the realities of incorporating a meatless diet into family life. The balance of meatless (dairy and nondairy) recipes here will allow you to move freely and at your own pace, exploring the style of vegetarianism that feels right to you and meets your family's needs. This is a guidebook, not based on any particular doctrine, that recognizes the importance of a flexible approach to making long-lasting, fundamental dietary changes.

Embracing a meatless diet is a step toward better health, and in that spirit we've gone out of our way to create dishes with a wholesome profile. It is a matter of fact that the good, whole, natural foods upon which this book is based are inherently flavorful and satisfying. There are some dishes here for splurging, but generally speaking, these recipes embrace today's attitudes and guidelines about healthy eating. Besides, there's a lot more to health than just what goes on the plate.

My Ten Rules for Feeding the Healthy Vegetarian Family

1. *Start early.* Our four kids have been vegetarians since day one, so a meatless diet is literally second nature to them. They grew up on salads, grain and bean dishes, meatless soups and veggie burgers. It isn't always so easy to make dietary changes once kids get older, so the sooner you can steer them in that direction, the better. However, if you haven't been able to start early, then . . .

2. *Start slowly.* Changing dietary directions mid-course can throw the family ship into chaos if you try to do it too quickly. It would not be wise to announce one day *OK guys, listen up. As of today, no more meat!* You'd have a mutiny on your hands. Start by serving one new meatless dish each week, gradually phasing out the meat or serving smaller portions of it.

3. *Stay familiar.* Don't derail your early efforts by serving anything too out of the ordinary. You might run into a great recipe for Tofu, Tahini, & Lentil Sprout Bake, but how is that going to sound to the kids? If your kids like chili, make them a meatless one. Or if they like pasta, serve lots of meatless pastas at first. Introduce new foods and ingredients slowly. When they ask about the dish you're serving, use the "It's just like . . ." line we do when the kids' friends eat over. [*It's just like the lasagne or whatever your mom makes, except it has no meat.*] Most kids will find comfort by the association. And a few wise guys will tell you their mom buys frozen lasagne.

4. *Seek variety.* One look at the vegetarian cookbook rack at your local bookstore is all the proof you need that there's almost no end to the ways you can prepare meatless meals. Kids like variety; it keeps them interested. By the same token, they like old favorites too. Your challenge is to serve up just the right amount of both. Over time, use new greens in salads. Vary your salad dressings. Serve homemade breads with your soups. Kids might try to moan about what they're missing out on. Your job is to focus on all the new things you *can* eat.

5. *Don't pressure.* Like I say, your kids might complain about missing certain foods. Some might disagree, but I think it's best not to put too much pressure on your kids to change their diets. Food can be, often is, an emotional security blanket. I don't think you can take that away without ill effects. An occasional hot dog or burger isn't the end of the world, and your willingness not to be dogmatic will encourage your children to be more accepting of the changes you would make.

6. *Work together.* Cooking with kids can be chaotic, and it isn't for everyone. But it can also be a lot of fun, and a wonderful learning experience for them and you. Keep in mind that a child will have a limited attention span in the kitchen, and if you don't plan and give them specific, age-appropriate tasks, they'll start stuffing dirty socks in the food processor if they get bored. Kids will be proud of the fact they pitched in on a meal, and they'll be more likely to eat the finished dish.

7. *Encourage input.* This is the equivalent of those signs you see on the back of trucks: HOW'S MY DRIVING? When you start changing over to meatless cooking, you should post the HOW'S MY COOKING? sign, at least in spirit. Kids are pretty good judges of what tastes good and what doesn't because they don't get bogged down in the intellectual aspect of food. (I'm serious. This has happened to me a number of times as a food writer: I try to convince myself that something tastes good either because someone else has said so, or because I'm very attached to the idea of liking it, perhaps because I've spent all day trying to make the idea work. But my taste buds won't let me lie.) Listen to what your kids say about your cooking, especially when you're changing over to a meatless diet. If they don't like something, don't take it personally. Ask them why: Salad dressing too sharp? The veggie burgers too bland? Steamed broccoli too mushy? Too many pasta dishes this week? If you give kids the idea you're doing your best to please them, they'll usually reward your efforts by giving new dishes a fair try.

8. *Avoid sanctimony.* In my mind, the worst disservice anyone can do to their kids or the rest of mankind is to let a vegetarian diet or lifestyle give rise to a holier-than-thou attitude. We can choose not to eat meat for any number of good reasons, but never to look better than someone else. We can find dignity with our choice. We can be serious students of meatless cooking. But our hearts should be open to those who don't share our own views.

9. *Lighten up.* I used to think I needed to be Mr. Cooks Everything From Scratch. I cooked that way mainly because I liked to, but there was also this image thing I had to maintain. But being Dances with Pots and Pans leaves you little time for a life, something that someone with four kids desperately needs. Nowadays, I don't feel like every veggie burger I cook has to be my own, and I'm not even above serving Tater Tots on the side if I don't feel like cutting and roasting potatoes. Any health food store and many supermarkets now carry a lot of good-quality convenience foods, meatless and healthy stuff. These foods tend to be a bit pricey, but you can learn ways to stretch them. Those little round tubs of black bean soup, for instance, are great when you add them to sautéed onions. We add extra cumin and coriander to the sauté, then stretch the soup with chopped canned tomatoes.

10. *Give thanks.* Say a little prayer of thanks before every meal for the bounty we have. At the risk of sounding like your fifth grade teacher, we really are fortunate to live in a country where we have access to so many good raw in-

gredients and where even the less fortunate of us are so much better off than much of the world's population. It's good for those around you to hear expressions of gratitude, and it can't hurt your karma either.

CREATING A PEACEFUL HOME FOOD ENVIRONMENT

Though this is primarily a book of recipes, I strongly feel that there's too much emphasis placed on recipes today and not enough written about the more subtle aspects of eating. What goes on behind the scenes in family kitchens often shapes our attitudes about food and cooking. So allow me a few more thoughts on the matter.

Because I write cookbooks, I've had plenty of opportunities to talk about my books with friends, the media, siblings, and complete strangers in the supermarket or on the street. And having done this for many years now, I'm amazed at how often these conversations—punctuated by parental sighs and moans of exasperation—turn to the subject of kids and food. Those talks, and the recognition that the way kids eat is a troubling issue for legions of parents, are some of the seeds from which this book has grown.

Typically, a parent will say to me, "How do you get your kids to eat asparagus?" (or broccoli, salad, chickpeas—you fill in the blank). At first, this question used to take me by surprise; I just didn't get it. If I've had food problems with my kids it has been getting them to *stop* eating. (*Ben! That's your fifth helping of salad and I haven't even sat down yet!* Ben: *Then hurry up and sit down!*) In addition, I've never set out to "get" my kids to eat anything: If they didn't eat, I figured they weren't hungry or were tired of eating pasta for the sixth night in a row.

Though it isn't new, this whole concept of getting your kids to eat something, whether it's brussels sprouts or chicken wings, against their own will and judgment is indicative of the wrongful approach parents sometimes employ in the daily struggle for sensible eating. This tactic very quickly turns divisive, making the dinner table a place of contention instead of a relaxed and nourishing family enclave.

I've written this book with the belief that while you can't make your kids eat anything without negative consequences, you can create the sort of healthy family food environment where kids are welcome in the kitchen, where their mealtime wishes are acknowledged, and where there is plenty of good, wholesome, and varied food around for the taking. I really believe in my heart that if you make an honest effort to create this sort of environment, things will fall into place and kids will develop good eating habits in the long run. I'm not saying that your kids won't go through a streak of wanting to eat nothing but pizza or cold cereal, despite your best intentions; you sometimes have to expect and accommodate those aberrations. And I'm not saying that your child will ever eat salad; he may not. I don't mean to sound cavalier, but so what if he doesn't? Frankly, I think what our kids do or don't eat is far less a concern than how adults deal with it. In the end, will it make a big difference if little Sam never learns to like broccoli? He'll still grow up strong, loving, and at peace with the world. Let's not lose sight of what's really important.

Inviting kids into the kitchen is not an easy thing for many parents. I know when I'm on some sort of deadline, or feeling irritated about something, it can be a real stress on me. Having kids in the kitchen can be chaotic, a challenge to our adult sense of order.

There are, as I have learned, both practical and emotional concerns to address if children are to share and participate in the kitchen. There are safety concerns, because of potentially harmful knives, appliances, and gadgets. There are logistical concerns, too: When both parents work, how can they find the time to cook happily with their kids? I've tried to cover all these areas throughout the book in the hopes of shedding light on family cooking.

Given half a chance, kids will choose to eat well. Provide them with good raw ingredients, variety, a little instruction, and your own enthusiasm, and you'll be amazed at what transpires. Listen to what your kids tell you about eating, their likes and dislikes, and do what you can to work with them so the kitchen, and mealtime, is always a source of joy.

Ken Haedrich
Stinson Lake
Rumney, New Hampshire

Snack Foods

You've heard of grazing? Well, if you have children then you already realize that even if they didn't coin the word, they no doubt invented the concept. I kid you not: When my four are at home, there's almost never a moment when one of them isn't in the kitchen trying to find something easy to eat. Graham crackers with peanut butter and honey, celery or carrot sticks, cheese and crackers, chips and dip, you name it. I keep threatening to buy each of them a feed bag and just strap it around their necks.

This chapter contains a few ideas for snack foods our kids like best, from butterless popcorn to good bread dipped in olive oil. Some are easy enough for kids to do on their own; younger kids will need some help. By all means, get your children into the kitchen as soon as they're willing; the earlier you can teach your kids to fend for themselves at snack time, the easier your life will be. I've known kids who are incredibly inept in the kitchen, self-conscious and dependent on Mom or Dad for all their food needs. When I see a child like that, I know that they've never been encouraged in the kitchen, never been nudged toward self-sufficiency. I think that's too bad for all concerned.

I will feel eternal gratitude for the person who invented popcorn; it has to be one of the greatest kid foods of all time. If you don't already have one, go right out and buy a good air popper. It's an inexpensive investment that will last for years and far safer than trying to pop corn over a burner. It's easy, too; with just a minimum of supervision for younger kids, your children can operate the machine themselves. Try our recipe. You'll be amazed how good popcorn can be with olive oil and nutritional yeast the way we do it here.

As for other snack hardware: Buy some Tupperware containers specifically for carrot and celery sticks. That way your kids will always know where to find them. These can be peeled and cut ahead; the kids can grab them when they need to. Keep washed grapes in another container (halved for very young kids). Make sure your kids know which knife to use for spreading peanut butter on crackers and celery sticks (not the paring knife). Show them how to use a cheese planer; it is safer than using a knife and in most cases can be used without supervision. And finally, encourage them to clean up and put stuff away when they're done. But don't expect miracles. I've been doing that for sixteen years now with little luck.

Sam's Simple Olive Oil and Good Bread Snack

One day my youngest son Sam and I were shopping at the food co-op in Hanover, New Hampshire. As I was heading for the cashier, I noticed that Sam was engaged in a lively discussion-cum-face feed with a young woman selling flavored olive oils. As fast as she could hand him chunks of rustic bread, he would dip them into one of her oils and wolf them down. When he'd all but exhausted the good lady's supply of bread, he came running to me, chin dripping with olive oil and flecks of rosemary, and begged me to buy a bottle. The frugal Yankee in me quickly calculated how many multiples I could make of her recipe if I simply threw the few ingredients together myself, but my son's enthusiasm easily won out. Besides, the woman had just given my kid dinner; buying a bottle of her oil was the least I could do.

That original bottle is long since history, but Sam and the rest of us have carried on the tradition. Not that this is anything very original; I imagine people have been dipping their bread in olive oil for some thousands of years. And most better Italian restaurants today serve this as a matter of course. But the tradition is worth noting because it is a healthy snack, kids like it, and you can put it together in just a few minutes if you have the right ingredients on hand—namely good bread, olive oil, rosemary, and garlic.

There are no specific quantities per se; they will be determined by the number of people you are serving. Pour some olive oil into a bowl; it needn't be the most expensive or extra virgin, and in fact the darker, stronger-tasting oils are liable to pack more flavor than many kids like; our standard brand is Berio, which might not be the choice of connoisseurs, but we like it just fine. Stir in 1 or 2 cloves of very finely minced garlic or put it through a garlic press. Add chopped and crushed (with a rolling pin) rosemary to taste and a pinch of salt and freshly ground pepper.

For the bread, you will need either good rustic sourdough bread or homemade French or Ugly Breads (222); the latter, warm, is our favorite. Simply pull the bread apart into small rough chunks, dip it in the oil, and go for it. Add some grapes and olives and you've the makings of a feast.

And here's a tip from Sam: Put a few paper towels in your lap and keep one for your face. He knows what he's talking about.

Goodie Plate

We've been making goodie plates for as long as our oldest, Ben, has been able to ask for snacks. We think he invented the name—*doodie pate, doodie pate!*—but the precise origin may have slipped through the cracks in our parental memory, never to be retrieved. Nonetheless, a goodie plate in practice is a sort of antipasto of fruits, nuts, cheese, crackers, and other good things to eat. In spirit, it is a piece of edible art whose beauty is found primarily in the subtle sharing aspects of putting it all together and consuming the feast. An apple is a snack; an apple, peeled and sliced, served with wedges of cheese and a bunch of grapes, is a goodie plate. There is no recipe for a goodie plate per se, though I have listed some of our favorite additions below.

apple and pear slices, tossed in lemon juice

slices of Cheddar or Monterey Jack cheese

peanut butter

dark or golden raisins

other dried fruits: pitted dates, apples, figs, apricots, pears, or cranberries

coconut, dried or fresh chunks

pitted grapes

crackers

Toasted Sweetened Pecans (page 12)

fresh berries in season

sliced canned pineapple

tangerine sections

celery or carrot sticks

Our Favorite Tahini Dressing (page 44) for dipping vegetable sticks

*S*imply choose from among your favorites and arrange them on a plate. You can arrange items in free-form groups, in concentric circles, or like pie wedges. Loose items like peanut butter and leftover dressing are best served in little ramekins. Serve and enjoy.

Sam's Peanut Butter Balls

MAKES ABOUT TWENTY 1 1/4-INCH BALLS

I've called these Sam's Peanut Butter Balls, after my youngest child, but I could just as well have named them after any of the kids since this has always been one of the first recipes they've taken to. It's the perfect kid recipe: They love all of the ingredients and there's nothing to cook (unless you add the optional toasted seeds; Mom or Dad can do that ahead) and it isn't so fussy or precise that the kids can't do all the measuring. And then they get to roll them, the fun part.

1 cup salted natural peanut butter, smooth or chunky

1/3 cup mild honey, such as clover or orange blossom

2 teaspoons carob powder or unsweetened cocoa

big pinch of cinnamon

2/3 cup raisins

2 tablespoons plus 1/2 cup unsweetened shredded coconut (available at
    health food stores) or sweetened flaked coconut

*I*f you are starting with a new jar of peanut butter, make sure you stir it well to mix any separated oil back in.
        In a large mixing bowl, mix the peanut butter, honey, carob powder, and cinnamon with a wooden spoon until blended. Stir in the raisins and 2 tablespoons of the coconut. Refrigerate the mixture for 1 to 2 hours if possible.
    Using a spoon, scoop up small heaps of the mixture and gently roll them into 1 1/4-inch balls. It makes rolling easier if, once you have a rough ball, you roll the ball in coconut. Roll the balls in coconut a second time, then arrange them on a plate. Cover loosely with plastic wrap and refrigerate the balls for at least 30 minutes before serving.

Our Popular Butterless Popcorn

This is a scaled-down version of the best healthy popcorn you'll ever eat. We live just off a lake and in the summer, when we go to the beach, we bring at least one grocery sack of this and often more because all the kids we know—and many we don't—can't keep their hands out of the bags (it tends to get a little sandy as the day wears on). None of the kids care much about the way we make this, but the parents inevitably do. Our secret is a light coating of olive oil, just enough to make the nutritional yeast and seasonings stick. One of the tricks is to drizzle on the olive oil in such a way that you get a nice even coating on the popped corn; drizzle and toss, don't just dump it on. If you're really obsessed, you can keep a sprayer around with olive oil just for this purpose, but I'd be lying if I said that's how we do it. (With four youngsters, I've learned the hard way about the dangers of keeping sprayers around except under lock and key; on any given day I may end up spraying shampoo on my popcorn or olive oil on my dress shirts when I iron them.) Keep in mind that not all brands of seasoning salts are created equal; some of them like Spike—my favorite choice for popcorn—are salt-free. So use it accordingly.

16 cups (about $^1/_3$ cup dry) hot popped corn

$2^1/_2$ tablespoons light-tasting olive oil

3 tablespoons nutritional yeast

seasoning salt to taste (see headnote)

While the popcorn is still hot, drizzle the olive oil over it, tossing the popcorn to coat it thoroughly. Sprinkle on the nutritional yeast and seasoning salt, tossing well, and serve.

❧ Food for Thought ❧
A PERSONAL POPCORN QUIRK

In this day and age, it makes no sense not to own an electric air popper for popping corn, especially if you have kids. An air popper allows kids to make popcorn when they want, without the worry of being at the stove over a direct source of heat. Besides, air poppers are much more efficient than other stovetop methods; there are fewer duds.

Toasted Sweetened Pecans

MAKES 1 1/2 CUPS

It's probably a good thing that the cost of pecans is so astronomical, otherwise we'd be eating these like there was no tomorrow; as it is, we eat a lot of them. Besides just snacking on them out of hand, we mainly use these sweetened pecans on salads. They're often just what you need to balance the sharpness and acidity of salad dressing. Around the holidays we've given these to friends, packaged in decorative tins. For the baking impaired, keep in mind that they're even easier than making cookies and the response is no less enthusiastic.

2 tablespoons water

1/4 cup packed light brown sugar

1 1/2 cups pecan halves

Preheat the oven to 350° and very lightly oil a large baking sheet. Warm the water in a medium cast-iron skillet. Add the brown sugar and stir over medium heat for a minute or so, until the sugar granules have dissolved. Stir in the pecans, increase the heat slightly, and toast them for about 2 more minutes, stirring continuously; if you see the pan start to smoke—not steam—remove it from the heat.

Immediately scrape the pecans into a single layer on the baking sheet. Put the pecans in the oven for about 7 minutes to finish toasting the nuts and dry out the sugar. Transfer the baking sheet to a rack and cool the nuts completely, loosening them with a spatula after about 10 minutes. Store the cooled nuts in an airtight container.

❧ Food for Thought ❧
A PECAN PARTY PLATTER

These nuts are popular party fare, great as is but even better served with a bit of flair. They have a particular affinity for fresh sliced pears or apples and—of all things—blue cheese, an affinity that's the basis for one of my favorite salads (page 28). With that in mind, you can build a simple but satisfying party platter from these basic ingredients. Toss the sliced fruit in lemon juice so they lose color. The blue cheese can be served as a wedge, partially crumbled, or in a dip for the fruit. Add the Toasted Sweetened Pecans, some crackers and you're in business.

Mom's Hot Soy Milk

MAKES 2 SERVINGS

Almost all kids love a steaming cup of hot cocoa when they've been playing hard outside in the snow. But many parents today would just as soon have a tasty alternative without the milk and chocolate. Hot carob is one alternative, and I've recently discovered a great way to make it. Karen took a different route, straying from carob to almond and vanilla flavorings we buy at the health food store. Flavorings, unlike extracts, are not alcohol based, which some people prefer. She sweetens the soy milk with a touch of real maple syrup; 1 tablespoon per serving is just right. Then she adds a festive touch with a pinch each of cinnamon and nutmeg. The kids really love this and as for myself, who once couldn't go through a winter day without at least 2 cups of coffee or hot cocoa, I'm here to tell you this is as soothing as either, without the downside of caffeine.

> 2 cups plain (not flavored or sweetened) soy milk
>
> 2 tablespoons maple syrup
>
> 1 teaspoon almond flavoring
>
> 1 teaspoon vanilla flavoring
>
> big pinch of grated nutmeg
>
> big pinch of cinnamon

In a small saucepan, heat the soy milk, maple syrup, and flavorings, bringing them to a near simmer; do not boil. Cover and cool until it has reached a sipping temperature. If it has formed a surface skin, just skim it off. Divide between 2 mugs. Dust each serving with the spices and serve hot.

Fresh Raspberry Smoothie

MAKES 4 SERVINGS

Here's an easy one for raspberry lovers, a special shake to enjoy during the short fresh raspberry season. We take frigid milk and raspberries and blend them with a little vanilla and honey. It blends up smooth and sweet, looking the prettiest shade of deep raspberry red you've ever seen.

$^{1}/_{2}$ pint fresh raspberries

2 cups milk

dash of pure vanilla extract

2 to 3 tablespoons honey

Scatter the raspberries on a plate and put the plate in the freezer. Wait a few minutes, then pour the milk into a measuring cup and place it in the freezer also. About every 10 minutes, stir the milk. When it starts forming large frozen crystals—about the same time the raspberries are becoming frozen hard—transfer both of them to a blender. Add a dash of vanilla, perhaps 3 or 4 drops, and the lesser amount of honey. Blend until smooth, adding more vanilla and honey if you like. Divide among 4 glasses and serve.

Starters

I call this section Starters, but what we have here are dips, spreads, and little snacks that taste delicious whenever you choose to eat them. Sometimes, especially around the holidays, we'll serve one or more of these if we have friends over. We might put out an assortment of them instead of a meal, or just one or two if something more substantial will follow.

Everyone likes a good dip or spread, even more so if it is something a little different, a little inventive. Let's face it: We've all eaten enough of the sour cream-and-onion-soup-mix—type dip to last a lifetime. And most of us are just plain tired of the genre, or looking for something healthier to slide our cracker into.

Instead of heavy creamy bases, most of the dips in this section rely on vegetables or beans for their bulk and body. Then we add layers of flavor with a bit of cheese and herbs, or olives, capers, lemon juice, or tomato paste when they benefit from the addition of bold or concentrated flavors. It takes a little time for all of the flavors to mingle; that's why, whenever possible, you should let these sit for at least 30 minutes before serving. All should be refrigerated when you're holding them before serving, though they generally taste best when served at room temperature.

I can really appreciate a cook who takes the time to arrange a thoughtful presentation for a well-made spread. Though I'm guilty of it myself, I don't like it when someone unceremoniously slaps a plastic container of dip and bag of crackers on the table. It's much more gracious to use attractive bowls, put out little knives, and use appropriately sturdy crackers; call me fussy, but I'm always a little put off when I see shards of crackers in a mound of spread simply because there was no way for anyone to serve themselves properly. A little extra effort will dignify your efforts as the cook and let your guests know that you care about their comfort.

Sun-Dried Tomato and Olive Spread

MAKES ABOUT $^3/_4$ CUP

Nothing that starts with a lot of sun-dried tomatoes and olives can miss the mark entirely, correct? At least that's what I figured when I began throwing them in the food processor with a few other choice tidbits in pursuit of something good to toss with a bowlful of leftover pasta that beckoned to me from the fridge. I'd been barraged with enough sightings of packaged sun-dried tomato pestos—a great name if I ever heard one—to try my own hand. In any case, I chose not to call mine a pesto because it has so many uses beyond pasta. In addition to mixing it with pastas hot and cold, you can use it on crackers or toasts, to add sparkle to avocado sandwiches, mixed in with scrambled eggs or omelets, and on top of veggie burgers or individual small pizzas. The Parmesan cheese is optional; it gives you a slightly firmer, more spreadable dip (if you intend it for crackers), but it's not at all necessary.

12 oil-packed sun-dried tomatoes (see page 290 for instructions on
    making your own)

8 or 9 large pitted imported green olives

2 garlic cloves, coarsely chopped

3 tablespoons olive oil

1 or 2 teaspoons lemon juice

small handful of fresh basil leaves

salt and freshly ground pepper to taste

$^1/_4$ to $^1/_3$ cup freshly grated Parmesan cheese (optional)

Put everything in the bowl of a food processor, using 1 teaspoon of the lemon juice. Process to a finely textured spread, scraping down the sides of the bowl often. Taste, using a little more lemon juice if necessary. Transfer to a bowl, cover with plastic wrap, and refrigerate if you aren't using it right away.

Broccoli-Parmesan Dip

MAKES ABOUT 1 1/2 CUPS

This is very good, a vegetable dip I dreamed up for the kids starring one of their favorite vegetables. If you get tired of dips that use the same old routine—tons of sour cream and that sort of thing—this will be a welcome change. The main ingredient is broccoli, with just a pinch of cream cheese or Neufchâtel cheese to smooth it out and a little Parmesan for flavor. This is excellent on little toasts, rice cakes, or crackers, and it also makes a tasty pasta sauce (page 139).

1 pound broccoli (1 good-size head)

2 tablespoons olive oil

1 medium onion, chopped

2 garlic cloves, minced

juice of 1/2 lemon

1/2 cup freshly grated Parmesan cheese

1 ounce Neufchâtel cheese or cream cheese

1 tablespoon chopped fresh basil or 1 teaspoon dried

salt and freshly ground pepper

Cut the flowerets from the broccoli and peel the stalks. Coarsely chop the stalks, then put the flowerets and stalks into a steamer and steam for 6 to 8 minutes, until quite tender. Transfer the broccoli to a plate and let cool.

While it cools, heat the oil in a small saucepan and stir in the onion. Sauté over medium heat for about 7 minutes, until translucent, then stir in the garlic. Sauté for 30 seconds more, then remove from the heat.

Put the cooled broccoli, sautéed onion and garlic, lemon juice, and Parmesan cheese in the bowl of a food processor and process until very finely chopped. Add the Neufchâtel or cream cheese, basil, and salt and pepper to taste. Process again briefly until smooth. Transfer the dip to a serving dish. This is best if it has several hours to mellow in the refrigerator, but it can be served right away if you like.

Spiced Black Bean Dip

❧

MAKES ABOUT 2 CUPS

There's a commercial brand of black bean dip that my family and I really like. It is quite nicely seasoned and has a good texture. Still, I thought we could do a little better for less—the cost isn't one of its virtues—so we read the ingredient list on the label and got to work. If you've ever tried anything like this, you know how tricky it can be. You have to make plenty of educated guesses and read between the lines when necessary. And they always say stuff like "choice herbs and spices," which is really a great help. Despite these handicaps, I think we did a fine job with this; I think it's better than the original. The first time my son Sam tried it, he said that this stuff is great . . . AND HOT!

2 tablespoons flavorless vegetable or sunflower oil

1 large onion, chopped

2 garlic cloves, minced

2 teaspoons ground coriander

1 teaspoon ground cumin

1 teaspoon chili powder

1 15^1/$_2$-ounce can black beans, drained and rinsed

1^1/$_2$ tablespoons tomato paste

2 to 4 tablespoons pickled jalapeño peppers, to taste, plus some of the liquid from the jar, *or* 1 small can mild green chilies

few drops of Tabasco sauce (optional)

salt and freshly ground pepper

lemon juice (optional)

Heat the oil in a medium cast-iron skillet and stir in the onion. Sauté the onion over medium heat for 8 to 9 minutes, stirring often. Stir in the garlic and spices and cook the spices, stirring, for 1 minute more. Scrape the sautéed mixture into the bowl of a food processor and add the black beans, tomato paste, jalapeños, and about 1 tablespoon of the liquid from the jalapeño jar. Add a few drops of Tabasco, if you're using it, and salt and pepper to taste. Process the mixture to a smooth puree, scraping down the sides of the bowl if necessary. Taste, adding more salt and pepper if necessary. If it seems to need it, add several squeezes of lemon juice for more tang.

Creamy Onion and Sun-Dried Tomato Dip

~

MAKES ABOUT 1 CUP

Expensive they may be, but sun-dried tomatoes are worth the occasional splurge when you need to pack a lot of flavor into a dish. This creamy dip, made with Neufchâtel cheese, is a prime example. There are olives, basil, sautéed onions, and garlic here, but what really shines are those wonderful sun-dried tomatoes. I call for 8 or so, but you could easily use more of them, perhaps increasing the amount of Neufchâtel cheese also. Serve with a good sesame cracker or thin slices of toasted French bread. I was surprised that one of my kids who doesn't even like olives liked this dip. And another—Alison, my olive lover—went nuts over this. Leftovers are doubtful but they could be used to fill an omelet. Consider doubling the recipe for a party crowd.

1 1/2 tablespoons olive oil

1 medium onion, chopped

2 or 3 garlic cloves, minced

handful of fresh parsley

8 good-quality pitted green or black olives

8 oil-packed sun-dried tomatoes

small handful of fresh basil leaves or about 2 teaspoons dried

4 to 5 ounces Neufchâtel cheese or cream cheese, at room temperature

1/2 cup freshly grated Parmesan cheese

freshly ground pepper

Heat the oil in a heavy, medium skillet and stir in the onion. Sauté the onion over medium heat for about 8 to 9 minutes, until it begins to turn golden. Stir in the garlic and sauté gently for 1 minute more.

Scrape the sautéed mixture into the bowl of a food processor. Add the parsley, olives, tomatoes, and basil and process the mixture until it is finely chopped.

Put the Neufchâtel and Parmesan cheeses into a mixing bowl and blend them with a wooden spoon. Scrape the tomato mixture into the cheeses and blend thoroughly, adding pepper to taste. Transfer to a serving dish. Cover and refrigerate, but remove from the fridge about 30 minutes before serving.

Lentil Pâté or Tapenade

✷

MAKES ABOUT 1 1/2 CUPS

This is a wonderful, versatile dip, robustly seasoned with chili powder, paprika, and soy sauce. If you're having a party, it's a sure bet for vegetarians and nonvegetarians alike. And your kids will gobble it up. Serve it straight from the bowl for family, or mold it in a small bowl or loaf pan for a party, refrigerating thoroughly before turning it out. (For insurance, line your container with plastic wrap first.) Scatter the top with chopped olives, parsley, or chopped hard-cooked egg. If you really want to zip this up, use it as a base to make a lentil tapenade; simply add a handful of good-quality oil-cured olives. The tapenade is terrific spread on thin garlic toasts and both can be used to make spectacular pizzas. We also use this as a filling in lasagne, and it makes a good omelet filling, too. When I make this at my cooking classes, everybody loves it.

1 1/2 cups cooked lentils (page 42)

1 cup walnuts

2 tablespoons olive oil

1 large onion, finely chopped

2 garlic cloves, minced

1 teaspoon paprika

1 teaspoon mild chili powder

small handful of fresh parsley leaves

1 1/2 teaspoons soy sauce or tamari

small handful of pitted oil-cured olives (8 to 10), if making tapenade

a few squeezes of lemon juice

salt and freshly ground pepper

*I*f you haven't already, cook the lentils and set them aside to cool. Meanwhile, preheat the oven to 350° and toast the walnuts for 10 minutes. Set them aside to cool.

Heat the oil in a medium skillet and add the onion. Sauté over medium heat for 10 minutes, stirring often. Stir in the garlic, paprika, and chili powder and continue to cook, stirring, for 1 minute more. Scrape this mixture directly into the bowl of a food processor and cool.

When the nuts have cooled, add them to the processor along with the parsley. Process to a rough puree, then add the lentils and soy sauce. (To make the tapenade, add the pitted olives to the food processor when you add the lentils.) Process 5 to 10 more seconds, scraping down the sides if necessary. Taste, adding a squeeze of lemon juice and salt and pepper to taste. Process a few more seconds, until smooth but still slightly textured.

Cheese Grilled Pita Wedges with Mediterranean Relish

MAKES 4 TO 5 SERVINGS

All food should be this good. Here I take one of my favorite condiments, Mediterranean Relish, and serve it nacho style. But instead of the chips, I use cheese-filled pita bread brushed with olive oil and warmed in a skillet just until the cheese gets to that lovely oozing stage. The breads are cut into wedges and served on a platter with the dip and several garnishes. Kids might not go for the forward taste of the relish, but that leaves all the more for mom or pop. Besides, there are kid alternatives; see *Food for Thought*.

1 recipe Mediterranean Relish (page 194)

2 cups grated fontina, mozzarella, or Monterey Jack cheese

3 whole wheat pita breads, halved

olive oil to brush on the breads

handful of ripe cherry tomatoes, quartered

2 tablespoons chopped fresh parsley

Prepare the relish and set it aside in the saucepan; it will need to be reheated when you serve this. Get out a platter and a small serving bowl to put the relish in. Preheat the oven to 250°.

Evenly spread about $1/3$ cup of cheese in each half of bread. Heat a large cast-iron skillet. While the skillet is heating, lightly brush one side of each pita with olive oil. Place as many halves in the skillet—oiled side down—as will fit comfortably and warm them over medium heat for 2 to 3 minutes on each side; brush the second side with oil before you flip them. Transfer the breads to a baking sheet and keep them warm in the oven while you heat the other breads in the same manner.

When you are ready to serve, reheat the relish and put it in the small bowl in the center of your platter. Cut each half of pita into 3 wedges and arrange the wedges on the plate around the relish. Scatter the tomatoes and parsley on top of everything and serve at once.

❧ *Food for Thought* ❧

GRILLED CHEESE PITAS

Even if the kids aren't likely to go for this version of stuffed cheese bread—they won't relish the relish, you might say, like adults will—there are alternatives. Just heat up some tomato sauce and serve it in small bowls. Or put out their favorite salsa; there are several excellent ones you might try in the relish section of this book.

Artichoke Heart and Mint "Hummus"

MAKES ABOUT 1¹/₄ CUPS

Karen thinks this is better than traditional hummus, and for anyone who has trouble digesting chickpeas it may be the best-tasting alternative you're likely to run into. All I've done really is taken the basic hummus idea and adapted it to artichoke hearts. There's much less tahini than usual to preserve the delicate artichoke flavor, and a measure of mint and basil adds an unexpected lift to this spread. Serve with crackers, as a dip, or use with lettuce and cucumber slices as a pita sandwich filling. My kids think this is great, too.

1 14-ounce jar artichoke hearts, drained
small handful of fresh parsley leaves
small handful of fresh mint leaves or 1 teaspoon dried
small handful of fresh basil leaves or ¹/₂ teaspoon dried
pinch of cayenne (optional)
1 garlic clove, coarsely chopped
3 tablespoons tahini
1 tablespoon olive oil, plus a little extra for garnish
juice of ¹/₂ lemon
1 to 2 tablespoons water
salt and freshly ground pepper
paprika, for garnish

*P*ut the artichoke hearts, seasonings, and garlic in the bowl of a food processor and process until the mixture is finely chopped; stop the machine once or twice to scrape down the sides. Add the tahini, olive oil, lemon juice, 1 tablespoon of water, and salt and pepper to taste. Process again to make a smooth, slightly textured puree. Stop the machine again, taste, and adjust the seasoning as necessary, adding a bit more water if it needs a little thinning; it will be slightly firmer than traditional hummus. Transfer the mixture to a storage bowl or serving plate. Cover with plastic wrap and refrigerate if not serving right away. To serve, spread the mixture on a small plate, dust with paprika, and drizzle with olive oil.

Salads

I often wonder—when I see my kids shoveling down their dinner salads like there's no tomorrow—how salad got such a bad rap with kids. (In restaurants, the kids' frenzied, salad-eating ways have left more than one waitress slack-jawed.) I can only imagine that for many kids, once they get a whiff of the fact that salad is supposed to be good for them and the pressure's on to eat it and grow up healthy and strong, you can forget about it, Charlie. *No way am I gonna eat that rabbit food.*

I suspect many kids also suffer from Unimaginative Salad Syndrome. They've grown tired of that wedge of iceberg with a slug of bottled Russian dressing. When the cook is bored, the kids will be bored. You can count on that. But salad doesn't have to be boring, and this section is full of proof to the contrary. Salads at their best are crisp, cool, refreshing, and colorful. They're visually exciting, a feast for all the senses. And the dressing only enhances the excitement on the plate. Those are salads kids will eat.

Sometimes salad is the whole meal around here. About once or twice a month we do something we call simply "big salad." Big salad—or any other salad, for that matter—is a bit of an enterprise, but that's okay. Salad making doesn't have to be lengthy, mind you, but it must be careful. The lettuce must be washed and dried with care and all tired or wilted leaves discarded; besides eggshells in my egg salad, nothing turns me off like slimy greens. The greens should be gently torn into reasonable, mouth-size pieces. If I live forever, I'll never understand why some restaurants serve salad with lettuce leaves so large you'd have to be a horse to cram them in with one bite. Extras like toasted sunflower seeds, grated cheese, grated carrots, beets, and sliced cucumbers—all the sort of stuff we eat with big salad—should be arranged around the greens with care, not dumped unceremoniously on top. Dressing should be passed separately so each person can take as much or as little as they like.

These things are no longer a novelty item, but since I've only recently gotten one, this is the place to mention a salad spinner. Much as I love salad, I've never liked washing greens. Nor did I ever like drying them, laying all those leaves on paper towels and blotting up the excess water. The salad spinner that I got makes it all quite simple. You just rinse the leaves under running water, tear them into pieces, and put them in the spinner. You spin like crazy, the water flies off, and the lettuce is good and dry. If you don't own one, you might want to consider buying one. They save an awful lot of paper towels, too.

If you garden, then naturally you have the best salads of all. Or maybe you have half a garden or a good market garden down the road; any of these will give your salads a commensurate fresh appeal. Whenever possible, bring life to your salads by including the freshest seasonal produce that's available. Even if you don't have the room or inclination to garden, you can grow a few salad herbs right on your windowsill or in containers on the patio. If you have kids, snipping the fresh herbs and tossing them in the family salad can become their job. Invite kids to make salad with you. If they're reluctant salad eaters, it could change everything.

❧ *Food for Thought* ❧
LETTUCE TALK ABOUT WASHING GREENS

I direct these comments to the kids: I'll be honest, washing lettuce greens is one of my least favorite jobs in the kitchen. I feel the same way about washing greens as you probably feel about cleaning your room. But you still have to do it, right? And you still have to wash greens if you want to eat salad, so you might as well learn to do it right. If your mom or dad wants you to wash greens, try this: Ask them to get you a salad spinner. That's one of those big round plastic jobs with a basket inside. You put the greens in the basket and pull or turn the handle. The basket spins very fast and the water flies off the greens. Your next best bet is a plain clean cotton dish towel. You just lay the lettuce leaves right on the towel and blot the water off with another dish towel or a paper towel. Make sure you dab the leaves instead of pushing down hard on them. That crushes the lettuce. And be thorough because wet lettuce tastes weird and waters down the dressing.

Height of Summer Salad with Honey-Lemon Vinaigrette

MAKES 4 SERVINGS

Freshly grated carrots and beets, slices of sun-drenched tomatoes, crisp greens—here we take those easily found garden staples and dress them with a tangy lemon vinaigrette. Everything is arranged simply on a serving platter, in colorful tidy rows, then drizzled with the dressing. This makes a pleasant, light gardener's lunch or accompaniment to all your summer fare.

3 medium fresh carrots, peeled and grated

3 to 4 medium just-picked beets, grated

2 medium-large ripe tomatoes, sliced about 1/4 inch thick

1 smallish head Boston or red or green leaf lettuce, or a mixture of summer greens, washed

VINAIGRETTE

1/4 cup olive oil

2 tablespoons lemon juice

1 teaspoon apple cider vinegar

1 1/2 teaspoons honey

1/2 teaspoon Dijon mustard

1 tablespoon chopped fresh basil

1 tablespoon coarsely chopped fresh lemon thyme or 1 teaspoon fresh thyme

salt and freshly ground pepper to taste

If you have the time while you're preparing the vegetables and dressing, refrigerate the plate you'll be serving this on. Once the vegetables are prepped, arrange them in rows—or in any other artful style—on your serving plate. Prepare the vinaigrette by whisking together all of the dressing ingredients in a small bowl. Spoon the dressing over everything, then serve right away.

❧ *Food for Thought* ❧
OTHER COLORS ON YOUR PLATE

Of course, there's an abundance of fresh summer vegetables that would be more than welcome on a salad plate such as this one. Off the top of my head, I can think of steamed and cooled asparagus tips, strips of roasted peppers, steamed and cooled green beans, and golden cherry tomatoes, to name just a few.

Green Leaf Salad with Grapes, Pecans, and Blue Cheese

MAKES 4 TO 5 SERVINGS

When we want to put a few special touches on our basic green salad, here's one way we do it. The kids don't like the blue cheese part—Karen and I do—but all of us love the way the seemingly disparate ingredients work so well together. The tahini dressing is best here; my second choice would be the Sweet Poppy Seed Dressing on page 45.

1 large or 2 smaller heads green or red leaf lettuce

1 large carrot, grated

1 small red onion, halved and thinly sliced

handful of seedless green or red grapes, halved

Our Favorite Tahini Dressing (page 44)

handful of Toasted Sweetened Pecans (page 12), coarsely chopped

a little crumbled blue cheese (optional)

Wash and dry the lettuce leaves. Tear the leaves into bite-size pieces and place them in a wide salad bowl. Scatter the grated carrot over the lettuce, followed by the sliced red onion and grapes. Once the salad has been served, pass the dressing, pecans, and blue cheese for garnish.

Our Easiest Cucumber Salad

MAKES 5 TO 6 SERVINGS

Unlike the rest of my family, I'm not a big cucumber fan. But if you jazz them up a little bit—like we do here—I'm game. One of the things I like about this dish is how brainless it is and how few ingredients it requires. This is a good way to wake up the sluggish flavor of winter cucumbers or bring out the best in your homegrown ones. We begin by salting the slices and letting them sit for up to an hour to release excess juice (but if we're in a hurry—and we often are at mealtime—we skip this step). You'll notice a lot more liquid from really fresh cukes and understand why market cukes often taste dry. Then the slices are tossed with a mustardy vinaigrette and served right away or refrigerated if you have the time. Throw in chopped fresh summer herbs if you have some handy, but don't worry if you don't.

5 large cucumbers, sliced about $^1/_8$ inch thick (see *Food for Thought*)

$^1/_4$ teaspoon salt

$2^1/_2$ tablespoons red wine vinegar

2 tablespoons olive oil

$1^1/_2$ teaspoons Dijon mustard

freshly ground pepper to taste

small handful of chopped fresh parsley, basil, or dill

Put the cucumbers in a large bowl and sprinkle the salt over them. Toss well, cover, and refrigerate for up to 1 hour. Drain the cukes, then put them back in the bowl. Whisk the remaining ingredients in a small bowl and pour the mixture over the cucumbers. Toss well and serve, or cover and refrigerate until serving.

❧ *Food for Thought* ❧
THE WAX ISSUE

Whether or not the FDA approves of it, I can't stand the heavy coat of wax that comes on most market cucumbers (among other vegetables). That's why, unless I'm feeling incredibly lazy, I generally peel them first. In the summer, of course, when you buy locally the wax really isn't an issue, so don't worry about peeling them. Summer or winter, I sometimes like this fancy touch: I peel the cukes with my lemon zester, a handheld tool with a series of small holes at one end. You drag the zester down the peel and it takes the skin off in threads, leaving little raised green rows on the surface. It makes for pretty slices, something like a bicycle tire with big treads.

Yogurt Cucumber Salad

MAKES 4 TO 6 SERVINGS

Here's a standard for any table, vegetarian or otherwise, just the right side dish with a plateful of curry, a summer sandwich, veggie burgers, or sliced drop-dead ripe summer tomatoes. You can build a pita sandwich with it, using fresh greens, sliced vegetables, and sprouts. With as few ingredients as this, it's important that you use the freshest ingredients available.

1 large cucumber, peeled

2 cups plain yogurt

small handful of chopped fresh parsley

small handful of chopped fresh mint

pinch of salt

freshly ground pepper

pinch of cayenne

fresh lemon juice

Quarter the cucumber lengthwise, then slice the sections into bite-size pieces. Mix them in a bowl with all the ingredients except lemon juice, seasoning to taste. Stir in several squeezes of fresh lemon juice to taste. Serve at once, or cover and refrigerate until serving.

Greek Tomato and Feta Salad, Coronis Style

꒜

MAKES 4 SERVINGS

Our friends, Susan and Lawrence Coronis, tell me that the credit for this recipe goes to Lawrence's dad, a Greek immigrant. The recipe is deceptively simple; it depends on perfectly red-ripe summer tomatoes, without which it isn't worth even the minimal effort involved. The tomatoes are sectioned and doused with equal parts of olive oil and balsamic vinegar, this being the one point of departure for Lawrence and his father; the elder has always preferred apple cider vinegar, which I have yet to try and can't imagine I'd like as well. Tomatoes and dressing are then tossed with pieces of feta, basil, oregano, and garlic. I like to layer everything in the bowl simply because I find the sight of the individual elements so appealing, then toss it at the table. But there's a good argument for tossing the salad 20 or 30 minutes ahead, so the dressing has time to saturate the tomatoes and cheese. Susan emphasizes that almost as important as the salad itself is good crusty bread to eat with it to help sop up the juice; any good crusty bread will do.

1 1/2 pounds small ripe tomatoes

1/4 cup olive oil

1/4 cup balsamic vinegar

1/4 pound feta cheese, broken into large chunks

small handful of chopped fresh basil

1 tablespoon chopped fresh oregano or 1 teaspoon dried

1 garlic clove, minced

salt and freshly ground pepper to taste

Core the tomatoes and cut them into large bite-size wedges. Put the wedges in a salad bowl and pour the olive oil and vinegar right over them. Add the remaining ingredients either in layers or simply toss them right in; see the headnote. Cover with plastic wrap and serve within 20 to 30 minutes, tossing right before serving if you haven't already done so.

Avocado Lover's Potato Salad

MAKES 6 SERVINGS

This is a real hit with my gang; if yours loves avocados, the same will be true for you. It's a summer salad for the most part, dependent on good ripe tomatoes and tiny new potatoes. I just boil the potatoes right in their skins, then toss them with an avocado dressing you can make while the potatoes are cooling. Fresh chunked tomatoes, chopped red onion, and parsley round out the salad. It is served next to sliced tomatoes and a few leaves of tender summer greens. Note that you must use the smaller, pebbly-skinned Haas avocados, not the larger ones.

1 pound very small red-skinned potatoes, scrubbed

AVOCADO DRESSING
1/2 very ripe avocado, peeled and coarsely chunked

4 tablespoons olive oil

2 tablespoons lemon juice or 1 tablespoon each lemon and lime juice

small handful of fresh cilantro leaves (optional)

a few drops of Tabasco or other hot sauce

1 small garlic clove, coarsely chopped

salt and freshly ground pepper

water (optional)

ASSEMBLY
1 1/2 ripe avocados, peeled and cut into bite-size chunks

3 large ripe tomatoes, cored

1 small red onion, finely chopped

small handful of fresh parsley

2 to 3 tablespoons chopped pickled jalapeños (optional)

fresh lettuce leaves

Put the potatoes in a saucepan with plenty of salted water to cover. Bring to a boil then boil the potatoes until the point when a paring knife pierces easily to the center; the exact timing will depend on the size of the potatoes. Drain the potatoes, run cold water over them, then spread them on a large plate and let cool.

While the potatoes are cooling, make the dressing: Put the half avocado, oil, lemon juice, cilantro, Tabasco, garlic, and a little salt and pepper into a blender. Puree the mixture to make a thick dressing with a texture like mayonnaise; thin with a little water if necessary. Season to taste with salt and pepper.

If you like, you can pull-scrape the skins off the potatoes; if they're very small potatoes, it isn't necessary. In any case, cut the potatoes into large bite-size pieces and toss them in a bowl with the avocado dressing. Add the chunked avocado, one of the tomatoes (cut into bite-size pieces), the onion, parsley, and jalapeños if you're using them and toss gently, seasoning the salad to taste with salt and pepper.

To assemble the salad, arrange the fresh lettuce leaves around the edge of a serving platter. Thinly slice the remaining tomatoes and arrange them in a circle, slightly overlapping the lettuce. Put the potato salad in the center. Drizzle the lettuce leaves with a little lemon juice and olive oil, dust with fresh pepper, and serve.

Fresh Pea and Potato Salad with Mustard-Herb Vinaigrette

MAKES 6 SERVINGS

I use only fresh peas in the summer, when I can buy them at a local farmstand. The rest of the time the quality at the supermarket is pretty poor, since the sweetness of fresh peas disappears so quickly, in which case frozen *petits pois* are the better choice. This excellent cold potato salad is one way we enjoy the season's best sweet tender peas and small new potatoes in concert. The mustardy vinaigrette adds some zing to the potatoes and ties their flavor beautifully to the fresh delicate peas. The yogurt helps to stretch the dressing and make it creamier, but if you're on a dairyless diet you can simply leave it out. Fresh herbs are essential for the dressing.

1 1/2 pounds small red-skinned potatoes

1 pound fresh peas (in the pod)

1 small red onion, finely chopped

1 inner celery rib, finely chopped

MUSTARD-HERB VINAIGRETTE
3 tablespoons olive oil

2 tablespoons apple cider vinegar

1¹/₂ tablespoons Dijon mustard

3 tablespoons plain yogurt

2 tablespoons chopped fresh dill

1 to 2 tablespoons chopped fresh parsley

1 or 2 teaspoons chopped fresh mint

salt and freshly ground pepper

*B*ring the potatoes to a boil in a large saucepan of salted water. Boil the potatoes for 10 to 15 minutes, until they can be pierced easily with the tip of a paring knife; the exact timing will depend on the size of the potatoes. Drain the potatoes, run cold water over them briefly, then spread them out on a large platter to cool. If you like, you can peel-scrape the skins off, but if the potatoes are very small it isn't really necessary.

While the potatoes are cooling, shell the peas and drop them into a saucepan of lightly salted boiling water. Boil for 6 to 8 minutes, until the peas are tender; drain and transfer to a large mixing bowl.

Cut the potatoes into bite-size chunks and add them to the peas; add the chopped onion and celery.

Make the vinaigrette. In a small mixing bowl, whisk all of the dressing ingredients, adding salt and pepper to taste. Add the dressing to the potatoes and peas and toss well. Season the salad to taste with salt and pepper, then cover and refrigerate at least 2 hours before serving.

Sticks and Stones

MAKES 4 TO 6 SERVINGS

This is our take on Waldorf salad. The sticks are pieces of celery and apples; the stones, chopped walnuts and grapes. Instead of the traditional mayo dressing, we use a light coating of oil, apple juice concentrate or cider, and honey, with some poppy seeds (really tiny stones) thrown in for fun. If your kids don't like celery, you can decrease or eliminate it, increasing the amount of apples proportionately. This is great with veggie burgers, sandwiches, or baked beans.

1 or 2 celery ribs

1 large Granny Smith or other tart crisp apple

1 cup green grapes, halved

¹/₂ cup chopped walnuts

DRESSING

1 tablespoon apple juice concentrate or 1¹/₂ tablespoons apple cider

1 tablespoon olive oil

1 tablespoon lemon juice

1 teaspoon honey

1 teaspoon poppy seeds

pinch of cinnamon (optional)

*C*ut the celery into 1-inch crosswise pieces, then cut lengthwise into fat matchsticks; transfer to a bowl. Peel the apple or not, then cut in half. Place the halves flat side down and slice straight down into ¹/₄-inch-thick sections. Working around the core, cut the sections into fat matchsticks also; they don't have to be perfect. Toss with the celery, adding the grapes and walnuts.

Prepare the dressing. Whisk the dressing ingredients in a small bowl. Pour them over the other ingredients and toss to coat. Cover and refrigerate if not serving right away.

Bow Tie Pasta and Veggie Salad with Tahini Vinaigrette

MAKES 12 SERVINGS

This is the big, master recipe you'll need to make a crowd-pleasing pasta salad for a party. First, it can be easily halved, so if this seems like way too much, don't worry. Now, about those vegetables, this is just a sampling of what we generally put in, not the final word on the subject. You can try this as is, or tailor it to your kids' likes and dislikes. Starting with the sure bets, everyone in my family goes for the carrots, celery, red onion, pickles, and broccoli. Beyond the basics, I find it's the garnishes that can really make this a hit with adults and kids alike.

1¹/₄ pounds bow tie pasta, cooked until tender, drained

olive oil

6 cups broccoli flowerets, steamed until tender

2 cups cauliflower, steamed until tender

salt

1 small summer squash, cut into ¹/₄-inch dice

2 large carrots, peeled and grated

1 large green bell pepper, chopped

2 small red onions, finely chopped

2 celery ribs, finely chopped

1 cup diced dill pickles

large handful of fresh basil leaves

large handful of fresh parsley

freshly ground black pepper to taste

10 to 15 cherry tomatoes, halved (optional)

TAHINI VINAIGRETTE

¹/₂ cup olive oil

¹/₂ cup flavorless vegetable or sunflower oil

¹/₂ cup red wine vinegar

2 tablespoons tahini

1 tablespoon Dijon mustard

1 garlic clove, minced (optional)

¹/₄ cup water

GARNISHES

Your choice: grated Parmesan cheese, crumbled feta cheese, grated
    Cheddar cheese, balsamic vinegar, chopped olives, chopped pickles,
    sunflower seeds

Cook and drain the pasta, tossing it with a little bit of olive oil so it doesn't stick together while you prepare the remaining ingredients. Steam the broccoli and cauliflower, letting them cool in a large, shallow bowl. Salt them lightly, then set aside. Toss the remaining salad ingredients with the pasta. Mix in the broccoli and cauliflower.

Make the vinaigrette. Whisk all of the dressing ingredients in a medium bowl and pour them over the salad, tossing to coat everything well. Taste and correct the seasoning as necessary; this likes lots of pepper and fresh herbs. Refrigerate the salad until ready to serve, tasting again. It might need a few splashes of vinegar or water, especially if it has been several hours since you've made it. Serve in a big pretty bowl with the garnishes on the side. If you're serving this as a whole-meal salad rather than a side dish, arrange an assortment of fresh crisp lettuce greens and a ring of thinly sliced tomatoes around the perimeter of each plate before serving.

Couscous-Tomato Salad with Sweet-and-Sour Dressing

MAKES 6 SERVINGS

Here is a welcome idea for tomato season: gorgeous, curry-golden couscous mixed with fresh tomatoes, vegetables, and a lemon-honey vinaigrette. It makes a good picnic dish or potluck contribution. Just be sure not to add the tomatoes until the very end, lest they end up looking and tasting rather drab.

$2^1/2$ tablespoons olive oil

2 teaspoons mild curry powder

$3/4$ cup instant couscous

$1^1/2$ cups water or vegetable broth

$1/8$ teaspoon salt

$1/3$ cup dried currants

2 tablespoons finely chopped red onion

1 small green bell pepper, finely chopped

2 tablespoons finely chopped parsley

2 tablespoons finely chopped fresh mint or $1/2$ teaspoon dried

3 tablespoons lemon juice

1 tablespoon honey

salt and freshly ground pepper

4 medium ripe tomatoes, cored and sliced, or 2 cups cherry tomatoes, halved

Heat $1^1/2$ tablespoons of the oil in a small saucepan and stir in the curry powder. Cook over medium-low heat for 30 seconds, stirring, then stir in the couscous, water, and salt. Bring to a boil, cover, then turn the heat to low. Cook for 1 minute, then remove from the heat and set aside for 5 minutes. Transfer the couscous to a bowl, fluffing it with a fork. Stir in the currants, onion, green pepper, parsley, and mint. Cool.

Whisk the lemon juice and honey in a small bowl and pour it over the couscous. Taste the couscous, tossing in the remaining tablespoon of oil. Add salt and pepper to taste. Cover and refrigerate until serving.

Just before serving, add the tomatoes and toss again.

Couscous Salad with Corn, Tomatoes, and Avocado

~

MAKES 6 SERVINGS

We depend on instant couscous a lot in the summer because it can be prepared so quickly without heating up the kitchen. Here we combine it with fresh scraped corn, juicy summer tomatoes, and chunks of ripe avocado to make a popular summer salad. Great with sandwiches, grilled vegetables, or steamed and buttered green beans, this also makes a filling full-meal salad for up to 4 adults.

1^1/$_4$ cups instant couscous, regular or whole wheat

1^2/$_3$ cups water

^{1}/$_4$ teaspoon salt

4 tablespoons olive oil

1 medium onion, finely chopped

3 ears of corn, shaved (about 2^1/$_2$ cups kernels)

1^1/$_2$ teaspoons mild chili powder

1^1/$_2$ teaspoons ground cumin

2 tablespoons red wine vinegar

juice of ^{1}/$_2$ lemon

1 small green bell pepper, chopped

2 to 3 tablespoons chopped fresh parsley or cilantro

2 large ripe tomatoes, halved, seeded, and coarsely chopped

1 ripe avocado, peeled and chunked

Put the couscous in a large, heavy skillet and toast over medium-high heat, stirring, for 3 to 4 minutes. While the couscous toast, bring the water to a near boil in a small saucepan and stir in the salt. Carefully (the steam will rise quickly) pour the water over the couscous. Stir quickly, then cover and remove from the heat. Set aside for 10 minutes undisturbed, then fluff with a fork.

Heat 2 tablespoons of the oil in a large nonreactive skillet. Add the onion and sauté over medium heat for 7 to 10 minutes, stirring often. Stir in the corn and add enough water to cover it. Bring to a boil, salting the corn lightly, and cover. Gently boil the corn for about 5 to 7 minutes, until tender. Remove the lid and boil off the liquid. When the pan is almost dry, stir in the spices. Continue to cook the corn, stirring, for 1 minute more. Scrape the corn mixture into a small bowl and cool to room temperature. Meanwhile, uncover the couscous and fluff it with a fork.

When the corn is cool, stir in the vinegar, lemon juice, and remaining 2 tablespoons of oil. Pour over the couscous and toss well. Mix in the green pepper and parsley. Cover and refrigerate, or serve at room temperature, tossing the tomatoes in now. (Wait on the tomatoes if you're refrigerating the salad.) Pass the avocado separately when you serve the salad.

Barley, Black Bean, and Pepper Salad

MAKES 4 TO 6 SERVINGS

Barley makes an excellent foundation for a grain salad, but it must be cooked carefully lest you wind up with mush (see *Food for Thought*, page 180). Here we toss the barley with black beans, red onion, fresh cilantro, and a few other good things to give it a slight southwestern or south-of-the-border feel, accented by a garlicky lime-and-jalapeño vinaigrette. If tomatoes are fresh and in season, chunk some up and toss them in at the last moment before serving. For the sake of convenience I've used canned black beans here, but by all means use your own cooked dried beans if you are so inclined; fresh is always better. This is substantial enough to make a whole-meal salad, but can also be a great addition to a summer salad plate.

1 cup barley

2 cups water

$^{1}/_{4}$ teaspoon salt

1 small red onion, finely chopped

1 red bell pepper, finely chopped

2 tablespoons chopped fresh parsley

2 tablespoons chopped fresh cilantro

1 19-ounce can black beans, drained and well rinsed (about $1^{1}/_{2}$ cups)

DRESSING

$^{1}/_{4}$ cup olive oil

1 tablespoon lime juice

1 tablespoon lemon juice

1 tablespoon red wine vinegar

1 teaspoon tomato paste

1 garlic clove, minced

2 tablespoons minced pickled jalapeño peppers

$1/4$ teaspoon paprika

$1/2$ teaspoon each cumin and ground coriander (optional)

salt and freshly ground pepper

At least 2 hours ahead, cook the barley. Combine the barley, water, and salt in a medium saucepan. Bring to a boil, reduce the heat, and cover. Cook the barley over very low heat for about 35 minutes, until the water is absorbed. Remove from the heat and let it sit undisturbed for 15 to 20 minutes, then fluff the barley with a fork to keep it from clumping. Set aside to cool.

While the barley cools, put the onion, pepper, and herbs in a mixing bowl with the black beans. Set aside.

Make the dressing by whisking together the oil, lime and lemon juices, vinegar, tomato paste, garlic, jalapeños, and paprika. Put the cumin and coriander in a small skillet and dry-roast them over medium heat, stirring, for about $1^{1}/2$ minutes, just until they start to smoke. Whisk them into the dressing.

Add the barley to the bowl with the vegetables and herbs. Toss well, then add the dressing and toss again until everything is well coated. Season the salad with salt and pepper to taste. Serve at once, or cover and refrigerate until serving.

Great Northern Bean and Broccoli Salad

MAKES 6 SERVINGS

This is a family favorite with pizza and pasta dishes. When we serve it with either, they tend to become one (the salad spooned on top of the pizza or tossed with the pasta), delicious proof of how compatible this salad is with other foods. I don't want to sound elitist about my beans, but I think the Great Northerns—big white beans—are a lot of what makes this salad so good; small white beans will do, but the texture of the Great Northerns is superior here, somewhat softer and more tender. They seem to soak up more of the vinaigrette. Since the beans can take on a lot of *oomph*, I like to add an extra teaspoon of mustard to the dressing when I make this. My kids love broccoli; the original version didn't have any, but since I've started adding it, we never have any leftovers.

$^1/_2$ pound dried Great Northern beans, cooked

3 cups broccoli flowerets, steamed until barely tender

1 medium green bell pepper

1 small red onion, finely chopped

1 medium grated carrot

$^1/_4$ cup finely chopped parsley

1 recipe Tomato Balsamic Vinaigrette (page 44)

grated Parmesan or Romano cheese or croutons, for garnish (optional)

*P*ick over and rinse the beans. Put them in a pot with plenty of water. Bring to a boil, boil for 2 minutes, then remove from the heat. Cover and set aside for 1 to 2 hours. Drain the beans, cover with more water, and bring to a boil. Simmer the beans, partially covered, for 35 to 45 minutes, until just tender. Drain and set aside, reserving the water for soup stock.

Combine the beans, broccoli, vegetables, parsley, and vinaigrette in a large bowl; toss to mix. Let the salad sit at room temperature up to 30 minutes before serving, but refrigerate if it will be much longer. If you like, pass a small bowl of grated Parmesan or Romano cheese or croutons for garnish.

Lentil and Feta Cheese Salad

MAKES 6 SERVINGS

You see variations of this salad appearing in cookbooks a lot these days, for one good reason: the combination is excellent. One good recipe in *The Greens Cookbook* (Bantam, 1987) by that super-good cook Deborah Madison uses squares of roasted peppers, which is a great trick if you've the time and inclination. She also uses those expensive small French lentils, but all I've ever used are your basic lentils and nobody's ever held it against me. One of the keys here is lots of fresh herbs—think summer picnic salad—but don't let that stop you from whipping this up in January; instead of fresh mint, I've dumped the contents of a mint tea bag (dried mint) into it and the result was fine, if not exactly summery.

$^1/_2$ pound lentils

1 bay leaf

1 celery rib, finely chopped

1 small green or red bell pepper, finely chopped

4 scallions, whites only, thinly sliced

1 ripe tomato, cored, seeded, and diced

1 small carrot, grated

small handful of fresh parsley, minced

small handful of fresh basil, minced, or 2 teaspoons dried

small handful of fresh mint, minced, or 1 to 2 teaspoons dried

DRESSING AND GARNISH

5 tablespoons olive oil

2 tablespoons red wine vinegar

2 tablespoons lemon juice

1 teaspoon Dijon mustard

1 or 2 garlic cloves, minced

1 teaspoon honey

salt and freshly ground pepper

1 cup crumbled feta cheese or other mild cheese, cubed

Rinse the lentils and place them in a medium saucepan with the bay leaf and about 3 to 4 inches of lightly salted water. Bring to a boil, then boil gently for about 22 to 25 minutes, removing the lentils from the heat just when they are tender but still a bit firm (see *Food for Thought*). Drain in a colander, then rinse briefly with cold water. Drain again for a minute or so, then transfer the beans to a good-size mixing bowl. Discard the bay leaf. Toss the lentils with the vegetables and herbs and set aside while you make the dressing.

Whisk the dressing ingredients in a small bowl, adding salt and plenty of black pepper to taste. Scrape it over the lentils and toss well. Cover and refrigerate the salad for at least 1 hour before serving. Right before serving, taste and add more olive oil to lubricate everything and perhaps a splash or so of vinegar. Pass the cheese separately when you serve the salad.

❧ *Food for Thought* ❧
WATCHING OUT FOR LENTIL MUSH

Of all the beans we commonly cook with, lentils demand the most precise cooking: Within a matter of minutes they can go from al dente—perfect for a salad like this—to *hasta la vista,* mush city. You've got to watch them like a hawk, setting your timer for 22 or 23 minutes (once they reach a boil), checking them every couple of minutes beyond that point. The trick is to taste 2 or 3 spoonfuls before you determine that they're done, and don't be surprised if the results aren't uniform. If most of them are just tender, with a few acceptable chewy ones here and there, get them off the heat at once. Drain and rinse. If you wait until there are no chewy ones, many will be overcooked.

Fresh Cranberry-Ginger Vinaigrette

MAKES ABOUT 1 CUP

Here's a New England–style original, a sweet-tart salad dressing made from fresh cranberries and maple syrup. It's an excellent choice when you'd like to add a fruity accent to your salads, and the deep, near plum color—especially against bright salad greens—makes it especially appropriate for festive, preholiday meals. The cranberries give this a slightly grainier texture than you may be used to, but it isn't the least bit offensive or obtrusive. Notice that you can use apple or orange juice to give the dressing a subtle shift of emphasis. It was with the orange that Karen and I first tasted the inspiration for this dressing at a fine dinner prepared by the chefs-in-training of the New England Culinary Institute in Essex Junction, Vermont. This would be the perfect dressing for a salad of cold sliced cooked beets. Shake or whisk well just before serving.

$^1/_3$ cup fresh cranberries

$^1/_4$ cup pure unfiltered apple juice or orange juice

3 tablespoons balsamic vinegar

2 tablespoons olive oil

$1^1/_2$ tablespoons maple syrup

1 teaspoon grated fresh ginger

Put all of the ingredients in a blender and process until liquefied; the mixture will, however, retain flecks of cranberries. That's fine and unavoidable. Transfer to a serving container. Cover and refrigerate until serving.

Our Favorite Tahini Dressing

つつ

MAKES ABOUT 1 1/4 CUPS

Tahini makes an excellent smooth and creamy salad dressing. This one has been in the family for at least ten years; you might call it the house dressing. Sometimes we won't make it for a while, but we always go back to it because it is just so dependably good and popular. If I had a dime for every person who asked for the recipe, I'd be a rich man. The only point of controversy is the garlic; some of us—myself included—love it; some would rather leave it out. Though this is primarily a salad dressing, there seems to be no end to the things my kids pour this over, virtually anything we eat with it at the same meal—crackers, pasta, steamed broccoli, you name it. This will thicken in the fridge if you have any leftovers; simply thin it with a little water.

1/2 cup tahini

1/2 cup water

1/4 cup red wine vinegar

1 tablespoon flavorless sunflower or olive oil

2 teaspoons Dijon mustard

1 teaspoon tamari

1 or 2 garlic cloves, minced (optional)

1/3 cup chopped fresh parsley

freshly ground pepper to taste

Put all of the ingredients in a medium bowl and whisk to blend; the correct consistency of the dressing is like heavy cream, perhaps a tad thicker. You can thin it, if necessary, with a little water or thicken it with an additional spoonful or two of tahini. Cover and refrigerate until using.

Tomato Balsamic Vinaigrette

つつ

MAKES ABOUT 1/2 CUP

Balsamic vinegar used to be just for the very hip, but now it's become almost a standard item in the American pantry. And why not, since kids like it too; the natural sweetness of balsamic vinegar appeals to them. Here's a salad dressing most of my kids enjoy very much. Not only do we use it on salads, but it is the spark in the Great Northern bean salad we love with pizza (page 40). It works beautifully with the chopped tomato; fresh is best, but if I have a few tablespoons of canned crushed tomatoes in the fridge that need to be used up, I'll use that instead.

$^1/_3$ cup olive oil

2 tablespoons balsamic vinegar

1 tablespoon red wine vinegar

1 teaspoon Dijon mustard

1 garlic clove, minced

2 to 3 tablespoons finely chopped fresh tomato or canned crushed tomato

2 teaspoons chopped fresh basil or $^1/_2$ teaspoon dried

pinch or two of salt

freshly ground pepper

Whisk everything together in a mixing bowl. Taste and adjust the seasoning. Refrigerate if not using soon.

Sweet Poppy Seed Dressing

MAKES ABOUT 1 $^1/_4$ CUPS

This quick, zippy-sweet blender dressing has become one of our most popular in recent years. It's also proven to be one of the most versatile. In addition to using it with tossed salads, it often takes the place of mayonnaise dressing in coleslaw and potato salads, thus cutting out much of the calories and fat. It has just the right amount of sweetening, enough to please the kids but not so much that it turns off the adults. Try it. This recipe is adapted from one in a very fine book titled *May All Be Fed* by John Robbins (William Morrow, 1992).

$^1/_4$ cup olive oil

$^1/_4$ cup flavorless vegetable or sunflower oil

$^1/_4$ cup coarsely chopped red onion

$^1/_4$ cup red wine vinegar

2 tablespoons maple syrup or honey

1 teaspoon Dijon mustard

2 tablespoons poppy seeds

*P*ut everything except the poppy seeds in a blender and blend for about 10 seconds on high speed until smooth. Pour into a serving bowl and whisk in the seeds. This keeps 2 to 3 days in the refrigerator.

Good Coleslaw

MAKES 6 TO 8 SERVINGS

We make coleslaw a couple of different ways, with and without dairy products. Without, we use the basic formula here, but instead of the yogurt and mayo we dress it with Sweet Poppy Seed Dressing (page 45). Start with about one-third cup of dressing, toss well, then add more to taste. The version below is rather more traditional, made with a good portion of yogurt to replace some of the mayonnaise. For more color, use up to 2 cups red cabbage if you have some on hand.

7 to 8 cups thinly sliced cabbage

1 large carrot, peeled and grated

2 tablespoons minced fresh parsley

1 to 2 tablespoons minced red onion

$^1/_2$ to $^2/_3$ cup cold plain yogurt

$^1/_2$ cup mayonnaise

1 teaspoon Dijon mustard

1 teaspoon sugar

$^1/_2$ teaspoon celery seed

$^1/_4$ teaspoon salt, plus more to taste

freshly ground pepper

*M*ix the cabbage, carrot, parsley, and onion in a large bowl. In another bowl, whisk the yogurt, mayonnaise, mustard, sugar, celery seed, and salt. Pour the dressing over the cabbage and toss thoroughly. Add additional salt and pepper, to taste. Cover and refrigerate if not serving right away.

Soups

Soup is a gift. It warms us to the core, welcomes all manner of leftovers, forgives both the heavy and light hand. And it stretches the cook's budget. How many other dishes can you say that about? Soup is a puttering affair: You add, taste, season, stir, and smell. Repeat. Good soup makers know how to putter. They don't rush. They know that soup things need to mingle and mellow before the flavor's really there.

Vegetarian soups have every bit as much flavor and character as meat and fish soups, they just have a different sort of character and flavor, derived from the plant kingdom. Aromatic vegetables—onions, leeks, celery, sometimes garlic—provide the foundation flavors of good vegetarian soups. Grains and pastas add body. Beans, greens, root vegetables, and purees add texture and color. Fresh or dried herbs provide highlight and nuance.

To make good meatless soups, you have to think like a soup maker. Soup makers are always on the lookout for new ways to add flavor to soups. When they put a bowl of leftover mashed potatoes in the fridge, they automatically think how well that would thicken the next day's soup, made with the water the spuds were cooked in. Soup makers put aside likely soup-bound leftovers in one corner of the fridge and then use them. Not surprisingly, most of the good soup makers I know are bread bakers; homemade soup and bread is the best of home-cooked meals.

Here is a collection of soups I think your family will enjoy as much as we have. Most are hearty, meant to be eaten in the cold weather months, but there are a few lighter ones suitable for summer. If you have young children, I've noticed that one of the quickest turnoffs for most little kids is vegetables that are cut too big; just the sight of them can scare a youngster away. Even if they can't express it, kids know that they can choke on big chunks of vegetables. So, especially if you have small children, take the time to cut everything reasonably small. As the kids get older this is less of a concern, but monster veggies are always in bad taste, if you ask me.

Vegetable Stock

MAKES ABOUT 2 QUARTS

When it comes to meatless stocks, vegetarians face what I like to call The Long-Standing Vegetarian Soup Conundrum: how to make deep-flavored soup stocks without the benefit of beast or fowl. A good stock can make or break a soup, add life to risotto, or perk up your stews.

I do use commercial bouillon cubes, but my first choice is always a home-made stock. Homemade tastes better than anything canned, cubed, or powdered. And besides, I occasionally like the puttering activity of making stock.

Most cooks agree upon a basic foundation of flavor-enriching vegetables and herbs for a good vegetarian stock. They are onions, leeks, garlic, celery, carrots, parsley, and bay leaves. The consensus, however, ends about there with the question of whether or not the vegetables require a preliminary sweating in oil or butter. Some say it isn't necessary: Just throw everything into a pot of water and bring to a boil. In my own experiments I've found that gently sautéing the onions and leeks in a little butter or oil helps to bring out their natural sweetness, which makes the stock more flavorful. The object is to soften the vegetables at this point—not brown them—over relatively low heat so they release moisture gradually. Browning will make the stock quite dark, with a caramelized taste. That's okay for, say, a French onion soup or winter squash bisque. But it would overpower a delicate soup.

Anyway, here is my basic meatless stock recipe, followed by a few suggestions for other vegetables not included in the basic recipe.

$1^{1}/_{2}$ tablespoons olive oil

2 medium leeks

1 large onion, chopped

3 bruised garlic cloves, with the skins on

10 cups cold water

2 celery ribs, chopped

2 large carrots, peeled and chopped

handful of fresh parsley, stems included

1 large or 2 small bay leaves

salt

*H*eat the oil in a large soup pot. Cut the leaves off the leeks where the green turns to pale, then snip off the root. Halve the leeks lengthwise, almost all the way to the root end, then fan the leeks and thoroughly rinse them under running water. Chop coarsely, then stir them into the pot with the onion. Sauté over medium heat for about 10 minutes, stirring often. Stir in the garlic and sauté another minute.

Add the remaining ingredients to the pot and simmer, uncovered, for about 30 to 45 minutes. It should reduce by one-third to about half. Salt the stock incrementally as you go. Use just enough to get an idea how the flavor is developing, but always undersalt as reduced stocks can turn quite salty. Strain, cool, then refrigerate the stock. It will keep about 2 days in the fridge (once cold, the fat can be skimmed if you like) or for several months in the freezer (divide between small leftover containers).

Quick Mushroom Broth

MAKES ABOUT 5 CUPS

Dried mushrooms make it possible to create a quick, deeply flavored broth suitable for vegetable soups and vegetarian stews. It also makes a delicious broth for cooking grains; I use this to make risotto—which almost always depends on meat or chicken stock—and the complex, woodsy flavor makes it the perfect liquid for cooking wild rice. If you have a personal favorite wild mushroom, by all means use it; I generally buy little bags, which weigh almost an ounce, labeled "exotic blend," a combination of porcini, cèpes, oysters, and shiitakes. They aren't cheap, but you can wring a lot of flavor out of them, so I feel like the cost is justifiable. Even if I'm not planning to make anything else with this broth, I like to keep it on hand in the winter when I crave something hot to drink—namely coffee—but I want to avoid the caffeine, which makes me a little bit crazy.

1 tablespoon olive oil

1 medium onion, chopped

1 celery rib, chopped

❧ *Food for Thought* ❧
STOCK OPTIONS

No stock in my book would be complete without the addition of potato peels—or just plain potatoes, peels and all. Some stock pundits hold that only the peels are suitable, on the grounds that whole potato chunks will break down, release their starch, and make the stock somewhat cloudy, all of which is true. On the other hand, how often does it really matter? I could perhaps think of one or two times when a potato-clouded broth might be a cause for concern (like when I have Julia over for dinner). But I can think of many more when the extra flavor and body would be perfectly wonderful. Try it both ways and see which you prefer.

In addition, here are a few other ingredients you might add to the stock as it starts to simmer:

Summer squashes—These have a subdued flavor, but they're especially welcome in summer stocks when they're taking over the garden.

Winter squashes—Use mainly the stringy seeds and not the flesh, which falls apart and tends to dominate the broth.

Tomatoes—Ripe, peak-of-summer tomatoes add color, flavor, and acidity to the broth. Appropriate for many summer soups.

Fennel—Bold and predominant. Use primarily for a fennel soup or some seafood stews. Use the stalk and outer leaves.

Mushrooms—Dried, you can toss in a few as the soup simmers. They add a deep, woodsy note. Fresh ones should be sliced and added with the garlic; the result is more tame than with dried, but still clear.

Eggplant—Adds body and its own distinctive flavor to the broth. Add cubes of it just before the garlic and sauté-stew 3 to 4 minutes, covered, before adding the water.

Stay away from *cabbage, cauliflower,* and *brussels sprouts,* as they give broth an off flavor and aroma.

As for herbs, fresh are best, but as with everything that goes into stock, no one flavor should predominate. It's hard to use too much parsley. A little chervil, oregano, thyme, and basil are all excellent. Dried herbs can also be used, though in moderation.

6 cups water

1 ounce dried mushrooms

1 small carrot, grated

1 teaspoon soy sauce or tamari

small handful of fresh parsley, including the stems

1 bay leaf

1 vegetable bouillon cube (optional)

salt to taste

*H*eat the olive oil in a medium saucepan. Stir in the onion and celery and sauté over medium heat, stirring occasionally, for 7 minutes. Add the remaining ingredients and bring the stock to a simmer. Simmer gently, covered, for 10 minutes, then remove from the heat and let stand for 30 minutes. Strain the stock, pushing as much liquid as possible out of the vegetables. Cool, then store the stock in the refrigerator in a covered container if you aren't using it right away. It will last about 3 days in the fridge, but it may be frozen for a month or more.

Noodles and Broth

MAKES 3 TO 4 SERVINGS

This is our simplest soup, the one we make when we don't really want to make soup. The idea is to fix a quick stock with whatever is on hand—potatoes, celery, carrots, a bay leaf—cut into chunks and thrown in a saucepan with some water. No need to dice everything up just right. The stock is simmered for about 20 minutes, strained, then strengthened with a little tamari and part of a bouillon cube if you like. Once the broth is ready, you just cook some pasta right in it and serve. This is really wonderful if you or someone you love isn't feeling well; it's a real soul soother.

scrubbed potatoes

celery

a small onion

carrots

a little cabbage

a little fresh parsley

1 bay leaf

salt

1 teaspoon tamari

1 unsalted vegetable bouillon cube (optional)

2 to 2¹/₂ cups short pasta of your choice

*P*ut 6 cups of water in a medium saucepan and add 6 to 7 cups assorted roughly chunked vegetables from the list above; throw in any little odds and ends of vegetables from your fridge that you might have around. Add the parsley, if you have some, and a bay leaf. Add a bit of salt to the pot and bring to a boil. Reduce the heat slightly and simmer the stock, partially covered, for about 20 to 25 minutes. Strain the broth—I just lift out the vegetables with a big skimmer—and add the tamari to the broth. If you like the flavor as it is, fine; if you'd like it a bit stronger, add part or all of the bouillon cube.

Add the pasta to the broth and boil gently until the pasta is tender. Serve hot.

❧ *Food for Thought* ❧
AND WHEN YOU'RE REALLY IN A RUSH . . .

. . . forget the vegetables entirely and just use the bouillon cube. Yes, this barely even deserves to be called cooking, but when you're really pressed to get something on the table or there's hardly anything in the larder but a lonely bouillon cube, it works. We call these bouillon noodles, and we've served them more than I care to confess. A little grated Parmesan cheese will jazz them up if there's some handy.

Peasant Soup

MAKES 8 TO 10 SERVINGS

People often ask me: *How do you come up with your recipes?* Here's a good example. Karen and I had eaten an uninspired version of peasant soup at a local restaurant. Still, we liked the idea of a peasant soup, so we started a lively dialogue about how you'd make a soup if you really were a peasant. Peasant fare, we reasoned, must rely heavily on the basic larder and be absent of any pretense and finesse. A peasant wouldn't lose any sleep over seasonings; neither would we. Just the basics. And a little soy sauce (these were Asian peasants). So instead of the usual presautéing of onions and such, Karen just threw every-thing into the pot and started simmering. I was doubtful. Wouldn't the soup have a raw onion taste? (It didn't.) Would the broth be wimpy, like the disap-pointing version I mentioned above? (It wasn't.) And, more importantly, would the kids go for it? (They did.)

12 cups water

$^1/_3$ cup lentils

2 cups finely chopped onions

4 medium carrots, peeled and thinly sliced

2 cups green beans, cut into $^3/_4$-inch pieces

4 cups (about $^1/_4$ head) finely shredded cabbage

10 smallish all-purpose potatoes, peeled

1 teaspoon salt, plus more to taste

2 tablespoons tomato paste

1 tablespoon dried basil

1 tablespoon tamari or soy sauce

freshly ground black pepper

*P*ut 4 cups of the water, the lentils, and chopped onions in a large soup pot and bring to a boil. Gently boil for 10 minutes, covered. Add the remaining 8 cups of water, the carrots, green beans, and cabbage. Grate 2 of the potatoes and add them to the soup with 1 teaspoon of salt. Cover and cook the soup at a gentle boil for 15 minutes. While the soup cooks, cut the remaining 8 potatoes into bite-size cubes.

Add the rest of the potatoes to the soup. Stir in the tomato paste, basil, tamari, and black pepper to taste. Simmer the soup until the potatoes are ten-der, seasoning to taste with more salt if necessary. Serve hot.

❧ *Food for Thought* ❧
PEASANT SOUP DU JOUR

I love this soup just as it appears here, but it would be silly to be overly protective and dogmatic about it: Peasant soup is, by its very nature, utilitarian. So don't be afraid to scour the fridge for leftovers that could find a happy home in a peasant soup. You may not end up with the exact same soup, but you'll still end up with good soup. There's a knack to using leftovers and tidbits in a soup like this, acceptable limits, if you will. Puttering with soup is like raising a child: You want to enhance and guide but preserve its own special nature. I wouldn't, for instance, add a lot of crushed tomatoes or tomato puree; that would give the soup a decidedly tomato base, something that's all too common with soup. Part of the charm of this soup is that the tomato paste builds flavor into the broth without being overt. Your best choice is little bowls of leftover cooked greens, or a few fresh greens you might chop and add to the simmering soup. Some leftover ratatouille would work, a bit of chopped summer or winter squash, a parsnip, or odd piece of celery. Or a scoopful of cooked grain or leftover noodles. Keep it simple and subtle.

Mushroom Barley Soup

MAKES 6 SERVINGS

Here is a mushroom soup the kids will eat since most of the mushrooms go incognito; some of them are sliced and sautéed separately so they can be added to individual portions if your kids don't want them. The soup is delicious, the broth light, fragrant, and restorative, just the sort of thing you need when you're feeling under the weather. You needn't make a separate stock either, because with a full pound of fresh mushrooms in the soup, there's plenty of good flavor here already. If your kids have never tried barley before, this is a good introduction; it softens right up in the hot broth, like the noodles in alphabet soup.

1 cup pearl barley

10 cups water

1 pound mushrooms

3 tablespoons olive oil

1 cup chopped onions

^{1}/2 cup finely chopped celery

2 bay leaves

2 garlic cloves, minced

^{1}/2 teaspoon salt

2 tablespoons tamari

freshly ground black pepper to taste

^{1}/4 cup chopped fresh parsley

^{1}/8 teaspoon cayenne (optional)

Cook the barley: Combine the barley and 2 cups of the water in a small saucepan and bring to a boil. Lower the heat, cover, and cook over very low heat for 30 to 35 minutes, until all of the water is absorbed. Remove from the heat and set aside.

Put about ^{3}/4 pound of the mushrooms in the bowl of a food processor and finely chop them, scraping down the sides if necessary. Reserve. Thinly slice the remaining mushrooms and set them aside.

Heat 2 tablespoons of the olive oil in a large soup pot. Stir in the onions, celery, and bay leaves and sauté over medium-high heat for about 7 minutes, until the onions are translucent. Stir in the garlic, then add the finely chopped mushrooms. Sauté the mushrooms for 2 to 3 minutes, stirring often, then add the remaining 8 cups of water, salt, tamari, black pepper, and reserved barley. Bring the soup to a near boil, then simmer for 10 minutes.

While the soup simmers, heat the remaining 1 tablespoon of oil in a medium skillet. Stir in the sliced mushrooms and sauté them for 3 to 4 minutes, until they're nicely browned. Stir the mushrooms, parsley, and cayenne into the soup about 5 minutes before serving. Or stir the mushrooms into individual portions if your kids don't eat them.

❧ *Food for Thought* ❧
KIDS AND KNIVES

Conventional wisdom has it that kids and knives don't mix. Just mention the two in the same breath and parents grimace: Scenes of a mad dash to the emergency room flash across the mind.

While I don't recommend giving very young children access to sharp knives—that would be just plain foolish—I think many older kids are unduly denied the pleasures and benefits to be had from early knifesmanship because of exaggerated parental fears. From a kid's point of view, there's a lot to be gained from using a kitchen knife, things like hand-eye coordination, self-confidence, and the sheer bliss of pitching in and entering that often mysterious and closeted world of Things Only Adults Do.

My children have grown up in the kitchen, so all of them had an early interest in knives, an interest I tried to engage from the very start. Even when they were very young, I would let them cut vegetables with a sharp knife, my own hands guiding theirs. Gradually, very gradually, I let them graduate up to easy basics like slicing celery on their own; celery is good about sitting still, and being so long it lets you keep your cutting hand well back from your guiding hand. Today, my sixteen-year-old son, Ben, can handle almost any cutting job.

Of course, you're the best judge of whether your child is ready to use kitchen knives. Because children develop at their own pace, there is really no right time to begin using knives, nor is it something I would ever suggest pushing a child into if he showed no interest. A lot of kids never even pick up, let alone learn to use, a kitchen knife until they graduate from college (and then they learn pretty quickly).

Most adult knives are too big for kids, so if your children want to use knives make sure to buy one or two that fit comfortably into a small hand. Steak knives are good for beginners. Be aware that they will need your guidance and vigilance when they are cutting. Vigilance means keeping a watchful eye, not hovering over like a nervous Nellie, a habit that's bound to backfire. Demonstrate some of the basics and explain to them that vegetables should always rest on one of their own flat surfaces when you cut them; demonstrate how to make a flat surface on a potato. Also show them how to curl their fingers under when they cut so they don't expose their fingertips to the blade.

Feeling comfortable with kitchen knives is an essential part of becoming a confident, contributing cook. Help your kids to respect knives and use them efficiently and safely, and you'll be teaching them a valuable lesson.

Cream of Fresh Tomato Soup

MAKES 4 TO 5 SERVINGS

There's no cream, or even milk, in this creamy fresh tomato soup (you can use canned tomatoes in the winter months, if you like). The creaminess comes from cooking potatoes with the broth, then pureeing the soup before serving; the starch in the potatoes gives it a silken texture. This soup produces its own flavorful stock as it cooks, though I like to add a vegetable bouillon cube (or use vegetable stock) for depth of flavor; if you're feeding this to someone who is accustomed to the flavor of chicken broth in a soup like this, you should consider that option. If you're serving this in summer, fresh basil or other chopped fresh herbs make a fragrant garnish. A tablespoon of fresh shaved corn is good, too, or Roasted Pepper and Sweet Corn Relish (page 190), or plain yogurt. Herb croutons are also excellent. My kids like this soup very much.

2 tablespoons olive oil or unsalted butter

1 medium onion, finely chopped

2 celery ribs, finely chopped

1 garlic clove, minced (optional)

$^1/_2$ teaspoon paprika

3 cups water or Vegetable Stock (page 48)

2 medium all-purpose potatoes, peeled and diced

1 vegetable bouillon cube (optional)

1 small bay leaf

salt

4 medium-large ripe tomatoes, peeled, cored, seeded, and coarsely chopped, *or* 1 28-ounce can crushed tomatoes in puree

freshly ground pepper to taste

juice of $^1/_2$ lemon

freshly chopped basil, dill, or oregano, for garnish

grated Parmesan or Romano cheese, for garnish (optional)

Heat the oil or butter in a medium nonreactive soup pot. Add the onion and celery and sauté, stirring often, for 7 to 8 minutes, until the onion is translucent. Stir in the garlic right at the end if you are using it and the paprika. Sauté another 30 seconds, then add the water, potatoes, bouillon cube, bay leaf, and salt to taste. Bring the soup to a boil, cover, then simmer for about 15 minutes, until the potatoes are tender. Add the tomatoes and pepper, cover, and simmer for about 7 or 8 minutes more. Remove the soup from the heat and let stand for 15 minutes.

Working in 2 batches if you have a smaller processor, process the soup to a smooth puree. Reheat the soup, stirring in the lemon juice. Taste the soup and correct the seasoning if necessary. Serve hot, sprinkling each portion with the chopped herbs. Pass the cheese separately if you're using it.

VARIATION: To make a Curried Cream of Fresh Tomato Soup, add 1 teaspoon of mild curry powder to the sauté when you add the paprika.

Tomato-Dill Soup

MAKES 10 SERVINGS

This, our favorite quick tomato soup recipe, makes a lot of soup, perhaps more than you think you might need. But there's logic to the largesse. First, we wanted to use up the entire 2 cans of tomatoes that you have to open; that requires a certain amount of water to give the soup the right flavor and texture. Then there are the leftovers; there are more ways to recycle this soup than you can shake a stick at. You can simply freeze half for later. Or you can serve it on successive days with hot pasta and Parmesan cheese, with cooked brown rice or barley stirred in, for simmering Cornmeal Dumplings (page 163), or transformed into a hearty bean soup with several cups' worth of cooked white beans or chickpeas. I like a soup with stretch and this is one of the most versatile in that department. The balance of canned tomatoes is important here: one each of puree and crushed. All of one or the other throws off the textural balance. Like many dishes made with tomatoes, this benefits from some sitting time off the heat if you can swing it, which helps mellow the sharp edge of the tomatoes and allows the flavors to mingle.

3 tablespoons olive oil

2 cups finely chopped onions

4 celery ribs, finely chopped

3 quarts water

1 vegetable bouillon cube, salted or unsalted

1 28-ounce can tomato puree

1 28-ounce can crushed tomatoes in puree

1 tablespoon soy sauce or tamari

1 tablespoon balsamic or red wine vinegar

4 teaspoons dried dill weed

1 teaspoon salt, plus more to taste

freshly ground pepper to taste

*H*eat the oil in a large nonreactive soup pot. Stir in the onions and celery and sauté over medium-high heat, stirring occasionally, for about 8 minutes. Add the remaining ingredients and bring the soup to a simmer. Hold the soup at a near simmer for about 20 minutes, stirring occasionally. Taste and correct the seasoning as necessary. If possible, turn off the heat and let the soup sit for an hour or more, then reheat and serve.

Curried Yellow Split Pea and Winter Squash Soup

MAKES 8 SERVINGS

Most split pea soups are green, seasoned with ham bones, pretty predictable; this is none of the above. First, the color is a gorgeous tawny-gold, thanks to the combination of yellow split peas and orange squash. Instead of ham, the predominant seasoning is curry powder, an unexpected but delightful accent to the peas and squash. Despite the fact that this is a very filling soup—really a meal in itself with perhaps just bread or salad—my kids always ask for second and third helpings. This soup was awarded one of the highest possible kid compliments by my youngest son, Sam: "When are you going to make this again?" You should be able to find the yellow split peas at your local supermarket.

4 tablespoons olive oil

1 large onion, finely chopped

2 celery ribs, finely chopped

1 garlic clove, minced

4 teaspoons mild curry powder

approximately 9 cups water

$1^{1}/_{2}$ cups cubed winter squash

2 cups yellow split peas

1 bay leaf

1 teaspoon salt, plus more to taste

1 teaspoon sugar

1 tablespoon tomato paste

lemon wedges

chopped fresh parsley, for garnish

croutons, for garnish (optional)

*H*eat 3 tablespoons of the olive oil in a large heavy soup pot. Stir in the onion and celery and sauté over medium-high heat, stirring occasionally, for 7 to 8 minutes. Lower the heat, then stir in the garlic and sauté for 30 more seconds. Add the remaining tablespoon of oil and the curry powder and gently sauté for 30 seconds; keep stirring even if the pan seems dry.

Add the water, squash, split peas, bay leaf, and salt to the pot. Bring the soup to a near boil, then lower the heat. Partially cover the pot, then simmer the soup for about 1 hour, until the split peas are completely tender to the point of falling apart. Remove the soup from the heat and discard the bay leaf.

Using a food processor, process the soup to a fine puree, putting no more than about 2 or 2 1/2 cups into the machine at a time; use less if you have a small machine. As you puree the soup, either pour it into another pot to finish heating it or transfer it to a bowl temporarily. Put the pureed soup back on the stove over low heat and stir in the sugar and tomato paste. Taste the soup and add more salt if necessary. Simmer the soup for 5 more minutes, then serve hot with the lemon wedges, parsley, and croutons on the side; a little lemon juice gives the soup a pleasant lift.

❧ *Food for Thought* ❧
A SHORTCUT VERSION AND A FEW WORDS
ON BEHALF OF CANNED PUMPKIN

If you don't have any fresh squash in the house, reach into your pantry and pull out a can of plain pumpkin or squash. Then just add 1 cup of it to the soup when you puree it; even though it is already pretty smooth, the texture of the soup is best if you puree the squash in batches with the soup itself. My Official Position on canned squash is that it doesn't have the same flavor and appeal as fresh, but My Real Life Cooking Position is that I use the stuff often enough myself and, like canned tomatoes, the quality can be quite good. Most folks run into the problem of what to do with the leftover squash from the can, but there's actually quite a lot you can do with it. I like it in muffins and pancakes, quick breads, yeast breads, other soups, and stews.

Tortellini Gazpacho

ॐ

MAKES 6 SERVINGS

I can't tell you whether gazpacho is technically a salad or a soup—I've seen it called both—but I can tell you that it tastes wonderful with the addition of cheese tortellini. Thus made, it is less like any soup or salad than a pasta dish with a dressing of moist cold tomato sauce. No matter how you slot it, this is a dish to contend with; my kids can finish off the whole batch without batting an eye. Gazpacho needs fresh ripe tomatoes and the dish essentially requires that you take the extra few minutes to blanch the tomatoes to remove the skins. Try to make this at least a couple of hours before you plan to serve it so the dish has time to chill. Check the balance of seasonings once or twice as it chills, adding more salt, pepper, and vinegar if necessary. The tortellini go into the gazpacho about half an hour before the dish is served so they absorb some of the juice but don't become saturated, so time their cooking accordingly. This is a meal in itself, accompanied by good warm bread and a simple dessert, like fresh berries with a dab of Yogurt Cheese (page 291).

$^1/_2$ pound ripe tomatoes

$1^1/_2$ cups V-8 juice

1 large cucumber, peeled, seeded, and diced

1 medium green or red bell pepper, finely chopped

1 small red onion, finely chopped

2 small inner celery ribs, finely chopped

2 to 3 tablespoons red wine vinegar

2 tablespoons lemon juice

juice of $^1/_2$ lime

2 tablespoons olive oil

1 to 2 tablespoons chopped fresh basil

1 to 2 tablespoons chopped fresh parsley

salt and freshly ground pepper to taste

2 to 3 tablespoons finely chopped pickled jalapeño peppers (optional)

10 ounces cheese tortellini

Bring a pot of water to a boil and lower the tomatoes into the water for about 30 seconds. Transfer the tomatoes to a bowl with a slotted spoon and let them cool long enough to handle. Slip the skins off the tomatoes. Core, halve, and seed the tomatoes, then chop coarsely. Transfer the chopped tomatoes to a glass or pottery bowl and stir in the V-8 juice, cucumber, pepper, onion, celery, vinegar, lemon and lime juices, olive oil, herbs, salt and pepper, and jalapeño pepper. Cover and refrigerate the gazpacho for at least 2 hours.

About an hour before you plan to serve the gazpacho, bring a pot of salted water to a boil. Add the tortellini and cook them according to package directions. Drain and cool, tossing with a spoonful of olive oil and vinegar. About 20 to 30 minutes before serving, gently toss the tortellini with the gazpacho. Refrigerate until serving.

Tortellini, Spinach, and Chickpea Soup

MAKES 8 SERVINGS

A crowded, minestrone-style soup, this is just right on a cold night with a loaf of garlic bread and a tossed salad. To keep it simple, use canned chickpeas (drained and well rinsed). If you can't find good-looking fresh spinach, there's no harm in substituting a box of chopped frozen spinach. Don't add the tortellini until about 10 minutes before you plan to serve the soup so they don't get too soft.

    3 tablespoons olive oil

    1 large onion, chopped

    1 celery rib, chopped

    2 garlic cloves, minced

    8 cups water or Vegetable Stock (page 48)

    2 bay leaves

    1 large carrot, peeled and finely diced

    1 19-ounce can chickpeas, drained and rinsed

    1 28-ounce can crushed tomatoes in puree

    $^3/_4$ teaspoon salt, plus more to taste

    10 ounces fresh spinach, washed, stemmed, and chopped, or 1 10-ounce
        box frozen chopped spinach

    2 tablespoons chopped fresh basil or 2 teaspoons dried

    1 tablespoon chopped fresh oregano or 1 teaspoon dried

    8 ounces cheese or other favorite tortellini

    freshly ground pepper to taste

*H*eat the olive oil in a large nonreactive soup pot. Stir in the onion and celery and sauté over medium-high heat for about 7 minutes, until the onion is translucent. Stir in the garlic, sauté another 30 seconds, then add the water, bay leaves, and carrot. Bring the soup to a boil, then lower the heat and simmer for 10 minutes, until the carrots are tender. Stir in the chickpeas, tomatoes, salt, spinach, and herbs, then simmer the soup, partially covered, for about 10 minutes, until the spinach is tender. (If you are using frozen spinach, simply drop the entire block of spinach right into the pot and let it cook apart.)

About 10 minutes before you plan to serve the soup, add the tortellini. Simmer for 5 to 8 minutes, until the tortellini are tender. Correct the seasonings, adding the pepper and more salt if necessary.

Mary's
(White Bean, Broccoli, and Pasta) Soup

MAKES 6 SERVINGS

Have you ever loved a dish so much that you almost loved it to death? That happened to us and Mary's Soup a few years back; we just made it so much and liked it so much that we overdosed on it. So we took a sabbatical of several years, only to find that, though it may need an occasional break, true love never dies. Though the recipe is our own, what is certain is that Karen first tasted the inspiration for this soup at a Mary's restaurant in Miami nearly twenty-five years ago. Once you've tasted this, you'll understand how it could foster a lifelong love affair. This is not to say that it is a complicated soup, but there are no shortcuts here. This is a hefty, filling soup; a salad is the only accompaniment you'll need. For planning purposes, you'll have to make the mashed potatoes or stock before you plan to serve this so you have the potato broth that you'll need.

1 cup small dried white beans or Great Northern beans

1 large head broccoli

2 tablespoons olive oil

1 cup chopped onions

2 garlic cloves, minced

6 cups potato broth (from mashed potatoes, page 93) or Vegetable Stock
(page 48) made with potatoes

1 teaspoon dried basil

1 teaspoon salt

freshly ground pepper to taste

1/2 pound tagliatelle or other flat noodles

freshly grated Parmesan cheese, for garnish (optional)

*P*ut the beans in a pot and cover with water by about 2 inches. Bring
to a boil, boil for 2 minutes, then remove from the heat. Cover the
beans for 1 hour, then drain. Put the beans back in the pot and cover
with 8 cups of fresh water. Bring to a boil, reduce the heat to a simmer, and
cover partially. Cook the beans at an active simmer for about 1 hour, until tender. Drain, reserving the bean water.

Cut the broccoli into flowerets, reserving the thick stalks. Peel and dice the
stalks, setting aside both the stalks and about 4 cups of flowerets.

Heat the olive oil in a large soup pot. Stir in the onions and sauté over
medium-high heat for 5 minutes. Stir in the garlic and broccoli and sauté 2
minutes more over medium heat.

Add the potato broth, beans, and 2 cups of the bean water to the pot. Simmer for 10 minutes over medium heat, then stir in the basil, salt, and pepper.
Simmer for 1 minute more, then remove from the heat. At this point the soup
can sit at room temperature for up to 1 hour and in fact will benefit from the delay. Or you may proceed right away. Either way, begin—or continue—to heat
the soup when you put the water on for the pasta. The trick is not to overheat
the soup and turn the broccoli to mush.

Bring a pot of lightly salted water to a boil. Add the noodles and cook until
tender according to package instructions; drain. Put some noodles in each
bowl and cover with plenty of hot soup. Serve at once, passing the Parmesan
cheese separately if desired.

Creamy Mushroom and Wild Rice Soup

MAKES 6 SERVINGS

Good mushroom soup needs lots of mushrooms, more than you might think,
or else the flavor just isn't there. I've looked at many recipes and invariably
they call for a separate mushroom stock, sometimes made with a variety of

dried mushrooms. You can, of course, use some mushroom stock (page 49) for the liquid here, but I think the results are just as good and the recipe less intimidating if you just start with 2 pounds of regular white mushrooms. My supermarket sells big budget packs in this size, so the cost is reasonable. I call this a creamy soup, but there's no cream or milk. I just puree everything to get the creamy texture, reserving a few spoonfuls of the sliced sautéed mushrooms to stir back into mine and Karen's portions; the kids don't like pieces of mushrooms. As for the wild rice, it's a perfect match to the woodsy flavor of the mushrooms but by no means mandatory. Cooked barley is also good instead of the wild rice, or you may use almost any other cooked leftover grain you have in the fridge.

1/3 cup wild rice

6 1/4 cups water

salt

3 tablespoons olive oil

1 large onion, finely chopped

2 celery ribs, finely chopped

2 or 3 garlic cloves, minced

2 pounds mushrooms, cleaned and thinly sliced (see *Food for Thought*)

1 vegetable bouillon cube

2 all-purpose potatoes, diced

1 small carrot, finely diced

1 bay leaf

1 teaspoon fresh thyme or 1/2 teaspoon dried

1 tablespoon tamari, plus more to taste

1 teaspoon balsamic vinegar

freshly ground pepper to taste

*P*ut the wild rice and 1 1/4 cups of the water into a small saucepan. Salt the water lightly, then bring it to a boil. Lower the heat and cook the rice at a gentle boil for about 40 minutes, until the water is absorbed. The rice will still be chewy when it is done. Set aside.

Heat the oil in a medium soup pot. Stir in the onion and celery and sauté over medium-high heat for 7 minutes. Stir in the garlic and mushrooms, salt lightly, then cover and cook the mushrooms for 2 minutes, until they release their liquid. Uncover the pot and continue cooking the mushrooms until most of the liquid has evaporated. If you want some mushroom pieces in the finished soup, take a few spoonfuls out now and set them aside.

Add the remaining 5 cups water to the pot along with the bouillon cube, potatoes, carrot, bay leaf, and thyme. Salt the soup lightly, then cover and let the soup simmer for about 15 minutes, until the potatoes and carrots are tender.

Remove the bay leaf from the soup. Transfer the solids and about $1^1/_2$ cups of the broth to a food processor and process to a smooth puree. Stir the puree back into the soup pot, then season the soup to taste with the tamari, balsamic vinegar, pepper, and salt. Stir the wild rice into the soup shortly before serving and heat just long enough to heat it through.

❧ *Food for Thought* ❧
'SHROOM SERVICE

Do yourself a favor and only buy good-looking mushrooms. They should be fresh, firm, and white. Tired mushrooms are never a bargain: You have to cut away to salvage good flesh and they end up costing you in time and frustration. Good mushrooms don't need to be, really shouldn't be, rinsed under running water. That only makes them waterlogged and, even worse, makes them slippery and difficult to handle on the cutting board. Just wipe off any dirt with a dry paper towel. I've little patience for less-than-perfect stems; if they're dry or caked with dirt I just pull and discard them. And if the caps are just starting to get tired, here's a little-known trick: Remove the stems and reach inside the cap. You'll find a little flap of skin on the inside edge. Just pull it up gently and you'll peel some of the skin off the cap. Keep doing this until the cap is peeled.

Winter Squash, Bean, and Pasta Soup
∽
MAKES 6 TO 8 SERVINGS

Based on some of the wonderful versions of pasta e fagiole I've eaten, this is a soup for cold weather and hearty appetites. You should try to start it early on a weekend—the smell alone will make your day—then let it sit in a cool spot until dinner; the flavor is more complex and developed if you don't eat it right away. If you're a bread baker, make some good grainy rolls or Ugly Breads (page 222) to go with it; sometimes it's fun to spend the better part of a cold, wet day working on dinner, maybe even inviting some friends over on the spur of the moment. Much as we all like this, there's almost universal agreement that it isn't the same without the Parmesan cheese to sprinkle over the top. Resist the temptation to use canned beans here; cooking the dried beans slowly is what gives this soup such a lovely, flavorful broth.

$^1/_2$ pound dried cannellini beans, rinsed

3 tablespoons olive oil, plus more for garnish

1 large onion, chopped

1 large green pepper, chopped

3 celery ribs, chopped

2 medium carrots, halved lengthwise and sliced

2 garlic cloves, minced

10 cups water

1 bay leaf

$1^1/_4$ cups squash, canned or fresh pureed

1 cup chopped canned tomatoes in puree

$1^1/_2$ teaspoons dried basil

1 teaspoon dried oregano

$^1/_2$ teaspoon crushed dried rosemary

salt and freshly ground pepper to taste

$^1/_2$ pound fettuccine, broken into small pieces, or spiral noodles

$^1/_2$ cup chopped fresh parsley

red wine or balsamic vinegar, for garnish

freshly grated Parmesan cheese, for garnish

Rinse the beans and put them in a medium pot covered with about 3 inches of water. Bring the water to a boil, then boil uncovered for 2 minutes. Remove from the heat, cover, and set aside for 1 hour.

Meanwhile, warm 3 tablespoons of the olive oil in a large soup pot. Add the onion, pepper, celery, and carrots and sauté over medium heat, stirring, for 10 minutes. Add the garlic, sauté 1 minute more, then add the water and bay leaf. Once the beans have finished soaking, drain and add them to the pot. Bring the soup to a boil, reduce the heat to an active simmer, and cook the beans, partially covered, until very tender, about $1^1/_2$ to 2 hours.

Stir the squash, tomatoes, and herbs into the soup. Add some salt—about $^1/_2$ teaspoon for starters—and a generous amount of pepper. Gently simmer the soup for 30 to 45 minutes more, tasting it now and then to adjust the seasoning; a dense soup like this needs a fair amount of salt to bring up the flavor. Also, if the soup starts to become too thick, thin it with additional water as needed; this is a puttering-type soup if ever there was one.

About 20 minutes before you plan to serve this, bring a large pot of water to a boil. Cook the pasta until tender; drain and toss with a touch of olive oil to keep it from sticking. Stir the parsley into the soup, then serve the soup in large bowls with a big scoop of pasta in each bowl. Pass the olive oil, vinegar, and cheese at the table.

❧ *Food for Thought* ❧
WHEN FOOD FRIGHTENS, CONSIDER SCALE

If you've ever had occasion to visit a first-grade classroom as an adult, you've probably experienced a joltingly odd relationship to scale: Everything seems so small, so shrunk down to size. Your head swims in the clouds, well above the top of the blackboard, the desks are impossibly tiny, and the shelves are on the floor. Imagine if you had to conduct your daily life on this scale, how bothersome and intimidating it would be.

Yet that strangeness of scale is what many children have to face daily in the adult world of food. Simply put, food is often too *big* for them. Lettuce leaves look like palm fronds, steamed asparagus spears a forest felled by renegade winds. I was talking to one sympathetic mom who recalled a bowl of vegetable soup she had been served by the mother of a five-year-old. "I took one look at that soup and I thought of choking. All the vegetables were so big!" And if they looked big to an adult, can you imagine what they looked like to a five-year-old? Is it any wonder the child took one look at her bowl of soup and immediately lost interest?

When adults encounter resistance to food from their children, it would be wise to consider whether the issue is scale. Though they're seldom able to express it, kids are much more open to food that's clearly prepared with them in mind. Why do you think kids love tea parties? Sure, there's the dressing up and inviting the friends. But there's also the small teacups, dainty cookies, and other little finger foods they can relate to. The results can be dramatic when you begin to cook from a child's point of view. One of our family's little friends always said she hated onions, something we found curious because she would eat everything we served made with sautéed onions. Eventually we learned that her mom never chopped them small enough, often leaving them in big chunks. Another said she hated walnuts but relished the walnut cookies we made with finely chopped nuts. Chopping rendered them palatable for her.

No doubt another factor plays into this: the fact that many adults don't like to cut, chop, dice, and mince. Many of us are uncomfortable with sharp knives, for fear of being cut, and we don't like to spend any more time with them than necessary. While knives are always a potential hazard, a sharp knife—with a little practice—is quite safe and a pleasure to use. If you have a fearful relationship to your kitchen knives, it's time to get some pointers from a skilled friend or local chef. Most would be more than willing, even flattered, to give you a crash course in knife usage. Chefs are busy, so call between meals and try to set up a 10 minute lesson. Buy good knives and an automatic sharpener.

So whether you're making soup, salad, or anything for the kids, cut your cooking down to size. It might mean the difference between a meal that goes bang or bust.

Sandwiches Cold, Hot, and Wrapped

Sandwich making may not be a lost art, but it is certainly a dying one. There are pockets of resistance here and there—the odd deli or restaurant where all the pieces of the puzzle come together perfectly—but this is the exception, not the rule. Good vegetarian sandwiches may be the hardest of all to find; just piling a bunch of veggies on a bun isn't enough. The bread must have character; the mix of vegetables, balance; and the sauce or dressing should have enough punch to notice. Should the bread be toasted? A good meatless sandwich is the sum total of those little things, and those little things count.

Many people can't imagine what you put on a sandwich if you don't use cold cuts. Egg salad, perhaps. But what else is there? In this section we look closely at just how rich the possibilities are as we visit a broad spectrum of meatless sandwiches. Some will be familiar, but others, like Karen's Sunflower Seed Spread, you've probably not seen elsewhere, that is, unless you've eaten here for lunch. Many are served on bread, others on rolls, French bread, or burger buns. And a handful are wrapped in flour tortillas; burritos and quesadillas are essentially sandwiches also, and here we'll explore some of those as well.

Perhaps more than any other feature of a sandwich, the bread should be of notable quality. It's generally the bread that makes the first impression, so impress it should. If you have the time and inclination to make your own bread, wonderful; if not, look around for the best bakery bread you can find. Happily, today there's a rapid rise in the number of artisan bakers plying their wares in this country, and they can be found in most cities of any size as well as smaller communities. Most of them make superior sourdough breads and these breads are the building material of a really good sandwich. If you don't have a bakery nearby, check with your local health food store. Or contact a bakery in your region; many do a brisk business shipping to regular customers by UPS.

A Simple Vegetable Sandwich on Whole Wheat

MAKES 1 SANDWICH

One of the advantages of always having your own fresh whole wheat bread around is the way it serves as such a fine inspiration for sandwich making: I see that dark loaf of sesame seeded bread sitting there, and I just want to pile it to the sky with fresh vegetables and the perfect dressing. Our vegetable sandwiches change with the seasons and mood, but there are some regulars that tend to show up no matter the weather; that's what this sandwich is all about. Toast the bread, if you like, but slather both pieces with tahini dressing. If the dressing is on the thin side, put some in a small bowl and stir a small spoonful of fresh tahini into it; that will thicken it right up. (If you're plumb out or don't want to make it, use your favorite mayonnaise or thick salad dressing.) I grate the carrot right over the bread, add the cucumber slices, then the rest. The sun-dried tomato is optional and certainly not worth running out to the market for, but if you have some in the fridge, it's a good way to spark up the sandwich. In the summer, I would generally use fresh tomatoes instead. Serve with a bunch of grapes.

> 2 slices 100% Whole Wheat Bread (page 224) or other favorite bread
> Our Favorite Tahini Dressing (page 44)
> 1 small carrot, grated
> several very thin slices of green or red bell pepper
> salt and freshly ground pepper
> 9 or so thin cucumber slices
> 2 oil-packed sun-dried tomatoes
> small handful of fresh parsley leaves

*T*oast the bread if you like, then spread both slices generously on one side with the dressing. Cover one piece of bread with the grated carrot and sliced peppers, then salt and pepper to taste. Arrange the cucumbers over the peppers. Put the tomatoes and parsley on the chopping board together and chop them very finely. Sprinkle over the sandwich, then cover. Slice and serve.

❧ *Food for Thought* ❧
BEYOND THE BASICS

The eating gets rather indelicate when you try to put everything *and* the kitchen sink on a vegetable sandwich, but if you're moderate you could also add any of the following: several thin slices of cheese or crumbled feta; other fresh herbs, like basil; thinly sliced radishes; several pitted olives, chopped with the parsley and tomato; even a few toasted nuts. Have fun.

Karen's Sunflower Seed Spread

MAKES ENOUGH SPREAD FOR 5 TO 6 SANDWICHES

This is one of my favorite things to make a sandwich with, especially on toast with tomato, lettuce, and a smear of mayo. We've been making this for so long that the exact origins are a bit hazy at this point; it had something to do with a sunflower seed dressing we were making in the blender that got too thick. I've never come across anything quite like it outside our home. We begin by toasting sunflower seeds and lightly coating them with tamari. These are finely ground and then blended with a tahini sauce like the one you'd use to make hummus or baba ganouj and some chopped celery and onion. It can be used right away, but if you can let it sit in the refrigerator for an hour or two, all the better. The sunflower seed meal absorbs moisture like a sponge, so you'll have to loosen the consistency by stirring in some water each time you use it. This is also great on crackers as a sort of sunflower seed pâté.

2 cups raw hulled sunflower seeds

2 tablespoons tamari or soy sauce

1/2 cup tahini

1/4 cup lemon juice

$^{1}/_{2}$ cup water

1 garlic clove, minced

1 celery rib, finely chopped

1 tablespoon minced onion

salt and freshly ground black pepper

oast the seeds in a large heavy skillet over medium to medium-high heat for 8 to 10 minutes, stirring almost nonstop, until lightly browned. Transfer to a bowl and immediately mix them with the tamari, stirring well to coat all the seeds. Spread the seeds out in a single layer on a baking sheet and cool to room temperature.

As the seeds cool, whisk the tahini, lemon juice, water, and garlic in a small bowl until smooth. Set aside. Put all but $^{1}/_{4}$ cup of the seeds in a food processor and process to a fairly fine meal. Transfer to a bowl and scrape the sauce over it. Add the celery, onion, and reserved $^{1}/_{4}$ cup of seeds and mix well. Season the spread to taste with salt and pepper. Cover and refrigerate if not using the spread within 15 minutes. If the spread firms up as it sits—and it probably will—mix in water a tablespoon at a time to reach the desired consistency.

Veggie and Herb Sandwich Spread

MAKES ENOUGH FOR 4 SANDWICHES

This delicious sandwich spread—full of fresh vegetables and herbs—can be made with cottage cheese or, for vegans, with a sort of tofu cottage cheese you make in the food processor. Both ways are excellent. It makes a wonderful sandwich if you use good whole grain bread, fresh lettuce, and sliced tomatoes. I also love it on crackers; a crock of this at a party would be a major way station for the vegetarians you've invited. If you think of anything else that would be good in here, add it; that's pretty much how I developed this. You might be able to interest the kids in this one, but I'm guessing it will more likely be one for the adults in your life. It isn't absolutely necessary to drain the cottage cheese as I recommend, but it does give the spread a slightly drier consistency. The sun-dried tomatoes, although optional, add a nice spark.

$^{3}/_{4}$ pound cottage cheese

1 small onion, minced

1 medium carrot, grated

1 celery rib, finely chopped

2 radishes, finely chopped

$^1/_2$ small green bell pepper, finely chopped

2 tablespoons chopped fresh parsley

2 tablespoons Basic Pesto (page 289) or 2 tablespoons chopped fresh basil
plus 2 tablespoons freshly grated Parmesan cheese

$^1/_4$ cup oil-packed sun-dried tomatoes, finely chopped (optional)

salt and freshly ground pepper

red pepper flakes

*B*efore you start preparing all the vegetables, put the cottage cheese in a medium strainer and cover it with a piece of foil. Suspend the strainer over a bowl to catch the liquid and put a heavy can on top of it. Refrigerate for at least 1 hour.

Meanwhile, prepare the remaining ingredients and put them in a mixing bowl. Cover and refrigerate. Once the cottage cheese has drained for an hour, combine it with the remaining ingredients and mix well. Season to taste with salt, pepper, and red pepper flakes. If you have time, cover and refrigerate for an hour or two so the flavors have a chance to mingle. Serve on sandwiches or with crackers.

Grilled Eggplant Sandwiches: One for Adults, One for the Kids

MAKES 4 LARGE OPEN-FACE SANDWICHES

This is the ultimate in fun summer grilled food, a big, two-handed grilled eggplant sandwich. I offer you two versions: one with portobello mushrooms and a special herb sauce for the adults, and the basic model for the kids, made with their favorite store-bought tomato sauce. I love both of them myself. There's a fair amount of grill cooking to do here, so the grill cook has to be organized and on his or her toes. I suggest you grill all the eggplant slices first and keep them warm in the oven or just reheat them in a skillet. Then do the mushrooms and tomatoes at the same time.

OLIVE-HERB SAUCE

a good fistful of parsley (about 1 cup packed)

6 to 8 fresh basil leaves

1 garlic clove

9 or 10 good-quality pitted oil-cured olives

scant $^1/_2$ cup olive oil

1 to 2 teaspoons lemon juice

salt and freshly ground black pepper to taste

TOPPINGS AND ASSEMBLY

12 slices of grilled eggplant (see note below)

6 ounces grilled portobello mushrooms (see note below)

small ripe tomatoes (1 per adult sandwich), grilled

a good store-bought tomato sauce for the kids' sandwiches ($^1/_4$ cup per
      sandwich)

1 long loaf of French bread, halved lengthwise and crosswise

olive oil, to brush on the bread

$1^1/_2$ cups grated cheese; choose from fresh Parmesan, mozzarella, fontina
      (my favorite), or a combination (optional)

*P*repare the sauce by adding all sauce ingredients to a food processor. Process to a smooth consistency. Refrigerate. Make a fire and grill the eggplant as directed. Move the slices to the warming area of your grill or place them on a large baking sheet and keep them warm in a low oven. Grill the mushrooms and tomatoes at the same time; transfer them to heatproof plates and keep them warm also. Warm the tomato sauce for the kids' sandwiches and have it standing by. When you are ready to assemble the sandwiches, brush the insides of each slice of bread with a little olive oil and grill those sides until the bread is warm, 2 or 3 minutes.

To make the kids' sandwiches (do those first so you can enjoy your own), spoon a generous helping of sauce on each piece of bread you need. Layer 3 overlapping eggplant slices over the sauce and dampen them with a touch more sauce. If you are using it, sprinkle a little of the cheese over the top and put the sandwich on the grill. Cover for a minute or so, to start the cheese melting, then serve.

For the adult sandwiches, warm the bread as above, then spread the insides with several spoonfuls of the herb sauce. Layer the eggplant slices over the sauce, then cover each one with mushrooms and 2 pieces of grilled tomato. Cover with cheese, if you are using it, and warm the cheese as above. Serve at once.

VARIATIONS: If you are ambitious enough, you can add a layer of sautéed or grilled onions to the sandwiches; my son Ben likes it that way.

NOTE: *To grill eggplant slices,* cut rounds (of unpeeled eggplant) no less than 1/2″ but no greater than 3/4″ thick. Mix a clove of finely minced garlic with several tablespoons of olive oil. Brush both sides of the eggplant with the oil and place on the grill over hot coals; salt lightly. Turn the slices every minute or so, but try not to play with them too much or they'll fall apart. Brush with more oil as needed, and move them away from the hottest part of the grill if they start to blacken. The slices are done when they're soft and tender, after several minutes on each side.

To grill portobello mushrooms, first trim off the stem and brush off any dirt with a dry paper towel. Slice the cap(s) into 3/4″ slabs and toss gently with minced garlic and 2 to 3 tablespoons olive oil in a large bowl. Grill over hot coals, turning as necessary, until tender; salt to taste. If you like, lightly brush with balsamic vinegar (reduced by half in a small nonreactive skillet) as they grill.

Grilled Baguette of Eggplant, Artichoke Hearts, and Red Onions

MAKES 2 SERVINGS

I love an inspired sandwich; to me, it is one of the best meals you can have. The inspiration for this one came directly from a refrigerator, *my* refrigerator, full of not-too-unusual odds and ends; you'd probably have the same stuff on hand, except for the dressing, which can be made in a jiffy. Though a large slice from a good sourdough loaf would be fine, I like a toasted baguette that's slathered with the dressing, then layered with overlapping slices of pan-fried eggplant, quartered artichoke hearts, red onion, and parsley. The dressing can be omitted if you're not inclined to make it. But if you do use it, it should be on the thick side; an extra tablespoon or two of tahini will thicken it right up. A dusting of crumbled feta cheese finishes the sandwich beautifully if you happen to have some on hand. My son Ben loves this.

2 tablespoons olive oil

4 slices of eggplant, cut a generous 1/2 inch thick

salt

6 or 7 canned artichoke hearts, quartered and blotted dry on paper towel

1 baguette, about 12 inches long, halved lengthwise

Our Favorite Tahini Dressing (page 44)

half a lemon

1 small red onion, thinly sliced

small handful of fresh parsley leaves, finely chopped

2 tablespoons finely crumbled feta cheese (optional)

*H*eat the olive oil in a large, heavy skillet and add the sliced eggplant. Fry the eggplant for 3 to 4 minutes on each side, until lightly browned, over medium-high heat, lightly salting the slices after you turn them. If the pan smokes too much, cover it. When the eggplant is almost done, push the pieces aside and add the quartered artichokes to the pan. Heat, stirring, for 1 minute, then remove the pan from the heat leaving everything right in the pan.

You can serve this sandwich with or without the top piece of bread. Whichever you choose, quickly toast the bread under the broiler or in a toaster oven. Spread about 3 to 4 tablespoons of tahini dressing over the bottom half of the baguette. Layer overlapping slices of eggplant on the bread, followed by the artichoke hearts. Squeeze a little lemon juice over the artichokes, then top with plenty of sliced onion and parsley. Top with the cheese and other half of the bread, if you're using them. Serve at once.

❧ *Food for Thought* ❧
ARTICHOKE HEART MINUTIA

I'm partial to canned artichoke hearts because I simply don't like messing with fresh ones. The taste is fine, but to eliminate the slightest possibility of the tinny taste you sometimes get with canned food, I always do this: First, I drain them well—just dump them right into a colander—then I halve them and put them flat side down on a plate lined with paper towels. The towels soak up any excess liquid in the chokes so they don't taste wet when you bite into them. Use this step no matter how you're going to prepare them—in a frittata, marinated for an antipasto, or in pasta dishes.

Tempeh Barbecue, Avocado, and Monterey Jack Burritos

MAKES 4 SERVINGS

Burritos and other wrapped foods are all the rage, a measure of our nation's affinity for food that's fast, carefree, and almost impossibly versatile. New Hampshire's a long way from where the real burrito action is—California and points west—but the good news is that any gringo with a notion to can make a great burrito, no matter where you call home. Here's one burrito I especially like, a filling meal-in-a-wrap starring the somewhat meatlike tempeh barbecue. I dress it up with a popular supporting cast—chunks of avocado, red onion, grated carrots, and Monterey Jack cheese—but there's really almost no end to what else you might include; use your imagination, and whatever sounds good to you and yours. Serve with corn chips and salsa; the Tomatillo and Roasted Pepper Salsa Verde (page 187) would be splendid.

1 recipe tempeh barbecue (page 82)

4 flour tortillas

6 ounces grated Monterey Jack (or pepper Jack) cheese

1 large carrot, grated

1 medium red onion, finely chopped

sour cream

1 ripe avocado, cut into small chunks and dressed with a little lemon juice

1 ripe tomato, cored, seeded, and finely chopped (optional)

small handful of chopped fresh parsley

If you haven't already, prepare the tempeh barbecue; it should be hot or at least quite warm when you assemble the burritos, so reheat it at the appropriate time. To assemble the burritos, one at a time, thoroughly warm a tortilla in a hot skillet. As the tortilla heats, sprinkle some of the grated cheese over it. Let it rest briefly, then slide the tortilla out of the pan and onto a plate. Spoon a not-too-modest helping of the barbecue down the center of the burrito, then top with some of the grated carrot and red onion. Dot with sour cream and add chunks of avocado and tomato, if you're using it. Garnish with parsley. Fold a little of one side over the filling, then roll the burrito up perpendicular to the first fold. Serve right away.

Oriental Tofu Reuben

⌒

MAKES 1 SANDWICH

The same peanut sauce that we use to make sesame peanut noodles is the secret ingredient to this oriental Reuben, though the similarities between this and the real McCoy, I admit, begin and end with the sauerkraut and the grilling. Plain tofu on a sandwich can be pretty boring, to say the least. So we do a few things to make it less so, first pressing out the excess water, then breading and lightly pan-frying it so it tastes a little like tofu tempura. We layer that with the sauerkraut, a generous smear of the sauce, and grill it in the skillet. More sauce is served on the side to dip the sandwich in. My daughter Alison, who loves sauerkraut, adores this sandwich, so if your kids go for sauerkraut this might be a hit with them, too.

    1 recipe peanut sauce (page 150)

    2 or 3 slices of extra-firm tofu, cut a generous $1/4$ inch thick

    tamari, to brush on the tofu

    fine dry bread crumbs

    1 tablespoon flavorless vegetable oil

    $3/4$ cup sauerkraut

    2 slices of rye or other whole grain bread

    $1/2$ tablespoon butter or olive oil

If you haven't already, prepare the sauce and set it aside. Assuming you've purchased a pound of tofu, you can cut the slabs of tofu from either the larger or smaller of the sides, depending on the size of your bread and how much tofu you will need. In any case, fold a paper towel in half and place the tofu slabs on it. Place another doubled paper towel on top and press on the tofu with your palms, firmly enough to express the excess water but not so hard that you break the tofu. Repeat this process with fresh paper towels one or two more times, then set the tofu aside on a plate.

Lightly brush both sides of the tofu with tamari, then coat each side with bread crumbs. Heat the vegetable oil in a medium skillet, preferably a nonstick one. Add the tofu and fry over medium heat until golden brown, about 2 minutes on each side. Transfer the tofu to a plate. Squeeze the excess moisture out of the sauerkraut, then quickly add it to the skillet, stirring just long enough to heat it through. Remove from the heat.

To assemble the sandwich, layer the tofu on one piece of the bread and smear with about 3 tablespoons of the sauce. Cover with the sauerkraut and the other piece of bread. Butter both pieces of the bread or brush them with olive oil and grill the sandwich in a hot skillet for about 2 minutes on each side. Serve with potato chips, a pickle, and extra sauce on the side.

Avocado Reuben

⟋⟍

MAKES 2 SANDWICHES

For years now, both Karen and I have been in the habit of ordering Reuben sandwiches in restaurants, asking the waiter to please hold the corned beef, a request that's been met with every possible response from "I'll try" to near hostility. So I can't believe I didn't think of this delicious alternative myself—replacing the meat with avocado slices—until a friend recently told us about a similar sandwich she'd eaten in a vegetarian restaurant. It's optional, but Russian or Thousand Island dressing—either on the sandwich or served with it—is a great touch. It is worth mentioning—having eaten a lot of soggy restaurant Reubens in my day—that you should drain the sauerkraut before you begin and heat it as I describe below.

1 1/2 cups sauerkraut

Dijon mustard

4 slices of good rye or pumpernickel bread

4 thin slices of Swiss cheese

1 avocado, sliced

salt and freshly ground pepper

Russian or Thousand Island dressing

2 tablespoons unsalted butter or olive oil

Drain the sauerkraut and put it in a small nonreactive skillet over medium heat. Heat for about 2 minutes, stirring occasionally, to cook off any excess liquid that clings to the sauerkraut; you don't want to dry it out. Assemble the sandwiches as follows: Smear a little mustard over a piece of bread, then cover with 1 piece of the cheese. Layer on half of the sauerkraut and half of the avocado slices; salt and pepper the avocado slices to taste. Dab a tablespoon or so of the dressing over the avocado, then cover with another slice of cheese and another slice of bread. Butter the exposed sides of the bread or brush them with olive oil and grill the sandwich for about 3 minutes on each side in a hot skillet.

Alternatively, you can leave the dressing off the sandwich and serve it on the side. Serve with potato chips and sliced dill pickles.

Tempeh Barbecue Sandwich Topped with Coleslaw

MAKES 4 SERVINGS

This is different, but really worth trying. We have several things going on here: a "meaty" sandwich filling made from tempeh cooked in barbecue sauce. That goes on a good bun—your own or somebody else's, but it must be somewhat sturdy—and a pile of coleslaw on top. That's the cool-refreshing-crisp counterpart to the hot-spicy filling. (The slaw can go on the side if piling it on top of the sandwich strikes you as misguided.) Really, no matter how you make this, it is a pretty sloppy sandwich to eat, but a better hot one you'd be hard-pressed to find. Don't forget the potato chips.

1 tablespoon flavorless vegetable oil

1 medium onion, finely chopped

1 cup water

2 teaspoons tamari or soy sauce

1 8-ounce package tempeh, cut into very thin strips

3/4 cup vegetarian barbecue sauce (available in health food stores)

4 sturdy whole grain buns, homemade (page 225) or store-bought

3 cups coleslaw (page 46)

Heat the oil in a large nonreactive skillet. Add half of the onion and sauté over medium heat, stirring often, for 5 minutes. Stir in the water and tamari. Add the tempeh and bring to a boil. Boil for several minutes, stirring occasionally, until there's just a small amount of water left in the pan. Stir in the barbecue sauce.

Continue to heat, stirring, until the sauce is hot; if it seems too thick you can thin it with a little water. Meanwhile, toast or grill the buns you're using. Put the bottom halves on serving plates and spoon the tempeh over them. Top with some of the remaining onion. Pile the slaw on top or serve it on the side, then top with the other half of the bun. Eat up!

Scrambled Egg, Black Bean, and Cheese Burritos

MAKES 4 SERVINGS

There's almost no end to the way you can prepare a burrito like this using scrambled eggs as your basic filling and point of departure. These are real handy when you're in a hurry, and even though I'm not crazy about canned beans, I don't mind using them occasionally for this sort of quickie, especially when you need so few. (As I always say, just make sure the beans are drained and really well rinsed.) If you have the time, these are great with Red Rice (page 158) but if you're really flying, a bag of corn chips will do, with guacamole on the side. Have all the ingredients prepped and standing by before you begin scrambling the eggs. And bear in mind that these don't hold, so just serve them right away as they come out of the skillet.

4 soft flour tortillas

$1^{1}/_{2}$ to 2 cups grated sharp Cheddar cheese

8 eggs, lightly scrambled with 2 tablespoons chopped fresh parsley or
   cilantro

$^{1}/_{2}$ cup cooked black beans, warmed

$^{1}/_{4}$ cup green bell pepper, finely chopped

$^{1}/_{2}$ cup Fresh Tomato Salsa, store-bought or homemade (page 188)

Heat a large cast-iron skillet and lay one of the tortillas in it. Grate a little cheese over the surface, then spoon some of the scrambled eggs down the center, followed by a small handful of the beans, a tablespoon of pepper, and a big spoonful of salsa. When the tortilla is good and hot and the cheese is soft, slide it onto a plate. Roll the tortilla up and serve right away.

Apple, Sauerkraut, and Pepper Jack Quesadilla

⌇

MAKES 1 SERVING

This is sort of like an apple Reuben, quesadilla style. There are some obvious ways you might vary this, like using sliced pears instead of apple and Cheddar cheese for the pepper Jack. Within those general guidelines, you can't go wrong.

$^2/_3$ cup sauerkraut, drained

butter or olive oil

1 large tortilla or flatbread (I prefer the whole wheat kind)

Dijon mustard

$^1/_2$ to $^2/_3$ cup grated pepper Jack cheese

4 or 5 peeled apple slices

Heat the drained sauerkraut in a small saucepan over medium-high heat until most of the excess liquid has evaporated. Set aside.

Gently heat a large, heavy skillet, brushing it with a little butter or olive oil. Lay the tortilla in the pan and brush it with a little Dijon mustard to taste. Sprinkle the cheese over the entire surface, then cover half of it with the sauerkraut. Lay the apple slices over the sauerkraut, then fold the quesadilla in half, pressing down gently with a spatula. Let the quesadilla heat for 1 minute, then flip and heat another minute. Slide it onto your plate and eat hot.

Corn, Roasted Pepper, and Avocado Quesadillas

⌇

MAKES 4 SERVINGS

Quesadillas are food of a moment, which makes them perfect for snacks or a simple dinner. Here's a summer quesadilla, filled with fresh corn relish, chunks of avocado, and smoked Cheddar cheese; it's perfect with tortilla chips and glasses of fresh iced lemonade. (If you don't have the relish on hand and don't feel like making it, you can take this shortcut: Shave the kernels from 2 good-size ears of corn and put them in a skillet with just enough lightly salted water to cover. Bring to a boil, then cook for about 5 minutes, until all of the water cooks off. Transfer the corn to a bowl and add pepper to taste and a teaspoon of olive oil. Forget about the roasted peppers; stir a few tablespoons of chopped fresh green bell peppers into the corn.) If your kids aren't crazy about smoked Cheddar, just use regular sharp Cheddar or Monterey Jack.

4 large whole wheat flour or corn tortillas

1 cup Roasted Pepper and Sweet Corn Relish (page 190)

1 ripe avocado, peeled and cut into small chunks

1^1/$_2$ cups grated smoked Cheddar cheese

salsa, to serve on the side

Assemble all of the ingredients near the stove and get out your largest cast-iron skillet. Preheat the skillet over medium-low heat and lay one of the tortillas in the pan. Quickly spread about ^{1}/$_4$ cup of the relish over half of the tortilla. Dot the relish with some of the avocado chunks, then sprinkle some of the grated cheese over the filling; we generally just grate it right over the pan rather than pregrating it. It's faster. Fold the uncovered half of the tortilla over the covered half and press lightly with a spatula. Let it heat for about 45 to 60 seconds, then carefully flip it over and heat the other side for another 45 to 60 seconds. When the cheese is melted, it's done. Serve at once, cut into wedges, or hold them on a baking sheet in a warm oven while you make the others.

Salad Burritos

MAKES 4 TO 6 LARGE BURRITOS

Our kids love salad almost any way we serve it, but they're really into a wrapped burrito salad; there's something special about having it *their way*, and it reminds them of eating out because we borrowed the idea from their favorite Mexican restaurant. It takes a little effort to prep all the ingredients, perhaps 20 minutes of busy work; a second pair of hands helps. After that, it's all assembly. These can be eaten out of hand, even wrapped in foil for a picnic if they don't wait too long. By far our best way, however, is served at once, topped with chili sauce and eaten with fork and knife. We keep it simple when we do these: just a big bowl of corn chips on the side. Steamed corn on the cob is great, too.

6 large flour tortillas (sometimes called *wrapping* size)

8 ounces grated Cheddar or Monterey Jack cheese

1 head crisp lettuce, cleaned, leaves thinly sliced

2 to 3 ripe avocados, cut into bite-size chunks and tossed with a little
    lemon juice

1 small can pitted black olives, drained and chopped

1 large green bell pepper, finely chopped

1 medium red onion, finely chopped

1 15-ounce can black beans, drained and well rinsed (optional)

handful of cherry tomatoes, quartered

1 12–16-ounce jar favorite salsa

1 8-ounce container sour cream (optional)

Red Chili Sauce (page 196), heated (optional)

*B*efore you begin, prepare all the filling ingredients and arrange them on the work counter in separate piles. Clear away the clutter so the assembly can flow easily; in a frenzy of burrito assembly, you want to avoid accidentally shaking vanilla extract or some such thing in your burrito.

Warm the tortillas one at a time in a hot skillet; take care not to overheat them beyond the warm-and-flexible stage to the hot-and-brittle stage. Slide the hot tortilla onto a large plate and sprinkle with some cheese. Next, add little bits of any other filling you like. Keep everything in a row down the center but in a little from the edge. Fold one end over the filling just slightly so stuff doesn't fall out the end, then roll the burrito up. Put the burrito on a plate and serve as is or with some of the chili sauce spooned over the top.

Pumpkin and Wheat Germ Burgers

MAKES 6 BURGERS

Pumpkin gives this latest addition to our burger repertoire a pretty golden orange color. Karen literally threw these together one day with nothing but a few leftovers and some choice selections from the herb shelf. They contain no eggs or other dairy products, and to help bind them we use wheat germ, an excellent, nutrient-dense food with a pleasant nutty flavor. They're a cinch to prepare, nothing to precook or sauté. Serve these on burger buns, homemade (page 225) or good store-bought ones, with all the usual condiments and fixin's.

1 cup fine dry bread crumbs

$^1/_2$ cup toasted unsweetened wheat germ

$^1/_2$ cup extra-firm finely crumbled tofu

$^1/_2$ cup finely chopped onion

$^1/_2$ cup canned pumpkin or squash

$^1/_4$ cup very finely chopped walnuts

2 tablespoons finely chopped fresh parsley

1 teaspoon dried basil

$^1/_2$ teaspoon dried oregano

$^1/_2$ teaspoon paprika

2 tablespoons olive oil, plus a little extra for frying the burgers

$^1/_4$ cup water

*C*ombine everything in a large bowl and blend well with your hands until the mixture holds together. Form into patties; you can cover and refrigerate the patties at this point, if you like, for up to 24 hours.

Heat 1 to 2 tablespoons of oil in a large skillet. Add the burgers and brown them over medium heat for about 2 to 3 minutes on each side. Serve hot.

Veggie Burgers

MAKES 9 BURGERS

Anybody who is a vegetarian long enough becomes, by necessity, a student of The Veggie Burger. You're served them at family reunions, you try them in restaurants, dig into new cookbooks hoping to find one that the kids and spouse will like. *Veggie burger* is the generic term for any nonmeat burger, though, like this one, they often contain more grain than vegetables. I've had some pretty good packaged ones, but for the most part if you want an exemplary burger, you really have to make it yourself. Here is one we've gotten high marks for over the years, a veggie burger made primarily of cooked bulgur, bound with diced potatoes and carrots, and well seasoned with a variety of dry herbs. It has no eggs or other dairy products.

2 cups water

$^1/_2$ teaspoon salt, plus a pinch

1 cup uncooked bulgur

1 cup walnuts

handful of fresh parsley leaves

2 tablespoons olive oil

2 medium onions, finely chopped

1 garlic clove, minced

8 ounces mushrooms, thinly sliced

$1^1/_2$ tablespoons tamari or soy sauce

2 medium potatoes, peeled and cut into $^1/_4$-inch dice

1 medium carrot, peeled and cut into $^1/_4$-inch dice

$^1/_4$ cup instant or regular rolled oats

1 teaspoon dried basil

1 teaspoon dried oregano

$^1/_2$ teaspoon dried thyme

$^1/_2$ teaspoon crumbled dried sage

freshly ground pepper to taste

bread crumbs, for coating the burgers

flavorless vegetable or sunflower oil, for frying the burgers

Bring the water and $^1/_2$ teaspoon salt to a boil in a medium saucepan. Add the bulgur and bring the water back to a boil. Reduce to a simmer, cover, and cook the bulgur over low heat for 16 to 18 minutes; it shouldn't take any longer than that for all the water to be absorbed. When it reaches that point, remove from the heat and set aside, uncovered.

Put the walnuts and parsley into the bowl of a food processor and process until they are finely chopped. Leave them right in the food processor.

Heat the olive oil in a medium skillet. Add the onions and sauté over medium-high heat for 7 to 8 minutes. Stir in the garlic, mushrooms, and a pinch of salt. Sauté, stirring, for 1 minute, then cover the pan and cook the mushrooms over medium heat for about 4 minutes. Stir in the tamari and continue to cook for another minute or so, until the liquid has turned to a glaze. Remove from the heat and scrape the mushrooms into the food processor with the nut mixture. (Don't rinse the pan.) Process the mixture again until the mushrooms are finely chopped and set aside.

Put the skillet back on the heat and add the diced potatoes and carrot. Add enough water to cover the vegetables by about $^1/_2$ inch. Bring the water to a boil, salt lightly, then cook the vegetables rapidly until they're very tender and the liquid has evaporated, leaving a thickish glaze; if necessary, add a little extra water so the vegetables can continue to cook.

Scrape the potato mixture, mushrooms, and bulgur into a large mixing bowl. Stir in the oats, herbs, and pepper. Mash and stir the mixture well until it forms nice cohesive patties. Shape into 9 patties, lightly coating both sides of each one with bread crumbs. Place the patties on a small baking sheet, cover with plastic wrap, and refrigerate for at least 1 hour.

When you are ready to serve these, heat several tablespoons of oil in a large cast-iron skillet; it should form a very thin layer on the bottom of the pan. Fry as many at a time as will fit comfortably in the pan until nicely browned on both sides; medium heat for about 3 minutes on each side should do it. Serve at once.

❧ *Food for Thought* ❧
BURGERS BEYOND BULGUR

Bulgur is not the only grain that makes a good burger; many others are good and a second grain can make a burger with added interest and flavor. If you'd like to try something different, you can replace some of the bulgur in this recipe with some leftover cooked brown or wild rice, millet, couscous, or barley, say, up to a total of 1 cup. The only problem with cold leftover grain is that it often lacks the right texture to mix well; warm grain has the right slightly sticky feel to make cohesive burgers whereas cold grain is more dry and separate. You can help the situation by scattering the leftover grain over the surface of the bulgur during the last 2 minutes of cooking to warm it up.

Simple Vegetables, Finger-Lickin' Good

One of the most frequent complaints I hear from parents is this: My kid won't eat his vegetables. To which I immediately respond: How are you preparing them? Personally, I can't think of any vegetable I don't like, but on the other hand, I've had a lot of vegetables prepared in ways I don't care for and one or two I simply loathe under certain circumstances. (Summer squash comes to mind. All restaurateurs, I will bet my shirt, own a copy of a privately published manual called "How to Make BIG PROFITS Serving Summer Squash to Your Vegetarian Customers." Tip #1 in the manual is "serve humongous pieces," which I assume vegetarians are to interpret as an act of generosity. The part about actually cooking and seasoning it must be scanty indeed.) I won't go near a restaurant summer squash anymore and probably never will, the point being, how you prepare veggies, especially for kids, makes a difference, a big difference.

I give credit to my own love for vegetables to my parents, who had the good sense not to force my siblings and I to eat any vegetables we didn't like, though at times I must admit I thought they were simply so square that they actually *believed* I'd eaten most of the peas on my plate when I'd just rearranged my pile and slipped a few onto the floor and kicked them under the table. Fortunately, even before I had kids I figured out that you shouldn't force them to eat anything—about the *only* thing I figured out about kids beforehand—so I've made it a point never to make them eat their veggies. Consequently, they love almost all vegetables and the ones they don't, we simply don't serve.

This section of the book covers all the vegetables my kids like. A few of the preparations are involved, but most are simple and don't take a lot of time. Some are steamed, others are roasted, still others baked, sautéed, and mashed. Mashed spuds, you may have noticed, have become quite the in food these days, with all sorts of extras added. We've made our own contributions to this tasty craze and think you'll like them.

Gone are the days when boiled-to-death vegetables were the bane of kids everywhere. Today we know that vegetables can be prepared in enticing ways that preserve their flavor and fresh appeal. These are vegetables kids will eat with relish.

Italian-Style Home Fries

MAKES 4 TO 5 SERVINGS

Home fries are one of the big guns in our arsenal against what seems like a perpetual war against hunger, a war that's escalated mightily as the kids have come into adolescence. And when you make home fries as much as we do, you naturally start thinking of ways to vary them, lest you die from home fry boredom. Here's one way that really stuck. Try them for breakfast or dinner, with warm Italian bread and a salad. You'll need to bake the potatoes the day ahead.

4 tablespoons olive oil

1 large onion, chopped

1 small green pepper, finely chopped

1 medium-size carrot, grated

1 clove garlic, minced

4 medium baked potatoes, skins on, cut into bite-size chunks

salt and freshly ground pepper

1 teaspoon paprika

$1^1/_4$ cups marinara sauce, homemade or store-bought

1 tablespoon chopped fresh basil or 1 teaspoon dried

Heat 2 tablespoons of the olive oil in a large, heavy skillet. Stir in the onion and pepper and sauté over medium heat for about 8 minutes. Stir in the grated carrot, sauté for 1 minute, then add the remaining 2 tablespoons of oil to the skillet. Stir in the garlic and potatoes and cook the potatoes, stirring often, for about 5 minutes, until heated through. Salt and pepper the potatoes to taste, then stir in the paprika to coat the potatoes. Heat the potatoes for another minute, then stir in the marinara sauce and basil. Cook the potatoes another minute or so, until the sauce is hot, then correct the seasoning. Serve hot.

Basil-Parmesan Mashed Potatoes

MAKES 6 SERVINGS

These got a big 10 rating—actually, 9³/₄ until he added his own decisive pinch of salt—from youngest son Sam, one of our resident mashed potato judges. (In case you aren't familiar with the rating system for mashed potatoes, 10 is the highest score possible, taking into account body, texture, flavor, and, apparently, precise amount of salt.) This was no small honor, given Sam's qualifications: Mashed potatoes is his favorite meal. He enters an almost trancelike state when he's eating them; nothing else on his plate matters or gets eaten, for that matter. Anyone who loves basil will love these, and that's just about everyone. Besides copious quantities of basil, there's a head of roasted garlic in here also. A head sounds like a lot, but roasting tones down the rough, raw edges so the flavor is subdued but on the other hand intensified, if that makes any sense. These are great with summer's best sliced fresh tomatoes or something else tomatoey, like ratatouille, and corn on the cob; you can't beat it!

1 recipe Roasted Garlic (page 109)

about 10 good-size all-purpose potatoes, peeled and coarsely chunked

salt

1¹/₂ cups tightly packed fresh basil leaves

¹/₂ cup freshly grated Parmesan cheese, plus a little extra for garnish

2 to 3 tablespoons olive oil

1¹/₂ cups hot milk

salt and freshly ground pepper to taste

If you haven't already, roast the garlic. In a large pot, cover the potatoes generously with salted water and bring to a boil. Boil the potatoes for 10 to 12 minutes, until tender. While the potatoes are cooking, combine the basil and Parmesan cheese in the bowl of a food processor and process until finely chopped. Set aside.

When the potatoes are tender, drain them (save the water for soup) and transfer to a large bowl. Grasping the garlic at the bottom of the head, squeeze the cloves out onto a plate and mash them with a fork. Add the garlic, 2 tablespoons of olive oil, and most of the milk to the potatoes and mash them; I like to start with a hand masher to work in the milk, then switch to an electric mixer to fluff them up. Add more of the milk, if you need it, and salt and pepper. Serve the potatoes hot, garnished with a little extra Parmesan if you like.

Dairyless Mashed Potatoes

MAKES 6 TO 8 SERVINGS

Karen always used to say that the one thing that would prevent her from becoming a confirmed and steadfast vegan was mashed potatoes. Simply the thought of going through life without an occasional promise of creamy mashed potatoes, whipped to a cloudlike fluff without the richness of milk and butter, seemed like more than my partner could handle. She'd gone the route of mashing them with potato water in a valiant attempt to put the issue to rest, but they just weren't the same, much more grainy than creamy. It was during one such attempt—*You're not making them with potato water again, are you, Mom?*—that she had the idea of substituting soy milk for the regular milk and olive oil for the butter. That was the breakthrough. What we found was that a combination of soy milk and olive oil and some potato water gives these mashed potatoes the creaminess your taste buds expect. No matter what else we are serving, we almost always serve these with Great Gravy (page 197) and corn.

12 medium all-purpose potatoes (about 10 cups), peeled and chunked

1¹/₄ teaspoons salt

2 tablespoons olive oil

³/₄ cup hot *plain* soy milk

¹/₂ cup potato water

freshly ground pepper

Put the potatoes in a large pot and cover with plenty of water. Add 1 teaspoon of the salt and bring to a boil. Boil the potatoes, partially covered, for 10 to 12 minutes, until tender. Drain, reserving the potato water; what you don't use in the mashed potatoes should be saved for soup.

You can either mash the potatoes by hand or in an electric mixer; the former will give you a slightly more textured version, the latter will be fluffier. In any case, transfer the potatoes to a large bowl and add the remaining salt, olive oil, and heated soy milk, mashing them with your tool of choice. Mash in the first $1/4$ cup of the hot potato water, then gradually add as much of the remaining potato water as necessary to make mashed potatoes moistened to your liking. Finally, blend in pepper to taste and adjust the salt if necessary. Serve at once.

Lumpy Mashed Potatoes with Kale

MAKES 6 SERVINGS

Most parent-cooks don't have a hard time getting the kids to eat mashed potatoes: They're predictably smooth, tasty, but not assertive, trustworthy. That's not always—and in some homes almost never—the case with greens. Greens are suspect in even the best of homes, a suspicion that follows many kids right into adulthood. Recently, my brother and his family came for a holiday visit. I had made what I thought was a gorgeous minestrone-type soup with tons of good stuff in it, including pieces of kale, which by serving time was deliciously tender after hours of stewing in the lovely broth. Anyway, my sister-in-law starts picking at the kale like someone had cut up used nylons and dropped them in her bowl, tossing the pieces aside on her plate. Even though I wanted to blurt, *Are you crazy?!* I kept my cool adult demeanor and calmly asked her—as if everyone who ate at my house always picked the kale out of the soup I served—why was she doing this? She simply said, "I don't trust greens." Indeed. I've learned as a father-cook that one good way to engender trust is to pair the known with the unknown and that is the driving philosophy behind this wonderful dish. There are two components: steamed, finely chopped kale and mashed potatoes with the skins on. You could probably take it from there but here is how I do it anyway. Serve anywhere you'd serve mashed potatoes, with butter or dairyless Great Gravy (page 197).

1 good-size bunch kale (about 10 packed cups stripped leaves)

7 medium all-purpose potatoes, scrubbed and diced

salt

3 tablespoons olive oil

1 large onion, finely chopped

2 garlic cloves, minced

freshly ground pepper

*I*f you haven't already, strip the kale leaves from their central stems. Put the leaves in your largest bowl and fill it with cool tap water. Agitate the leaves vigorously to loosen any grit or sand, then transfer the wet leaves to a large enameled pot. Add about ¼ cup of water to the pot, cover, and steam the leaves over medium-high heat for 10 to 12 minutes, until tender; don't turn the heat too high or all the water is likely to cook off and the kale will burn and stick to the pan. Drain the kale in a colander and set it aside. When it is cool enough to handle, chop it finely and set aside.

Meanwhile, put the potato cubes in a large pot with plenty of lightly salted water. Bring to a boil, then boil the potatoes until tender. Remove from the heat but leave the potatoes in their water for now.

Heat the oil in a large skillet and add the onion. Sauté the onion for 7 to 8 minutes over medium-high heat, stirring often, then stir in the garlic and sauté 1 minute more. Stir in the kale, coating everything well with the oil, until the kale is hot. Spoon ¼ cup or so of the potato water over the kale, cover, and keep it warm over the lowest possible heat.

Drain the potatoes, saving the broth. Put the potatoes in a large bowl and mash them well, either by hand or with a mixer; season to taste with salt and pepper, adding spoonfuls of potato water to give them the preferred consistency. Uncover the kale, turn up the heat, and boil off most of the free liquid, then add the mashed potatoes and fold everything together with a rubber spatula. Serve hot.

❧ *Food for Thought* ❧
SPEAKING OF SPUDS

There are richer ways to mash potatoes and other possible enticements if you deem them necessary. You can, of course, throw a tablespoon or so of unsalted butter into the potatoes while you mash them. Or use warm milk to moisten the potatoes, instead of the potato water. A little bit of grated Parmesan cheese is wonderful in this dish if you don't mind the extra fat and calories. In any case, don't even think about throwing out the potato water, which will make a wonderful soup or base for yeast bread—check out the Thick Potato and Onion Focaccia on page 228. In fact, though it may sound like a heavyweight combination, that focaccia and these kaled spuds make a wonderful meal together; you would have to make the spuds ahead so the potato water is available for the dough, but that's not a problem because this dish will reheat nicely. Incidentally, potato water goes sour very quickly if left at room temperature. If you leave it in the pot at room temperature overnight, you'll lose it. So refrigerate the stuff as soon as it has cooled down, and freeze it if you don't need it right away. To make an incredible soup broth, add your leftover potato water to the pot when you cook large or small white beans.

Garlic-Mashed White Beans and Potatoes

MAKES 6 SERVINGS

The last few years have brought us a plethora of garlic-mashed potatoes. You see recipes for them everywhere in the food press and they're featured on the menus of some very classy restaurants. Here's an extension of that idea, one that replaces more than half of the potatoes with white beans. It tastes glorious and it goes with many Italian dishes the all-potato version doesn't seem quite right with, such as pizza, which I love to serve it with. Basically, you cook white beans until they're almost tender, then add some potatoes and continue to cook until everything is soft and mashable. Then you mash the beans and spuds with garlic warmed in olive oil, using a little of the cooking water to give it just the right consistency. The mash is spread in a shallow casserole, coated with olive oil, and dusted with rosemary—and Parmesan cheese if you like—then baked until hot and lightly crusted. It's a simple, soothing side dish with a bonus: The cooking water makes the base for a terrific soup of your choosing. My oldest son Ben is particularly crazy about this dish; he loves to turn the leftovers into breakfast patties (see *Food for Thought*).

^{1}/2 pound small white beans or Great Northern beans

salt

4 medium all-purpose potatoes, peeled and chunked

3 tablespoons olive oil

1 or 2 garlic cloves, minced

freshly ground pepper

^{1}/2 teaspoon crushed dried rosemary

^{1}/2 cup freshly grated Parmesan cheese (optional)

Put the white beans in a large soup pot and cover with about 2 inches of water. Bring to a boil, boil for 2 minutes, then remove from the heat. Cover and let sit for 1 hour. Drain the beans, add enough fresh water to fill the pot by about half, then return the beans to a boil. Gently boil the beans, uncovered, for about 40 minutes, until almost tender. Add some salt to the water, then add the potatoes and cook about 20 minutes more, until the potatoes are very soft. Drain the potatoes and beans, transferring them to a large bowl. Keep the cooking water nearby. Preheat the oven to 425°.

Gently warm 1^1/2 tablespoons of the olive oil and the garlic for 2 to 3 minutes in a small skillet. The garlic should not brown; you're only infusing the oil with its flavor. Pour the oil and garlic over the beans and potatoes. Using a hand masher, mash them well, moistening the mixture with some of the cooking water as you mash; they should have a consistency like medium-firm mashed potatoes. Taste, seasoning to taste with salt and pepper.

Lightly oil a large, shallow casserole or gratin dish. Spoon the mash into the dish and even the top with a fork. Drizzle the remaining 1^1/2 tablespoons olive oil over the top and dust with the rosemary. Sprinkle on the Parmesan cheese if you are using it and bake for about 30 minutes, until heated through. Serve hot.

❧ *Food for Thought* ❧
BEAN MASH FOR BREAKFAST

I don't know which I love more, this served as is or turned into patties the next day. Both my son Ben and I love the leftovers, mixed with a little extra Parmesan cheese, for breakfast patties; aside from snowboarding, it is one of the few things that can get him out of bed early. We simply take the leftovers and mix them with a little extra Parmesan to help bind the patties, then coat the surfaces lightly with bread crumbs. Then we fry the patties in a little olive oil. They're great with eggs and omelets, if your diet allows, but more often than not I just have mine with a piece of toast; olive bread toast is my first choice. I like to smear hot bites right onto the bread and drizzle with a smidgen of olive oil. Now that's living!

And if that doesn't sound like your cup of tea, here's another idea: Freeze the leftovers and use them to thicken soups. Just stir it right into the hot soup. It will add body and flavor to any vegetable soup and is especially good with broccoli soup.

Spicy Red-Roasted Potatoes

MAKES 4 SERVINGS

Unadorned oven-roasted spuds are glorious as is, but here is a jazzed-up version when you want something more. The spark is provided by some chili powder, paprika, oregano, sun-dried tomato paste, and plenty of garlic. Tossed with a little oil, the seasonings cling to the potatoes, roasting up to a spicy russet-crusted splendor. Serve these with veggie burgers or any cabbage dish for brunch or dinner. The sun-dried tomato paste is something of a luxury and I don't buy more than a couple of tubes a year. However, a little goes a long way and you can't really duplicate the flavor with regular tomato paste. You'll find it in the Italian or gourmet section of the supermarket.

3 tablespoons olive oil

2 tablespoons sun-dried tomato paste

2 teaspoons oregano

$1^{1}/_{2}$ teaspoons paprika

1 teaspoon mild chili powder

2 to 3 garlic cloves, minced

1 small onion, halved and thinly sliced

6 medium red-skinned potatoes, scrubbed, dried, and cut into bite-size
    chunks

salt

*P*reheat the oven to 450° and lightly oil a large roasting pan or jelly
roll pan. In a large mixing bowl, blend the oil, sun-dried tomato
paste, oregano, spices, and garlic. Add the onion and potatoes and
toss well to coat them with the spice mixture. Salt the potatoes to taste, then
spread them in the roasting pan, leaving as much room as possible between the
pieces. Roast the potatoes for 25 to 35 minutes undisturbed, until tender, then
serve at once.

Smothered Potatoes

MAKES 5 TO 6 SERVINGS

This is a wonderful hearty winter dish we've been enjoying in one version or
another for years. It is essentially spiffed-up home fries, "smothered" in a sauté
of peppers, onions, tomatoes, sour cream, and cheese. You can add some zing,
if you like, with the addition of chopped pickled jalapeños. These are great for
a weekend brunch or dinner, with just a salad and corn on the side. Make sure
you bake the potatoes the night before.

4 tablespoons olive oil

1 large onion, halved and sliced

1 large green bell pepper, sliced

4 medium-large baked potatoes, cut into bite-size chunks

salt and freshly ground pepper

2 garlic cloves, minced (optional)

2 teaspoons paprika

1 teaspoon chili powder

1 large or 2 medium ripe tomatoes, cored and chunked

1 tablespoon red wine vinegar

3 to 4 tablespoons chopped pickled jalapeño peppers (optional)

1/3 cup sour cream or plain yogurt

1 to 1 1/2 cups grated sharp Cheddar cheese or Monterey Jack

*P*reheat the oven to 400°. Heat 2 tablespoons olive oil in a very large, heavy, ovenproof skillet. Add the onion and green pepper and sauté over medium heat for about 10 minutes, until the onion begins to turn golden. Scrape the vegetables into a bowl and set them aside, then put the skillet back on the heat.

Add the remaining 2 tablespoons oil to the skillet and stir in the potatoes. Sauté them over medium-high heat for about 5 minutes, until heated through; add salt and pepper to taste. Stir in the garlic, sauté 30 seconds or so, then stir in the spices and tomatoes. Lower the heat and stir the sautéed vegetables back in with the potatoes. Continue to cook the potatoes, stirring, 3 to 4 minutes more. Sprinkle the vinegar and jalapeños over the vegetables, then remove from the heat.

Dollop the sour cream over the top, then sprinkle with the cheese. Bake for about 10 minutes, until the cheese melts. Serve at once.

Mixed Mashed Roots

MAKES 6 SERVINGS

Here we mash one root vegetable that most kids like (carrots) and one they're often less familiar with (parsnips), as good an introduction to parsnips as any I'm aware of. Parsnips are one of the more challenging veggies to do in a kid-friendly manner, and here they sort of conveniently fade into the background, a sweet, faintly detectable note. The carrots add their own distinct flavor and a scattering of bright orange confetti that is as pleasing to the eye as it is to the palate. Boiling the vegetables produces a sweet, rich broth, which is used first to mash the vegetables with, then boiled down a little more to make a self gravy, the icing on the cake. If you're eating butter, you can always melt a tablespoon with the gravy before you serve it, but it's by no means necessary. Serve this with sautéed greens, corn, or anywhere else you serve regular mashed potatoes.

2 pounds (about 6 cups) all-purpose potatoes, peeled and cut into big chunks

3/4 pound (about 4 medium) peeled and thickly sliced parsnips

1 large carrot, peeled, quartered, and thinly sliced

1/2 teaspoon salt

2 1/2 tablespoons olive oil

1 cup finely chopped onion

2 garlic cloves, minced

¹/₄ cup finely chopped fresh parsley

freshly ground pepper to taste

*P*ut the potatoes, parsnips, and carrot in a large pot and add enough water to cover the vegetables; it should comfortably cover them, not just barely cover them. Stir in the salt and bring the water to a boil. Boil the vegetables, partially covered, for about 10 to 12 minutes, until all the vegetables are tender-soft. Remove from the heat.

While the vegetables cook, gently heat the olive oil in your largest nonreactive skillet. Stir in the onion and sauté over medium heat for 5 to 6 minutes, until golden; do not let it brown. Stir in the garlic and sauté for 15 seconds more. Turn off the heat.

Put the vegetable pot near the skillet and, using your largest slotted spoon, transfer the vegetables to the skillet. Using a hand masher, begin mashing the vegetables, gradually adding some of the vegetable broth as you mash; it may take as much as 1 cup of broth to give them the proper soft texture. Stir in the parsley and pepper. Cover the vegetables and leave them on the stove.

Bring the remaining broth back to a boil and boil until there's only about 1 cup of liquid left in the pot; you needn't measure it, but simply take note that it will be quite full bodied and intensely flavored. Briefly rewarm the vegetables if necessary and transfer the gravy to a serving container. Serve hot.

Mom's Baked Squash with Applesauce

MAKES 6 SERVINGS

This is my version of a dish my mom used to make often when we were kids. It is as simple as can be, but as a kid I can remember being so tickled and amazed by the fact that you could actually put applesauce inside a squash and serve it that way; it was a pretty cool thing to do, one of those consummate gestures that kids will occasionally brag about to show any doubters that their mom is the best cook in the world. *So there!* In time, of course, one realizes that what was once viewed as virtuosity was, in fact, closer to cleverness: Here was an attractive, delicious dish you could feed a big family with almost no effort. My mom used to make this with acorn squash and I still do. The size is perfect for a family, and it has a large enough cavity to hold a good amount of applesauce. If you can find another squash that fits the bill, fine; I have also used small calabaza squash and I imagine there are others I'm not aware of that would work. Mom parboiled her squash; I simply put it in a covered casserole with a little water. Then, when the squash is almost done, I fill the cavities with applesauce, top with a little brown sugar and cinnamon, and bake a few minutes longer. That's all there is to it.

3 acorn squash

4 tablespoons cider jelly, apple jelly, or red currant jelly (optional)

salt

4 cups applesauce

2 tablespoons packed light brown sugar

$1/2$ teaspoon cinnamon

Preheat the oven to 400°. Halve the squash from top to bottom and scoop out the seeds. Cut a small slice from each half on the outermost ribs so the squash will sit flat as it bakes and place them in a casserole or baking dish with a lid. Brush 1 tablespoon of jelly over the flesh of each, if you are using it, then sprinkle lightly with salt. Cover and bake for about 50 to 55 minutes, until the flesh is just tender. If liquid has settled in the cavities, spoon it out, then fill each cavity with applesauce almost up to the top. Mix together the brown sugar and cinnamon and sprinkle some over each half. Bake about 10 more minutes to warm the applesauce, then serve.

Garlic-Baked Squash

MAKES 6 SERVINGS

Squash is a wonderful carrier for all sorts of flavors, especially when the flavor is garlic. Kids are sometimes shy of the upfront, untamed taste of garlic, but winter squash is a wonderful way to mellow it without obscuring the flavor. Consequently, the kids love this one. It makes an excellent winter side dish and topping for our Squash Shepherd's Pie (page 176). Leftovers can be used to thicken and add flavor to vegetable soups and stews. Since the squash is cooked twice, it helps to bake it ahead, either the day or morning before you need it.

2 buttercup squash or other medium meaty and flavorful winter squash

$1/4$ cup olive oil; you may substitute part unsalted butter

2 to 3 garlic cloves, minced

salt and freshly ground pepper

*P*reheat the oven to 425°. Place the squash on a large baking sheet and bake until quite tender when pierced with a sharp knife; this might take as long as 1¼ hours, depending on the size of the squash. Remove from the oven and let cool. Halve the squash, scoop out and discard the seeds, and spoon the flesh into a mixing bowl. (If you aren't using the squash within 4 or 5 hours, cover and refrigerate.)

When you're ready to proceed, gently warm the oil (or oil and butter) in a large, heavy skillet. Add the garlic and sauté it gently, stirring, for 1 to 2 minutes; it may turn golden, but don't let it turn dark brown. Stir in the squash and turn up the heat. Cook until heated through, mashing the squash with a potato masher; add salt and pepper to taste. If the squash seems dry, which you would have noticed when it cooled, mash in a few tablespoons of water or vegetable stock to moisten it. Serve hot.

❧ *Food for Thought* ❧
SQUASH LOVES COMPANY

If you have a large oven like I do, it is energy-wise and cooking-efficient to bake something else along with the squash. So while the squash is going, throw in some spuds for dinner or home fries for the next morning, bake some apples for dessert, make a pie, or cook some beans (they'll cook just as well in the oven as they will on a burner). If you're baking something that might cook too fast at 425°—that pie, for instance—just turn the oven down a bit and cook the squash a little longer.

Mashed Sweet Potatoes

MAKES 6 SERVINGS

A good argument could be made for simply baking sweet potatoes and eating the flesh *au naturel,* and I know this for a fact because Karen and I have had some pretty good arguments on the subject. On the other hand, I personally think there's nothing like a touch of butter and a little milk to gild the lily just a touch. Heck, I've seen many regular mashed potato recipes, using just acres of butter and cream, that must make the folks at the American Dairy Association positively swoon, but these aren't like that. A tablespoon of butter goes a long way in this recipe, but if you're still not game, do try Karen's good vegan variation below. These are right at home with most pilafs, especially with cold applesauce on the side. They're also good with fried polenta slices served with gravy. And of course you should serve them for Thanksgiving dinner.

6 medium sweet potatoes or yams (about 3½ pounds)

1 cup regular or skim milk

1 tablespoon unsalted butter

2 tablespoons maple syrup or honey

juice of ½ lemon

⅛ teaspoon cinnamon

⅛ teaspoon grated nutmeg

salt and freshly ground pepper to taste

*P*reheat the oven to 450°. Pierce each of the sweet potatoes with a fork 2 or 3 times. Arrange them on a baking sheet and place them in the oven. Bake for 45 to 60 minutes, until the flesh is fork-tender. Slit the tops of the potatoes to let off steam and set them aside.

While the sweet potatoes are baking, warm the milk, butter, and sweetening in a large nonreactive skillet until the butter melts. When the potatoes are cool enough to handle, scoop the flesh into the skillet and mash it with a potato masher right in the pan. Mash in the lemon juice, spices, and salt and pepper. Heat the potatoes through and serve hot. If there's any delay in serving the meal, you can reheat them right in the pan.

VARIATION: Karen makes her vegan variation basically the same way as I do these, only using soy milk instead of the regular milk and substituting olive oil for the butter. They're great, too.

🌿 *Food for Thought* 🌿

AND IF YOU'RE THE STUFFING SORT . . .

. . . you can always stuff your sweet potatoes; everybody loves an individual stuffed potato. Prepare the potatoes as above, making sure you don't trash the skins when you're scooping out the flesh. That's a little tricky because sweet potato skins aren't exactly durable; in fact, they can be pretty flimsy. Anyway, save the best 6 skins and stuff each one generously, mounding it up over the top. Carefully place the halves on a baking sheet and put them back into a hot oven just long enough to heat the potatoes through. If you're looking for a pretty garnish, chopped walnuts or just a pinch of cinnamon looks good.

Roasted New Potatoes and Brussels Sprouts

MAKES 6 SERVINGS

Roasted potatoes have always been a big hit with my kids, so I was pretty sure this dish would score when the idea dawned on me: The kids love cabbage, so the thought of little cabbages in with their potatoes was instantly appealing. What I do is quickly sear the vegetables in a little oil over high heat to start them cooking and give the surface a little color. Then I spread them in a roasting pan and finish them in the oven. A large pan is important; you don't want everything piled on top of everything else or the veggies will steam-cook instead of roasting. It makes a difference in the flavor. These are good alongside the tomato and eggplant gratin (page 134) or tossed with pasta, among other ways.

1 pound brussels sprouts

1 pound small new potatoes

4 tablespoons olive oil

1 tablespoon chopped fresh rosemary or 1 teaspoon crushed dried

1 garlic clove, minced

salt and freshly ground pepper to taste

Preheat the oven to 450° and lightly oil a large roasting pan. Trim and halve the brussels sprouts, cutting off the stubby stems. Halve the new potatoes (or quarter them if they're not too small); the potato pieces should be no larger and perhaps a bit smaller than the brussels sprouts.

Heat 2 tablespoons of the olive oil in a large, heavy skillet. Add the brussels sprouts and let them sit, undisturbed, over medium-high heat, for 1 minute. Cook for another minute or so, stirring only once or twice. Transfer the brussels sprouts to the roasting pan. Heat the remaining 2 tablespoons olive oil and cook the potatoes in the same fashion, stirring only once or twice over the course of 2 to 3 minutes. Add them to the roasting pan. Stir the rosemary, garlic, salt, and pepper into the vegetables and roast them, uncovered, for 25 to 30 minutes, until tender. Serve at once.

Crusted Summer Squash and Tomatoes

MAKES 6 SERVINGS

Having expressed my family's overall lukewarm relationship with summer squashes elsewhere in this book, now I'm here to say this is one way they will eat them . . . and quite enthusiastically at that. In fact, the first time I made this my son Ben, young master of the double-edged compliment, said this "was the best thing I'd made in quite some time." Just fills you with confidence, right? One of the big selling points here is that crusty stuff on top, as my daughter Alison put it. I think it is key; you know how summer squash can cook up kind of soft and textureless? Well, the crusty topping—just bread crumbs, olive oil, and Parmesan cheese if you like—is the perfect counterpoint. The squash is deliciously bathed in the tomato juices and basil gives the dish a heady aroma. I think you'll like this, too. It is excellent with corn on the cob.

5 tablespoons olive oil

1 large onion, finely chopped

3 medium summer squash, halved lengthwise and cut into bite-size
  pieces

salt

1 garlic clove, minced

6 plum tomatoes or 2 large tomatoes, cored, seeded, and chopped

small handful of fresh basil, chopped

freshly ground black pepper

3/4 cup unseasoned bread crumbs or plain cracker meal

1/4 cup grated Parmesan cheese (optional)

Preheat the oven to 400°. Heat 3 tablespoons of the olive oil in a large nonreactive ovenproof skillet. Add the onion and sauté, stirring often over medium heat, for 5 minutes. Add the summer squash and 2 big pinches of salt and continue to sauté, stirring occasionally, for 5 minutes more. Stir in the garlic, sauté briefly, then add the tomatoes. Cook the vegetables for about 10 minutes, stirring often, until the tomatoes are quite soft. Stir in the basil, black pepper, and more salt to taste. Remove from the heat.

Using your fingers to do a thorough job, mix the crumbs, cheese, a pinch or two of salt and pepper, and the remaining 2 tablespoons of olive oil in a small bowl. Sprinkle the crumbs evenly over the top of the vegetables. Bake the dish for about 15 to 20 minutes on the middle rack of the oven, until the top is golden brown. Cool briefly, then serve.

Garlic-Baked Tomatoes with Fresh Herb Bread Crumbs

MAKES 6 SERVINGS

I'm never quite sure how my kids are going to react to fresh cooked tomatoes, but their enthusiasm for this dish really took me by surprise; the two older kids especially loved it. Funny, because sometimes my kids don't like chunky tomato things. Anyway, this is one of those dream dishes you could throw together in your sleep or with a brood at your heels: Just chunk a few fresh tomatoes, throw them in a skillet with oil and garlic, and bake. Top with crumbs, brown, and serve.

6 or 7 medium ripe tomatoes

2 tablespoons olive oil

2 garlic cloves, minced

salt and freshly ground pepper to taste

BREAD CRUMBS
5 slices firm-textured white bread (like Pepperidge Farm)

small handful of fresh basil leaves

3 tablespoons olive oil

salt

$1/2$ cup freshly grated Parmesan cheese

Preheat the oven to 450° and get out a large ovenproof nonreactive skillet. Core the tomatoes and cut each one into either 4 or 6 wedges, the latter if the tomatoes are on the large size. Add them to the skillet with the olive oil, garlic, and salt and pepper and toss well. Put the skillet on an upper shelf of the oven and bake for about 25 to 30 minutes; the tomatoes should be very soft and juicy.

While the tomatoes are baking, make the crumbs. Break the bread into large chunks and put it in the bowl of a food processor with the basil. Process the bread for 5 to 10 seconds, until it is broken into very small crumbs. Heat the olive oil in a large skillet and stir in the crumbs. Keep stirring for about 1 minute over medium-high heat, just until it looks like the crumbs have absorbed the oil evenly. Remove from the heat and salt them lightly to taste.

After the tomatoes have baked the initial 25 to 30 minutes, remove them from the oven and reduce the heat to 400°. Mix the cheese into the crumbs and spread the crumbs over the top of the tomatoes. Put the tomatoes back in the oven, this time on a lower rack, and bake another 5 to 10 minutes, until the crumbs are golden brown. Let the tomatoes cool about 10 minutes before serving; they're best if not too hot.

Roasted Garlic

MAKES 1 HEAD ROASTED GARLIC

If I have any regret in life, it's that I didn't taste roasted garlic until my fortieth year; I plan to make up for it in the second half of my life. The revelation came at a wonderful Mediterranean restaurant Karen and I visited in Gloucester, Massachusetts, a town we spend a good deal of time in every summer. The garlic was served simply, with warm, thick-crusted peasant bread and olive oil. And it was roasted to an almost buttery perfection: You could pluck the cloves out of the head and actually spread them on the bread. Later I spoke to the chef, who shared his simple guidelines for accomplishing this magic the way I describe here. Use roasted garlic in mashed potatoes and other vegetable purees; on toast or bread, as I mentioned; in tomato sauces, dips, and salad dressings. Try to think about doing this while the oven is already in use so you're not cooking this one tiny thing all alone.

    1 whole head of garlic, the fresher the better (summer/fall is the best
        time)

    olive oil

Preheat the oven to 400°. Peel any loose papery skins off the garlic, then slice off the top third of the head, exposing the individual cloves. Put the garlic in a small baking dish and rub a little olive oil over the exposed cloves. Put a teaspoon or so of water in the baking dish. Cover tightly with foil and roast the garlic for about 40 minutes. When done, the cloves will be golden colored and feel soft when pierced with the tip of a paring knife. Serve or use at any temperature.

Garlic-Braised Asparagus

MAKES 4 TO 6 SERVINGS

The season for good asparagus is so short, maybe four weeks in all, that we seldom make it past Asparagus 101, tossed with olive oil and garlic and braised in the barest amount of water. It doesn't come any better or easier than this. Fresh asparagus makes a lovely self broth as it braises and you won't want to waste it. If we are serving this with baked potatoes, one of Karen's tricks is to use a little extra water in the skillet when she braises it. We spoon this broth over the baked potatoes to moisten them. It adds a great flavor and a heck of a lot less calories than sour cream or butter. If you happen to have some on hand, the asparagus can be braised in light vegetable stock or simply crumble part of an unsalted bouillon cube into the water as it comes to a boil. Time this carefully.

1 pound asparagus

2 tablespoons olive oil

1 or 2 garlic cloves

salt

freshly ground pepper

Cut an inch off the bottom of each spear and discard it. If the spears are thick, the bottom should be peeled almost halfway up the spear with a vegetable peeler. If the spears are thin and tender, it won't be necessary. In any case, cut the tips off, then slice the remaining part of the spears into logs about 3/4 inch long.

In a large nonreactive skillet, heat the olive oil and stir in the garlic and the asparagus tips and logs. Sauté them for about 1 minute, stirring, over medium heat, then add water to almost cover. Salt the water lightly, then cover and cook the asparagus over medium heat for about 3 to 5 minutes, depending on the thickness of the spears. Sample one of the thickest pieces of asparagus as you near the end of the cooking time; it should be just tender, with no stringiness to the bite. When it is done, salt and pepper the asparagus to taste and serve it hot, right away, in its own broth.

❧ *Food for Thought* ❧
ASPARAGUS: THE AMBIGUOUS SPEAR

The handling of most vegetables is so much more clear than the mystery of how one is supposed to tackle an asparagus spear. There's little question where the peel of a spud ends and the flesh begins, and the same goes for a winter squash. When you trim a pepper, you can see the stem and those white ribs you excise with care. Not so the spear. We've been warned to avoid that tough, stringy base, but where does it turn from tender to tough? It's like the equator: You know it is there, but you can't see it. I used to follow this piece of cooking wisdom: Simply bend the spear in your hands and it will break at the right spot. All well and good, of course, but mine would break so close to center it ultimately felt like an exercise in adolescent logic, sort of like buying a new pair of blue jeans and turning them into cutoffs before you'd even worn them.

Ultimately, I found that I liked working with thick spears best and that the tough base is less of a problem than we make it out to be. Apparently, most of the stringiness is in the peel and it is easy to peel a thick spear with a vegetable peeler: Just run it right down the spear. I like to start about halfway down just to play it safe. Aside from that, I simply trim about 1 inch off the bottom of each stalk because it tends to be dry and tough in that extreme section. If you take care of those two areas, you'll be all set.

As for marketing, be sure to buy fresh, firm, unshriveled spears with tight tips; if the tips have started to open, don't bother. Refrigerate immediately and plan to use them within 24 hours if possible.

Simple Sautéed Cabbage

MAKES 5 TO 6 SERVINGS

We're all so seasoning conscious these days we sometimes forget how wonderful plain vegetables can be. A case in point is this simple cabbage sauté, one vegetable our family never gets bored with. There's no secret ingredient, no sleight of hand or special pan required, not even an onion or garlic. Just throw it in the pan and cook it. You can serve this as a main or side dish. We usually just start making toast, slicing tomatoes, pulling out leftovers, and end up having one of those dinner free-for-alls; this dish seems to precipitate that kind of casual dining. Actually, very often we eat this for breakfast.

2¹/2 tablespoons olive oil (you can use unsalted butter for some of the
oil)

1 smallish head of green cabbage, quartered, cored, and thinly sliced

salt and freshly ground pepper

1 large carrot, peeled and grated

*C*hoose your largest heavy skillet; if it isn't at least 12 inches, you should
probably use a couple of smaller skillets. Put the pan on high heat until it is good and hot, then add the oil and swirl it around so it covers the
pan. Add the cabbage and don't disturb it for about 30 seconds; while you are
waiting, season it with some salt and pepper. After 30 seconds, give the cabbage a stir. Keep stirring it every 30 seconds or so, turning the heat down after
about 3 minutes. Stir in the grated carrot. Continue to cook the cabbage over
medium heat, partially covered, for about a total of 15 minutes, stirring occasionally. If the pan starts to get very dry and the cabbage is sticking or turning
black, cover it tightly to trap some of the steam. Taste the cabbage as you cook
it, seasoning it to taste with salt and pepper. Serve hot.

P O S T S C R I P T :

Just when I thought I was the first one to ever think up such a simple, clever
way to prepare cabbage, I discovered a very similar recipe in one of Marcella
Hazan's cookbooks, *Essentials of Classic Italian Cooking* (Knopf, 1992). She
calls it "smothered cabbage." I should have known better.

Sautéed Baby Beet Greens with Lemon

MAKES 4 SERVINGS

The only time of year I bother to prepare beet greens is early summer when I
can find them fresh and tender at a local farmstand; that's when we really love
them, quickly sautéed in olive oil and garlic and served with a squeeze of lemon
juice. Since we have so much of it, I might toss in some lemon thyme as an af-
terthought, but it isn't necessary. In case you've never had them, baby beet
greens cook up sweet and tender in a matter of minutes, with a texture and flavor not unlike spinach. Probably because they're so soft and mild tasting, the
kids are big fans. I love a hot pile of them with freshly sliced tomatoes and crusty
bread. They're also good with almost any potato or grain dish. This recipe
serves 4 but can easily be multiplied; figure on ¹/2 pound raw greens per person.

2 pounds tender baby beet greens

2 tablespoons olive oil

1 garlic clove, minced

$^1/_2$ teaspoon fresh lemon thyme (optional)

salt and freshly ground pepper

half a lemon

*B*reak the stems off the greens at the base of the leaves and put the leaves in a very large bowl. Fill the bowl with cold water, agitating the leaves vigorously to wash off the grit. As best as possible, shake the water off the greens, then stack and cut them into approximate $^1/_2$-inch strips. Set aside.

Gently heat the olive oil and garlic in a large nonreactive skillet, stirring occasionally for 1 minute. Increase the heat, then stir in the leaves, coating them with the oil. Sauté the leaves over high heat for 3 to 4 minutes, until tender, adding the lemon thyme, if using, and salt and pepper to taste at the end. Transfer to a serving dish, drizzle with lemon juice, and serve at once.

Basic Kale

MAKES 2 TO 3 CUPS COOKED KALE, ABOUT 4 SERVINGS

One of the best vegetables available to us is one that most people know only as that curly stuff they garnish salad bars with; almost without fail, the kids who work at the checkout counters of supermarkets can't identify the stuff, nor can many adults, which is a pretty sad commentary on how narrowly many families eat. I've been crazy about kale all of my adult life; my family eats so much of it I'm surprised we haven't turned green. It has more bounce and body than many other greens, and the flavor needs only the tiniest nudge, like a pinch of salt and vinegar. It is a little bit of work to strip the leaves from the stems, but I've come up with a great solution: Have the kids do it. If you just approach them in an understanding manner (*Ben, did I hear you say you needed a ride to go snowboarding tomorrow?*) they'll be delighted to help you out. Use cooked kale in everything from lasagne to minestrone, with beans, in pastas, pilafs, and as a pizza topping. It goes with just about everything.

1 large bunch (about 2 pounds) fresh kale

salt

2 tablespoons olive oil

1 medium onion, finely chopped

red wine vinegar or balsamic vinegar

freshly ground pepper

*S*trip the kale leaves from their central stems, discarding the stems and putting the leaves into the biggest bowl you have. You needn't tear the leaves into small pieces because you'll be chopping them later anyway. Fill the bowl with cool water, then agitate the leaves briskly to loosen the sand and grit; the curly leaves are notorious for hiding sandy grit.

Transfer the leaves into a big nonreactive pot; the water will cling to the leaves and that's fine. As you put the leaves in the pot, add a sprinkle of salt several times to salt the layers. The water on the leaves should be enough to steam the kale, but just for insurance I like to add a bit of extra water to the pot, perhaps $^1/_2$ cup. Cover the pot, bring to a full head of steam, then reduce the heat to medium. Steam the kale for 10 to 12 minutes, covered, until tender. Drain in a colander and cool.

When the kale is cool enough to handle, gather it into a ball and squeeze out most but not all of the liquid. Transfer to a cutting board and chop coarsely.

To finish the kale, heat the olive oil in a large nonreactive skillet. Stir in the onion and sauté over medium heat for 6 to 7 minutes, until soft. Stir in the kale and heat through. Just before removing from the heat, sprinkle several teaspoons of vinegar over the kale. Add pepper to taste. Taste and correct the seasonings, then serve.

Sam's Simple Broccoli

I thought twice about even mentioning this because it seems so obvious, but no use keeping it a family secret; it was the turning point in the career of one young broccoli eater in our family and perhaps it will make a difference for someone you know. And the secret is this: lemon juice. We just squeeze it over the steamed broccoli.

*T*o make Sam's favorite broccoli, we take 1 very large or 2 smaller heads of broccoli, rinse them well, and cut off the flowerets. Then we peel and dice the stalks. Everything is placed in a steamer, lightly salted, and steamed for just long enough to make the broccoli tender, maybe 4 to 6 minutes; keep an eye on it because you want it to become fork-tender but not mushy-soft the way broccoli can get. The hot broccoli is quickly transferred to a bowl, salted and peppered to taste, and doused with the juice of half a lemon. It can be buttered or not, depending on your preference; Sam can take or leave the butter as long as you don't forget the lemon juice. Then we pile about half of the broccoli onto Sam's plate and divide the remainder between the rest of us!

Delicious Disguised Mushrooms

MAKES ABOUT 1 CUP

I imagine this is the case with most families, but there are some foods that Karen and I like that the kids simply won't touch; olives is one that comes to mind immediately; 3 of my 4 kids don't like them. I could puree, pound, stuff, or dress them up as reindeer and in the end they'd still be olives. Then there are other foods that the kids do like, or at least will tolerate, but they can't warm up to the texture, mushrooms for one. I won't share with you all of the creative comparisons our kids have ventured for sliced sautéed mushrooms because I'm reasonably certain that none of them would whet your appetite. However, I will share with you this recipe for disguised mushrooms. They're the perfect compromise because we can all still enjoy the flavor and the texture is not an issue. Disguised mushrooms are basically sautéed, food-processed mushrooms. They aren't served alone; they're always used *in* something. We regularly add them to soups, stews, grain dishes (like risotto), and tomato sauce and use them as a layer in casseroles (see the Neoclassical Polenta Lasagne, page 177, for instance). You'll find many uses for them. The wine is optional, but it adds a nice touch if you'd like to use it.

2 tablespoons olive oil or unsalted butter

1 pound sliced mushrooms

1 or 2 garlic cloves, minced

salt and freshly ground pepper

1/2 cup white wine (optional)

Heat the olive oil or butter in a large nonreactive skillet. Stir in the mushrooms, garlic, and a big pinch of salt and pepper to taste. Sauté the mushrooms over medium-high heat, stirring often, for 1 minute. Cover, reduce the heat slightly, and cook the mushrooms for 3 to 4 minutes, until tender. If you are using the wine, add it now and cook the mushrooms for about 2 to 3 minutes more, until most but not all of the liquid has cooked off. Otherwise, simply cook off most but not all of the liquid in the pan. In either case, when most of the liquid has cooked off, remove from the heat and scrape the mushrooms into a food processor. Cool briefly, then process

❧ *Food for Thought* ❧

DISGUISED FOOD: BEYOND MUSHROOMS

While I don't advocate turning everything to mush to keep the peace at the dinner table, using this puree tactic from time to time is fair play, in the best interest of all concerned. There are times when texture is all. It can make or break a dish. Almost none of my kids, for example, likes a chunky tomato sauce; I didn't like it as a kid either. But all of them love a smoothish sauce. There are kids who wouldn't touch chunks of cooked potatoes, but they'll scream for mashed potatoes. If your child doesn't warm up to a particular food, don't assume it's the flavor they're rejecting; it could be the shape or texture. Try reintroducing the food using a different approach; pureeing or mashing may be the way to go, especially with young kids. Vegetable soups are one of the best places to introduce pureed vegetables kids might not otherwise eat; sometimes it is as simple as putting your child's portion in the food processor and thinning it with a little liquid. For a kid who is squeamish about vegetables, that simple step eliminates all of the textural and visual hurdles. Eventually, when your child learns he is eating the same soup you are, he gets the message that these vegetables aren't really as bad as he thought they were and, with any luck, he'll be more likely to try them in other ways.

them until they are broken into a rough puree, scraping down the sides of the bowl as necessary. Transfer the mushrooms to a bowl to cool. Cover and refrigerate until using.

Garlic-Stewed Tomatoes and Green Beans

MAKES 6 SERVINGS

I get very excited about the first green beans of the summer season and this popular family dish is one of the main reasons. I'll make this three or four times before I even consider moving on to other green bean dishes. One of the little tricks here is to undercook the green beans just a wee bit, so when they go into the pan with the already stewing tomatoes they can finish cooking without getting too soft and have just enough time to absorb the lovely garlicky tomato essence. So watch those beans. Much as I prefer this as a summer dish, occasionally I will find half-decent-looking fresh green beans in the winter and I'll make it then. Because the fresh tomatoes of winter aren't what they should be either, I like to add a few big pinches of sugar and a splash of red wine vinegar near the end of the cooking. That helps some. I love this with fresh corn on the cob and boiled new potatoes, tossed with fresh parsley and a little butter or olive oil.

$1^1/_4$ pounds (about 6 cups) fresh green beans, trimmed, halved, and rinsed

3 tablespoons olive oil

2 medium onions, halved and thinly sliced

2 to 3 small garlic cloves, minced

3 medium ripe tomatoes, cored and coarsely chopped

salt and freshly ground pepper

2 tablespoons chopped fresh parsley

1 tablespoon chopped fresh basil or 2 teaspoons dried

2 teaspoons minced fresh rosemary or 1 teaspoon dried

Bring several quarts of salted water to a boil in a large pot. Add the beans and boil until almost tender. This may take as little as 5 minutes for small tender beans and up to 10 minutes for large ones. Drain and set the beans aside.

Heat the olive oil in a large nonreactive skillet. Add the onions and sauté over medium heat for 8 to 10 minutes, stirring occasionally. Stir in the garlic, sauté for 10 seconds, then stir in the tomatoes and salt them lightly. Cover and cook the tomatoes for about 10 minutes, until soft. Add pepper to taste and the herbs. Stir in the green beans, cover, and gently simmer them for about 5 to 8 minutes. Serve right away or let them sit in the covered pan for up to 30 minutes to absorb the flavor of the tomato broth. Reheat briefly and serve.

Main-Dish Vegetables

When vegetables are the focal point of the meal, we think of them as main-dish vegetables. The very words *main-dish vegetable* are liable to strike some as an oxymoron: Aren't vegetables always relegated to a position of lesser importance on the dinner plate? Not in a well-balanced vegetarian diet they aren't. Vegetables can be top dog, so to speak, and this chapter provides ample proof.

Main-dish vegetables can be stews like ratatouille; braises—we have a gorgeous fall braise here of kale, winter squash, and corn; or even meatless hashes, like our Potato and Eggplant Hash (page 121). The prominent features of main-dish vegetables are both quantity (there's enough for generous portions) and relative complexity (they tend to involve more elements, prep work, and longer cooking times than their simpler cousins in the previous section). Given their prominent position, the quality of the vegetables is key: Whenever possible, main-dish vegetables should be prepared in season. They'll taste best that way. True, almost everything these days is "in season" at any given time in most supermarkets. That's the miracle of modern transportation, I suppose. But it seems less miraculous when you compare closely: Those green beans you get in December are a far cry from the local ones you find in July.

If you have young children, the sooner you introduce them to the idea that vegetables can take center stage on the dinner plate, the better off you'll be. If you have older children who are used to a more traditional main dish, proceed slowly. Pick a vegetable they like and go from there. Most kids like potatoes; you might start with the Vegan Scalloped Spuds (page 125). The Baked or Grilled Vegetable Packets (page 129) would work for kids who like to do things their way because they get to choose what goes in their own packet. I believe that asking our kids to join in can be a big step toward warming them up to a vegetarian diet; the better they know their foods and the more they help with the cooking, the more excited they'll be about eating it.

Red Flannel Hash

You've heard of red flannel hash? If not, it's traditional corned beef hash with cooked chopped beets added. This version KO's the corned beef, replacing it with cooked bulgur, and it tastes great. Naturally, the beets turn everything a deep red color. This is wonderful for breakfast, with or without a poached egg perched on top, or as a main or side dish for dinner. Food snobs beware: This tastes heavenly with ketchup.

$1^1/_4$ cups water

$1/_8$ teaspoon salt, plus more to taste

$1/_2$ cup uncooked bulgur

4 medium beets, scrubbed

$1^1/_2$ tablespoons olive oil or flavorless vegetable oil

1 medium onion, finely chopped

2 medium all-purpose potatoes, peeled and cut into $1/_2$-inch dice

$1/_2$ teaspoon dried thyme or 1 teaspoon fresh

freshly ground pepper

Bring the water and salt to a boil in a small saucepan. Stir in the bulgur, return to a boil, then lower the heat. Cook over very low heat for 15 minutes. Remove from the heat but leave the lid on for 5 minutes more; fluff with a fork and set aside.

While the bulgur cooks, put the beets in a medium saucepan and cover with lightly salted water. Bring to a boil and cook for 20 to 25 minutes, until tender. Drain, cover the beets with cold water, and let stand for 5 minutes; slip off the skins. When the beets are cool enough to handle, cut them into $1/_2$-inch dice.

Heat the oil in a large skillet. Stir in the onion and sauté over medium-low heat for about 5 minutes. Stir in the potatoes and sauté for 2 minutes, stirring often. Add just enough water to cover the potatoes; salt lightly and bring to a boil. Cover and cook the potatoes for 7 to 10 minutes, until just barely tender. Check the water occasionally; you want to end up with just a little bit in the pan when the potatoes are cooked because it will help flavor the hash.

Stir the beets into the skillet and heat briefly. Stir in the bulgur until every-thing is uniformly mixed, add the thyme, then salt and pepper to taste. Serve hot.

Potato and Eggplant Hash

MAKES 4 TO 5 SERVINGS

The definition of hash has loosened up in the last few years and I'm glad to see it. In the old days, hash meant just hefty meat-and-potato concoctions, but nowadays it isn't unusual to run into good hashes made with vegetables or grains instead of meat. Here's a dinner hash made with a couple of my family's favorite vegetables, spuds and eggplant. The eggplant gets a Provençal-style treatment—with tomatoes, onions, and herbs—then, when it is starting to turn soft, cooked potatoes are stirred in and the dish is heated for a few minutes more. In the end the eggplant has pretty much cooked down to a delicious mush that coats the potatoes; it has just the right texture to make this a credible hash. If you're eating cheese, sprinkle some grated Parmesan over the top just before serving the hash. Serve this with marinated vegetables and grapes for dessert.

5 medium all-purpose potatoes, peeled and cut into bite-size cubes
salt
2 tablespoons red wine vinegar
2 1/2 tablespoons olive oil
1 large onion, chopped
1 medium green or red bell pepper, finely chopped
1 medium-large eggplant, peeled and cubed
2 garlic cloves, minced
1 cup chopped fresh tomatoes or crushed tomatoes in puree
2 tablespoons chopped fresh basil or 1 1/2 teaspoons dried
handful of fresh parsley leaves, finely chopped
freshly ground pepper
1/2 cup freshly grated Parmesan cheese (optional)

Put the potatoes in a large pot of cold salted water and bring to a boil. Gently boil the potatoes until they're just tender, then drain and spread them out in a large shallow bowl or casserole. Sprinkle the potatoes with the vinegar and set them aside.

Heat 1 1/2 tablespoons of the olive oil in a large nonreactive skillet. Stir in the onion and bell pepper and sauté the vegetables over medium-high heat for 6 to 7 minutes, stirring occasionally. Add the remaining 1 tablespoon of oil to the skillet and stir in the eggplant. Cover the skillet, reduce the heat slightly, and let the eggplant cook for about 6 minutes, stirring once or twice. Stir in the garlic, cover the skillet again, and cook for 2 minutes more. Stir in the tomatoes and herbs, cover, and let the eggplant stew gently for 5 minutes.

Stir the cooked potatoes into the eggplant, then taste the hash, adding salt and pepper if desired. Reduce the heat to low, cover, and let the hash warm through for 5 minutes before serving. If you're using the cheese, sprinkle it on right before serving.

❧ *Food for Thought* ❧
SALTED EGGPLANT: FACT OR FICTION?

I hate to break stride with my fellow cookbook writers, but I just don't get this business about salting eggplant before you cook it. Do you salt yours? I sometimes get the feeling that there are only sixty people in the whole world who actually do this and all of them happen to write cookbooks. I know, conventional wisdom has it that salting raw eggplant helps to draw out any bitter juices contained therein, a sort of aubergine facial. Back when I did occasionally salt, it seemed foolish: I'd draw out maybe a little liquid, but it never amounted to more than a spoonful. And even if it were a little bitter, I frankly never noticed it in my ratatouille. That's why I don't salt the eggplant here or in any other recipe in this book.

Eggplant and Chickpea Curry
MAKES 4 TO 6 SERVINGS

This, in the words of my son Ben, is *BAAAD*! Even my other son, Sam—who views eggplant as a menace to mealtime—will eat eggplant this way. One trick: Don't overcook the eggplant until it gets mushy to the point of near disintegration; my kids, at least, find that to be a real turnoff. Canned chickpeas are fine here. As I've said elsewhere, the texture of canned chickpeas is a bit too soft for my taste, but they're convenient and the flavor is pretty good; do remember to rinse them well under cold water. We serve this over couscous, but any other grain will do.

4 tablespoons olive oil

1 large onion, finely chopped

2 to 3 garlic cloves, minced

4 teaspoons mild curry powder

1 tablespoon finely minced fresh ginger

1 medium eggplant, peeled and cut into $^3/_4$-inch cubes

salt

3 large ripe tomatoes, cored and coarsely chopped, or about $1^1/_2$ cups
   crushed canned tomatoes in puree

1 tablespoon tomato paste

1 19-ounce can chickpeas, drained and well rinsed

freshly ground pepper

$^1/_4$ cup chopped fresh parsley or coriander

*H*eat 2 tablespoons of the oil in a large enameled soup pot or casserole. Add the onion and sauté over medium-high heat for 7 to 8 minutes, stirring often. Reduce the heat slightly and stir in the garlic, curry powder, ginger, and remaining 2 tablespoons olive oil. Add the eggplant and stir well to coat with the oil and spices. Salt the eggplant lightly, cover, and let the eggplant cook for 2 to 3 minutes.

Stir in the tomatoes, cover, and let the eggplant stew for 3 to 4 more minutes. Stir in about 1 cup of water and the tomato paste, stirring well to loosen any spices that may be stuck to the bottom of the pan. Simmer the curry for 5 minutes, uncovered, then stir in the chickpeas. Season to taste with salt and pepper, letting the curry simmer for another 5 minutes; if you need it, add more water, keeping in mind that this is supposed to be a relatively dry curry, not a very saucey one. A minute or so before serving, stir in the parsley. Serve hot over your favorite grain.

Braised Kale, Winter Squash, and Corn

MAKES 6 SERVINGS

I can't think of a finer example of simple, tasty vegetarian cooking than this colorful fall braise. We eat this throughout the fall and winter, using frozen corn once the fresh is done. If we are serving a couple of side dishes or bread, we'll eat this as is. But for a more substantial main dish we'll spoon it over pasta or a grain. This combination of vegetables creates its own good broth, so no stock is required; I just use water. The mushrooms are important to the flavor of the broth, but if your kids don't like them, do as I do and instead of finely chopping them, just cut them in half so they can be easily removed from individual portions.

1 large bunch kale (1 to 1^1/2 pounds)

2 tablespoons olive oil

2 medium onions, chopped

1 garlic clove, minced

^{1}/2 teaspoon mild chili powder

8 ounces mushrooms

2 cups water

1 teaspoon crumbled dried sage

^{1}/2 teaspoon salt, plus more to taste

1 medium butternut or Delicata squash, peeled and cut into bite-size
    chunks

1^1/2 cups freshly scraped corn kernels (frozen are also fine)

^{1}/4 cup coarsely chopped fresh or canned tomatoes

freshly ground black pepper

Strip the kale leaves from their stems, ripping them into smallish pieces. Place the kale in a bowl and cover with plenty of cool water. Agitate the leaves in the water, then transfer to a colander and set aside to drain.

Heat the oil in a large nonreactive soup pot or Dutch oven. Stir in the onions and sauté over medium heat, stirring often, for 8 to 9 minutes. Stir in the garlic and chili powder and sauté another minute.

Add the mushrooms, water, sage, and salt. Bring to a simmer and add the kale. Cover and simmer for 10 minutes. Stir in the squash and corn. Cover and simmer 10 minutes more, until the squash is barely tender. Stir in the chopped tomatoes and simmer 5 minutes more. Taste and correct the seasoning, adding more salt, if necessary, and pepper to taste.

❧ *Food for Thought* ❧
QUESTION: JUST WHAT DO YOU DO WITH AN EAR OF CORN?

When you *scrape* corn, you end up not with whole kernels, but the inner flesh of the kernels and corn juice or milk. It is more like a rough corn puree than distinct kernels, fine for soups and stews and other recipes where a corn kernel texture isn't critical. Anyway, to scrape corn, run a sharp knife lengthwise down the center of a row of kernels, essentially cutting them in half. Do this to all the rows, then, on the baking sheet, push the *back* of the blade of your knife down the row; you'll need to use some force. This will push out the flesh and milk. If you're going to be doing this often, I suggest you invest in a corn scraper, a little toothed device mounted on a board that you scrape the corn over; the stuff just falls right into your bowl.

Shaving is the term used for removing kernels from the cob with a sharp knife, not to be confused with *scraping*. Both methods are fairly messy—it's outside work, because corn juice and kernels fly everywhere—but lots of fun and well worth the effort. To cut the kernels from the cob, get set up outside in a comfortable spot, like the picnic table. Bring a sharp paring knife and a large baking sheet to catch the kernels. Grasp the corn's handle with one hand, holding it on the baking sheet at a 45° angle. With knife in your other hand, simply run the blade under the kernels, cutting down the length of the ear. It takes a little practice to use just the right amount of pressure so you're not cutting off too little or jabbing it too deep to a dead stop.

In any case, the season for fresh corn is so short you'll want to cut as much as you can while you can. We always cut the kernels off a dozen ears before the end of the season, bag it up, and freeze for Thanksgiving dinner. It's a nice reminder that summer will be here again before we know it.

Vegan Scalloped Spuds

MAKES 6 SERVINGS

One of our favorite potato dishes is a magnificently rich gratin called potatoes *dauphinois*, a casserole of potatoes cooked—like many good things French—in an unabashed quantity of cream and butter. They're absolutely wonderful and I still make them once in a while, but you'd hardly call them appropriate as a regular item in a healthy family diet. Enter Vegan Scalloped Spuds. Instead of cream, these vegan potatoes are baked in a delicate meatless gravy made from nutritional yeast. Obviously, they taste very little like the French original that inspired this dish—though the texture is similarly thick and creamy—but they're excellent in their own right. My kids are really into these; believe it or not, we usually *double* this recipe when the kids are really hungry and we're looking for a surefire cold weather meal. We seldom have leftovers. We like this with salad, corn, and hot French bread.

 1 recipe Great Gravy (page 197)

 8 to 9 cups (2¹/₂ to 3 pounds) all-purpose potatoes, peeled and thinly sliced

 scant teaspoon of salt or vegetable salt

 freshly ground pepper to taste

*P*reheat the oven to 400° and place a large ovenproof casserole or gratin dish in the oven to heat. Prepare the gravy if you haven't already; you can make it in a large soup pot if you like or transfer it to one when it is done. Add the potatoes to the gravy and turn the heat to medium. Add the salt and plenty of pepper and heat the potatoes, stirring often, for about 5 to 7 minutes; you aren't trying to cook the potatoes, just bring them up to oven temperature. Remove the gratin dish from the oven and spread a little oil in the bottom of it with a paper towel. Turn the hot potatoes and gravy into the prepared dish—a second set of hands is useful to scrape the pot—and level the top with a spoon. Cover the dish with foil and bake for 30 minutes. Remove the foil and bake another 20 to 30 minutes, until the potatoes feel tender when pierced with a sharp knife. Serve hot.

Gratin of Potatoes and Tomatoes

MAKES 6 SERVINGS

When you think potato gratin, you probably imagine some version of creamy scalloped potatoes, right? I used to think that way, too, and we ate accordingly. So once a month—okay, maybe it was twice a month—I would prepare potatoes *dauphinois*, that classic of French cuisine, made with enough cream to fill a horse trough. It was, in a word, extraordinary—not to mention extraordinarily caloric. At the rate I was going, I knew it wouldn't be long before I'd be buying ugly clothes from mail-order catalogs titled "Hip Duds for Big Guys." Today I'm happy to have replaced rich potato dishes, like potatoes *dauphinois,* with ones like this, a gratin moistened with a highly seasoned tomato sauce. I find it every bit as satisfying as my old favorites, healthy but still comforting and delicious. As a treat, Karen and I like to sprinkle chopped green olives over the adult portion of this dish.

8 to 9 cups all-purpose potatoes, sliced a generous $1/8$ inch thick

salt

4 tablespoons olive oil

$1^1/2$ cups finely chopped onions

2 garlic cloves, minced

1 28-ounce can crushed tomatoes in puree

2 tablespoons chopped fresh basil or 2 teaspoons dried

1 tablespoon chopped fresh oregano or 1 teaspoon dried

$1/2$ teaspoon red pepper flakes

freshly ground pepper

$1^1/2$ cups grated sharp Cheddar, provolone, or other melting cheese (optional)

$1/3$ cup finely chopped pitted green olives (optional)

$1/2$ cup fine dry bread crumbs

*P*ut the potatoes in a large pot with plenty of salted water to cover. Bring the potatoes to a boil and boil gently for no more than about 2 minutes; you don't want them to become tender, just a little softened. Drain, then carefully spread the potatoes on a platter or baking sheet to cool. Preheat the oven to 400°.

Heat $2^1/2$ tablespoons of the olive oil in a medium saucepan. Stir in the onions and sauté over medium-high heat for 7 minutes, until translucent. Stir in the garlic, sauté 15 seconds more, then add the can of tomatoes, herbs, and pepper flakes. Simmer the sauce for 5 minutes over medium heat, seasoning it to taste with salt and a little pepper. Remove from the heat.

Lightly oil a large shallow casserole or gratin. Spread one-quarter of the tomato sauce over the bottom of the dish and layer with about one-third of the potatoes. If you are using the cheese, sprinkle some on after each of the 3 potato layers. Spread another quarter of the sauce over the potatoes, then continue layering potatoes and sauce, finishing with the sauce. If you are using the olives, spread them over the top, then sprinkle the crumbs evenly over the surface. Drizzle the top of the casserole with the remaining $1^1/2$ tablespoons of olive oil.

Bake the potatoes for about 40 minutes, until heated through. Serve at once.

Crusted Artichoke Hearts and Tomatoes

MAKES 4 TO 5 SERVINGS

I love artichoke hearts, though I must tell you that I have a mental block about actually preparing them fresh; it is simply one of those things that if I had to prepare my own, I'd never eat them. Besides, I find that the quality of the canned artichoke hearts I buy—usually Progresso brand—is pretty good. And I generally use them in ways that minimize any quality gap that might exist. Here is one excellent example, a dish Karen and I occasionally enjoy. First I infuse the hearts with flavor by gently heating them in olive oil and garlic. Once that's done, I add some chopped fresh tomatoes to the pan and then some herbs to make the simplest of sauces for the artichokes to simmer in. Then everything is topped with a dusting of bread crumbs—or bread crumbs and Parmesan cheese, if you like—and quickly browned. Simple ingredients, good food. If your kids are fond of artichoke hearts, they'll probably like these.

2 14-ounce cans artichoke hearts, drained

3 tablespoons olive oil

4 garlic cloves, minced

3 large ripe tomatoes, peeled, seeded, and chopped

2 tablespoons chopped fresh basil

2 tablespoons chopped fresh parsley

salt and freshly ground pepper to taste

$^1/_4$ to $^1/_3$ cup fine, dry bread crumbs

$^1/_4$ cup freshly grated Parmesan cheese (optional)

Cut each of the artichoke hearts in half, laying them flat side down on a platter lined with a double layer of paper towels. Set aside for 5 minutes.

Over very low heat, stir $2^1/_2$ tablespoons of the olive oil and garlic in a large nonreactive ovenproof skillet. Add the artichoke hearts, flat side down, and gently warm them in the oil for 2 to 3 minutes, then carefully push them off into a pile to the side of the pan. Add the tomatoes to the skillet and increase the heat. Heat the tomatoes alongside the artichoke hearts, stirring occasionally, until they break down and form a sauce, about 3 to 4 minutes. Stir in the basil, parsley, and salt and pepper. Arrange the artichoke hearts over the sauce, turning them flat side up, and simmer for 1 minute. Remove from the heat and preheat the broiler.

Dust the artichoke hearts with the bread crumbs, or first mix the crumbs and cheese and sprinkle them over the top. Drizzle with the remaining $1/2$ tablespoon of olive oil and broil the dish until lightly browned on top.

VARIATIONS: A little wine gives the tomato sauce base an added dimension. If you like, add $1/3$ cup dry white wine to the tomatoes once they start to break down, heating the tomatoes a minute or so longer to cook off the excess liquid. A few chopped pitted olives are also a welcome addition to the sauce; stir them in with the other seasonings.

Baked or Grilled Vegetable Packets

MAKES 4 OR MORE SERVINGS

This is one of the best recipes I know for kids and vegetables, because the kids get to choose just how they want to make these. They can be as creative and daring as they want or they can stick with the tried and true; it's totally up to them, no pressure to be gourmets-in-training. Mom or Dad's job is to round up and help prep the veggies and seasoning ingredients. In summer, this is a blast because everything is so fresh. Winter puts some restrictions on you but not many. So get the stuff first. Corn on the cob can be cut into 2-inch sections (lean hard on the back of your knife—it will work). Tomatoes need to be chunked, green beans snapped. Lots of fresh herbs are important or dried if fresh ones aren't available. Basil and parsley are basics, but others are welcome, too. You need some "kickers" in there, too, to boost the flavor. My favorites are pesto, balsamic vinegar, perhaps a tad of butter, or a spoonful or two of vegetable stock or brothy soup if it is on hand. Add salt and pepper liberally; since you won't be tasting as you go, you will need to add it at the beginning. This is great camp food (see *Food for Thought*).

VEGETABLES

corn on the cob, cut into 2-inch sections

green beans, snapped into bite-size pieces

eggplant, cut into cubes

summer squash, halved lengthwise and sliced

plum or regular tomatoes, cut into large chunks, or tomato sauce, if your
     kids don't like big pieces of tomato

mushrooms, sliced

onions, finely chopped

broccoli, cut into flowerets

carrots, peeled and sliced

new potatoes, cut into bite-size pieces

SEASONINGS
salt and freshly ground pepper

fresh parsley, basil, and other fresh herbs

balsamic or red wine vinegar

olive oil and/or unsalted butter

brothy soup stock

pesto (about $1/2$ tablespoon per packet), optional

chopped garlic (1 small clove per packet), optional

*B*egin by making a fire if you are going to be grilling these or pre-
heating the oven to 425°. Tear off pieces of aluminum foil about 14
inches long; you will need 2 per person because they should be doubled up, especially if the packets are going on the grill. Put the flat, doubled
sheets in front of you at your work area and rub some oil in a big circle in the
center of each. Have everyone pile their favorite vegetables in the center of
their packet. Salt and pepper them lightly, then sprinkle them with herbs.
Bring up the sides a little so the liquid can't run out, and sprinkle each one with
vinegar and about a tablespoon of olive oil. Especially if you are using a high
proportion of potatoes, carrots, and broccoli, add a spoonful of water or soup
stock to help steam the vegetables. Dot with pesto and sprinkle with garlic, if
you're using them. Close up the packets, using a marker to indicate which
packet belongs to whom. Place the packets right on the shelf of the oven or on
top of the grill and cook them for about 30 minutes. To check them, carefully
open the top (watch out for the steam) and poke the veggies with a fork. Place
the packets on plates, open carefully, and dig in.

VARIATION: My son Ben came up with this idea: He tosses chunks of
tempeh in barbecue sauce, spiking them with a shake of cayenne. Let sit 15 to
30 minutes, then add them to your veggies before cooking. His father approves; it tastes good!

❧ *Food for Thought* ❧
CAMP-STYLE VEGETABLES

These vegetables in foil are a great camping idea, especially since it is always a challenge to eat good, healthy fresh food while you are camping. Since most of us camp in the summer, it is never a problem to buy local produce where you camp, unless of course you camp in Alaska. Just get an idea of how much of each vegetable you'll need before you go to the local farmstand and buy accordingly (get some fresh fruit while you're there, for dessert). Make your campfire with a circle of rocks around the outside. If you have a grill top, great; just put the packets on top. Otherwise, just snug your packets up next to the rocks near the fire and they'll cook in a jiffy. Make couscous while you are waiting.

Vegetable Kofta
⟋

MAKES ABOUT 34 BALLS, ABOUT 8 SERVINGS

I've loved these little Indian vegetable balls for almost as long as I can remember. I first had them at the Indian restaurants I grew up near in my native New Jersey, eventually learning to make them for myself. Since I've been with Karen, these kofta have become one of her signature dishes, one of the big family meals she does several times a year. She says it's a great special occasion dish to serve guests you might ordinarily do your best lasagne for. A distinct advantage of Karen's version, which was inspired by cookbook author Jeanne Lemlin, in her book *Vegetarian Pleasures* (Knopf, 1986), is that these are made without a common kofta ingredient, chickpea flour, which can be difficult to find. Instead, these are bound with bread crumbs and mashed potatoes, enclosing a variety of colorful vegetables. Serve Yogurt Cucumber Salad (page 30) on the side.

    5 medium all-purpose potatoes, peeled and cubed

    2 tablespoons flavorless vegetable or sunflower oil

    1 cup very finely chopped onions

    2 medium carrots, peeled and very finely chopped

    1/2 cup frozen baby peas

    1 tablespoon ground cumin

    1 tablespoon coriander

    1/2 teaspoon turmeric

pinch of cayenne

1 10-ounce box chopped frozen spinach, thawed

$1/2$ teaspoon salt, plus more to taste

$1/2$ cup fine dry bread crumbs, plus more for rolling the balls in

light flavorless vegetable oil, for deep-frying (we use sunflower oil)

cooked rice, to serve the kofta on

Kofta Curry Sauce (page 195)

*P*ut the potatoes in a large saucepan and cover with plenty of cold salted water. Bring to a boil, then cook the potatoes until they're very tender, about 10 to 12 minutes. Drain the potatoes, transferring them to a large bowl, and save the water for soup stock.

Heat the oil in a medium skillet. Add the onions and carrots and sauté over medium-high heat for about 7 to 8 minutes, until the onions are clear. Stir in the baby peas, sauté another minute, then remove the pan from the heat and set aside.

Combine the spices in a small skillet. Stir the spices over medium-low heat for about 2 minutes to take away the raw flavor, then pour the spices over the potatoes.

Squeeze most of the excess liquid out of the spinach and scatter it over the potatoes, then mash the two together with a potato masher until the spices are evenly incorporated. Stir the sautéed vegetables, salt, and $1/2$ cup of bread crumbs into the potato mixture, then set the mixture aside and cool to room temperature.

Using a well-mounded tablespoon for each one, shape the mixture into balls, rolling each one in bread crumbs. As you shape them, transfer the balls to a baking sheet. Cover the kofta with plastic wrap and refrigerate for at least 1 hour; they can be made up to 24 hours ahead.

Before you fry the balls, have the rice and sauce ready and standing by. Fill a medium cast-iron skillet about halfway with oil and turn the heat up to medium-high. Once the oil is hot, test a ball to see if the oil temperature seems right; the oil should start to bubble around the balls when they go in but not so madly that the exterior burns before the center is heated through. Set the oven on low to keep the first balls warm while successive batches cook and line a baking sheet with a grocery sack.

Place the balls in the fat, leaving enough room between them to turn them easily. Fry the balls until the bottom half is a deep golden brown, about 2 minutes, then roll them over and fry the other half for another couple of minutes. Using a slotted spoon, transfer the kofta to the lined baking sheet and keep them warm in the oven while you fry the rest of the balls. Serve the hot balls over rice, covered with the Kofta Curry Sauce.

Ratatouille of Poached Eggs

MAKES 4 SERVINGS

Making ratatouille in July and August is second nature to many of us; poaching eggs on top of it may not be. This dish is an obvious choice for a lazy summer brunch, perhaps a special meal you'd offer friends at your ocean retreat. It is a great way to use last night's leftover ratatouille. Serve it with any good crusty bread, corn bread, or garlic toasts (page 288).

3 tablespoons olive oil

1 large onion, chopped

1 small green bell pepper, coarsely chopped

3 garlic cloves, minced

1 small eggplant, peeled and cut into $^3/_4$-inch cubes

1 medium zucchini, cut into $^1/_2$-inch cubes

salt

2 cups cored coarsely chopped fresh tomatoes

handful of fresh basil leaves, finely chopped

2 tablespoons chopped fresh parsley

freshly ground pepper

balsamic vinegar or red wine vinegar

4 large eggs

optional garnishes: chopped pitted green olives, feta cheese, or Parmesan cheese

In a large nonreactive skillet, heat the olive oil and stir in the onion and pepper. Sauté the vegetables over medium-high heat for 7 minutes, until the onion is translucent, then stir in the garlic, eggplant, zucchini, and a big pinch of salt. Reduce the heat, cover, and soften the eggplant, stirring occasionally, for 4 to 5 minutes. Stir in the chopped tomatoes, cover once again, and simmer over medium-low heat for about 5 minutes more. Add the basil, parsley, more salt, and pepper to taste; simmer the dish for a few more minutes, adding a little balsamic vinegar or red wine vinegar, if it seems necessary.

About 5 minutes before serving, make 4 large depressions in the ratatouille. Crack the eggs into a ramekin one at a time, then slide each one into a depression. Cover the skillet and poach the eggs over low heat for 3 to 4 minutes, or until the yolk is done to your liking. Put a serving of ratatouille with an egg on top on each plate. Serve right away, passing the garnishes at the table.

Gratin of Eggplant, Tomatoes, and Peppers

MAKES 6 SERVINGS

This gratin, something like an eggplant Parmesan but easier to make, was inspired by a dish Karen had at a friend's house and came home very excited to try. I said *easier than* eggplant Parmesan, so I should begin there. Typically, you start eggplant Parmesan by dipping the slices in egg, breading them, frying them in oil, then smoking up the whole kitchen so badly the smoke detector goes off, right? Which is why I so like this method: You just brush the slices with oil, bread them, and bake. No smoke, no hassle, and you can prep the rest of the ingredients while the eggplant bakes. Instead of a tomato sauce we use fresh sliced tomatoes; needless to say, this dish is best in the summer, when the key ingredients are at their prime. The gratin bakes up moist and bubbly hot, the breading absorbing some of the liquid so it isn't overly runny. The cheese is optional; the dish tastes great even without it. Serve with a simple grain or warm crusty French bread.

1 bruised garlic clove

1 large or 2 medium eggplants

$^1/_4$ to $^1/_3$ cup olive oil

1 cup fine dry bread crumbs

4 large ripe tomatoes, thickly sliced

salt and freshly ground pepper

1 large green bell pepper, finely chopped

small handful of fresh basil, finely chopped

1$^1/_2$ cups grated mozzarella or fontina cheese (optional)

Get out a large gratin dish or shallow casserole and rub it with the bruised garlic. Oil the gratin dish lightly with olive oil and set it aside. Preheat the oven to 400°.

Slice the eggplant into $^1/_2$-inch-thick rounds and lightly brush both sides with oil. Lightly bread both sides of the eggplant in the crumbs, then arrange them on a large baking sheet. Bake for 20 to 25 minutes, until barely fork-tender.

When the eggplant is done, arrange half of the slices in the gratin dish. Cover with half of the tomato slices; add salt and pepper to taste. Cover with half of the peppers and half of the basil. Repeat the layering again: eggplant, tomatoes, peppers, basil. Cover with foil and bake for 35 to 45 minutes, until bubbling hot. If you're using the cheese, remove the foil, sprinkle on the cheese, and bake, uncovered, for the last 10 minutes. Let the dish sit at room temperature for 5 to 10 minutes before serving.

Artichoke, Pepper, and Olive Frittata with Mediterranean Relish

~

MAKES 6 TO 8 SERVINGS

Since none of my family are really big egg eaters anymore—an occasional omelet seems to be the favorite—I don't often do eggy dishes. But when I do, here's one I like very much, made with artichoke hearts, sliced green pepper, onion, tomato, and cheese (I like feta; the kids prefer Cheddar or Monterey Jack). Everything just goes into the one skillet, then the beaten eggs are poured over the top. It bakes very quickly, then you let it cool briefly and serve; it tastes good at any temperature. It can be eaten without it, but the relish adds some real personality.

2 tablespoons olive oil

1 medium onion, chopped

1 small green bell pepper, thinly sliced

1 garlic clove, minced

1 8-ounce jar marinated artichoke hearts, halved

small handful of pitted green olives with pimientos, halved (optional)

1 medium tomato, cored and chunked

freshly ground pepper

10 large eggs

$1/4$ teaspoon salt

$1/3$ cup crumbled feta cheese or other favorite cheese in small cubes

Mediterranean Relish (page 194), heated

Preheat the oven to 375° and get out a 10- or 11-inch cast-iron skillet. Heat the olive oil in the skillet and add the onion and pepper. Sauté over medium-high heat for 7 to 8 minutes, then stir in the garlic, artichoke hearts, olives, and tomato chunks. Heat, stirring, for about 2 minutes, just until the tomatoes start to soften. Add pepper to the vegetables to taste.

Break the eggs into a bowl and beat until they're frothy; beat in the salt. Stir the cheese into the skillet, then very slowly pour the eggs over the filling; do not stir. Let the mixture sit undisturbed for 1 minute, then transfer the skillet to the oven. Bake on the center rack for about 15 to 20 minutes, just until the eggs are cooked through (the frittata will start to puff). Cool the skillet on a rack for about 10 minutes, then slice and serve at any temperature with the warm relish. I like the frittata best slightly warm.

Pastas

Deborah Madison, she of *Greens* cookbook fame and my personal favorite vegetarian author, said it best in her wonderful cookbook, *The Savory Way: It's hard to remember what we did for quick and satisfying meals before pasta.* In fact, I do remember what we did: nothing. Our moms cooked then, back in the days when pasta meant spaghetti 98 percent of the time, lasagne and macaroni the other 2 percent.

Today, of course, we're a nation of inveterate pasta eaters. There are pasta cookbooks galore, and there seems to be no end to the way we'll combine all those wonderful shapes with just the right sauce.

While this may not be the most comprehensive collection of pasta recipes you'll come across in one cookbook, they come with my assurance that each one of them has passed the rigorous pasta meal standards as set forth by my own children and their friends. I won't go into all the details of said standards, but suffice it to say that each of these dishes is good for at least two generous helpings per child. None has any weird cheeses, exotic mushrooms, or strange stuff like that.

I think you'll find these recipes to be wholesome and healthy; most use a moderate amount of fat, and there's no lack of fresh vegetables and legumes here. For me, that's good enough. While we're on the subject of health, you may wonder why I don't make mention of whole grain pastas here, on the grounds that they're perhaps better for you than plain white pasta. Indeed, this may be true. But the plain fact is that my kids just don't like the whole grain pastas nearly as much. I think part of the problem with whole grain pastas is their flavor—kids seem to like the relative blandness of white pasta. Another part is texture; whole grain pastas tend to be grainy. This is especially noticeable with large noodles, like lasagne.

But whole grain pasta or white, I think you'll find something here both you and your kids will love.

Karen's Macaroni and Squash

⌇

MAKES 5 TO 6 SERVINGS

This is, without doubt, the most universally popular of our pasta dishes; everybody in our immediate and extended family loves this dairyless combination that looks for all the world like macaroni and cheese. When we first started making this we almost always used freshly baked squash. And in the fall, when we have tons of fresh squash on hand, we still do. But demand for the dish was so high that we started using canned squash when there was no fresh baked on hand. If the results aren't quite the same, they're still excellent and it makes the dish so much easier to prepare on the spur of the moment. Karen likes soy milk for the liquid here because it makes the sauce smooth and creamy. But water or vegetable stock also work well. To keep the meal simple, serve with applesauce and frozen cooked corn tossed with butter or olive oil.

1^1/$_2$ cups freshly baked winter squash or canned squash

3 tablespoons olive oil

1 large onion, chopped

1 or 2 garlic cloves, minced

1 pound dried elbow macaroni

1^1/$_2$ cups plain unsweetened soy milk

2 teaspoons Dijon mustard

1 teaspoon salt

freshly ground pepper

2 to 3 tablespoons chopped fresh parsley, for garnish

If you have not already and you're using fresh squash, bake the squash first; butternut and delicata are two excellent choices. When it is cool enough to handle, scoop out 1^1/$_2$ cups of the flesh and set aside. Bring a large pot of water to a boil for the macaroni.

Heat 2 tablespoons of the olive oil in a large skillet. Stir in the onion and sauté over medium heat for 8 to 9 minutes. Stir in the garlic, sauté for 30 seconds, then remove from the heat. Begin cooking the macaroni as soon as the water comes to a boil.

Put the squash, soy milk, mustard, remaining 1 tablespoon olive oil, and salt in a blender. Puree the mixture until it is smooth, then pour it into the skillet of sautéed onions. Heat the sauce, stirring, until it is bubbly hot; add pepper generously. When the macaroni is done, drain and immediately pour into the hot sauce. Mix the sauce and macaroni until coated evenly. If it seems to need it, add a few tablespoons hot water to the dish to make it more saucey. Serve at once, garnished with the parsley.

Broccoli, Basil, and Parmesan-Stuffed Shells

MAKES 6 SERVINGS

Like lasagne and ravioli, stuffed shells are a surefire crowd pleaser, especially where kids are considered. Here we offer a broccoli stuffing, flavored with lots of basil (fresh in summer, dried otherwise), Parmesan, and lightened with ricotta cheese. This is an excellent make-ahead dish for a party; it can be fully prepared up to 24 hours ahead, refrigerated, and baked the next day. (If the filling is cold, make sure you give it an extra 10 minutes in the oven.) We like these with garlic toasts (page 288) and a tossed green salad served with Tomato Balsamic Vinaigrette (page 44). In the summer, serve with hot buttered green beans or a cold green bean salad. I usually use our Everyday Quick Tomato Sauce (page 193) to make this.

1 1/2 pounds fresh broccoli, flowerets only

3 tablespoons olive oil

1 large onion, chopped

3 garlic cloves, minced

small handful of fresh basil leaves or 1 1/2 tablespoons dried

juice of 1/2 lemon

1 cup freshly grated Parmesan cheese, plus some extra for garnish

1 cup ricotta cheese

pinch of grated nutmeg

salt and freshly ground pepper

30 jumbo stuffing shells

2 quarts favorite tomato sauce, store-bought or homemade, heated

Steam the broccoli flowerets until they're tender, then spread them out on a couple of plates to cool. While the broccoli cools, heat the olive oil in a heavy, medium skillet. Stir in the onion and sauté for 8 to 9 minutes over medium heat, until light golden. Stir in the garlic and sauté for 20 more seconds, then scrape the contents of the pan into the bowl of a food processor. Add the basil and process for 5 seconds, then add the broccoli, lemon juice, and Parmesan cheese. Process again until the broccoli is finely chopped. Add the ricotta, nutmeg, and salt and pepper to taste and process again to mix. Don't overprocess the filling at this point; you want it to remain somewhat textured, not become entirely smooth. Transfer the filling to a bowl and season to taste a final time with salt and pepper.

Bring a large pot of salted water to a boil. Add a small spoonful of oil and the shells. Cook them according to package instructions until al dente. Rinse several times with cold water, drain, then place the shells on a double layer of paper towels. Preheat the oven to 400°.

Get out a large shallow casserole and spread half of the tomato sauce in it. Stuff the shells with the filling and place them in the casserole. Cover with the remaining sauce, then cover the casserole with foil. Bake the shells for about 35 to 40 minutes, until heated through. Serve hot, with extra grated Parmesan at the table for garnish.

Roasted Vegetable Ratatouille with Bow Ties

MAKES 6 SERVINGS

I love this—assorted roasted summer vegetables tossed with bow ties, a little Parmesan cheese, and balsamic vinegar. It doesn't, I suppose, qualify as a genuine ratatouille, even though we use the same vegetables. Ratatouille simmers, this roasts, and roasting tends to deepen and individuate the flavors, adding some crispy, slightly charred highlights in the bargain.

1 large eggplant, cut into $3/4$-inch cubes

3 small zucchini, sliced about $1/4$ inch thick

10 ripe plum tomatoes, cored and quartered lengthwise

2 small ripe tomatoes, coarsely chopped

1 large red bell pepper, thinly sliced

1 medium onion, coarsely chopped

2 garlic cloves, minced

$1/4$ cup olive oil

2 tablespoons chopped fresh basil or 2 teaspoons dried

2 tablespoons chopped fresh parsley

salt and freshly ground pepper

1 pound dried bow tie pasta

1 tablespoon balsamic vinegar

Roasted Tomato Sauce (page 143), optional

freshly grated Parmesan cheese, for garnish

*P*reheat the oven to 450° and get out 2 large shallow casseroles; oil them lightly. Two pans are better than one because if the vegetables are too crowded they'll simply stew in their own juices instead of roasting. Put all of the prepared vegetables in a very large mixing bowl and toss with the olive oil. Add the herbs and salt and pepper to taste. Divide the vegetables evenly between the 2 casseroles and roast for 1 hour, stirring them about every 20 minutes. (Note: if you are making the Roasted Tomato Sauce, start roasting the tomatoes about 15 minutes before you start the rest of the vegetables so you can work on the sauce while the vegetables finish cooking.)

When the vegetables are almost done, bring a large pot of water to a boil for the pasta. Cook the bow ties until al dente, then drain and transfer to a large serving bowl. Toss with the balsamic vinegar, then add the grilled vegetables and toss again. The sauce, if you are using it, can be served on top of individual portions or tossed with the bow ties and vegetables. Serve at once, with the cheese on the side.

Penne with Tomato-Basil Cream Sauce

MAKES 5 TO 6 SERVINGS

Generally speaking, we don't eat too many creamy pasta sauces in the summer, but here is one notable exception. I say summer—high tomato season—but given the increasing availability of good (if incredibly expensive) winter tomatoes, this is a sensational quick pasta dish anytime you can find ripe tomatoes and you're willing to pay the price. To make the sauce, chunked tomatoes are softened in a skillet with sautéed garlic and onions. Once the tomatoes exude a fair amount of juice, Neufchâtel cheese is added to the sauce, allowed to soften, then blended in with lots of fresh basil. How much basil? Can you ever use enough? This fusion of fresh tomato juices and creamy cheese make for a wonderful sauce whose consistency can easily be thinned with a bit of water if necessary. It couldn't be simpler or more delicious. We like to pass a bowl of grated Parmesan at the table when the penne is served.

3 tablespoons olive oil

1 large onion, chopped

3 garlic cloves, minced

2 pounds ripe juicy tomatoes, cored and cut into large bite-size chunks

salt

1 tablespoon balsamic vinegar

1 pound penne

6 ounces Neufchâtel cheese

lots of chopped fresh basil

freshly ground pepper

freshly grated Parmesan cheese, for garnish (optional)

*B*efore you begin the sauce, bring a large pot of salted water to a boil for the penne. In a large nonreactive skillet, heat the oil. Stir in the onion and sauté for about 7 minutes over medium-high heat, until it starts to turn golden. Stir in the garlic and tomatoes and salt the tomatoes lightly. Cover the skillet and let the tomatoes stew gently for about 5 minutes, until they're soft but not mushy. Stir in the vinegar. (You can start cooking the penne at this point.)

Break the Neufchâtel cheese into 7 or 8 chunks and scatter them over the tomatoes. Cover, turn the heat to *very* low, and let the cheese soften for 2 or 3 minutes. Whisk the cheese into the sauce, stirring in the basil and salt and pepper to taste. Simmer the sauce very gently, stirring, thinning it if necessary with a little water. Drain the cooked pasta and transfer to a pasta bowl. Cover with the sauce and toss well. Serve at once, with cheese if desired.

✺ *Food for Thought* ✺
THE QUESTION OF SKINS

Anytime you cook fresh tomatoes in a dish like this you end up with shriveled tomato skins. Is that a problem? All depends on your outlook. Most adults will either ignore them or simply eat them in spite of their paperlike texture. Kids—few of whom have experienced firsthand the added hassle of blanching tomatoes to remove the skins—might not cut you any slack. So if you think your children will have a problem with the skins, it might be worth the extra step of blanching the tomatoes first; just submerge them in boiling water for about 20 to 30 seconds. When they're cool enough to handle, the skins should peel right off. Then just cut the tomatoes in chunks and proceed as usual.

Fusilli with Roasted Tomato Sauce

MAKES 4 TO 5 SERVINGS

You can get tired of the same old red sauce after a while. That's why I was so psyched to discover this way of making tomato sauce, especially when I saw how much the kids liked it too. Oven roasting plum tomatoes does wonderful things to them. It deepens and concentrates the flavor, so what you end up with is very similar to a sun-dried tomato (check out the similarities between these and the oven "sun-dried" tomatoes on page 290). It even works well on less-than-perfect winter tomatoes.

2¹/₂ to 3 pounds ripe plum tomatoes

olive oil, to brush on the tomatoes

salt and freshly ground pepper to taste

1 pound dried fusilli

3 tablespoons olive oil, plus a little extra for the pasta

1 medium onion, finely chopped

1 garlic clove, minced

1 tablespoon chopped fresh basil or 1 teaspoon dried

tiny splash of balsamic vinegar (optional)

freshly grated Parmesan cheese, for garnish (optional)

Preheat the oven to 450° and lightly oil 2 large shallow casseroles. Core and halve the tomatoes lengthwise, then lay them in the casseroles, flat sides up, without crowding. Brush the cut surfaces of the tomatoes with a little olive oil, then lightly salt and pepper them. Roast the tomatoes for about 45 to 50 minutes, until they're quite shrunken and shriveled; the bottoms will likely char a bit, but that's fine as it adds nice flavor. Set aside.

Bring the pasta water to a boil and begin adding fusilli. As the pasta cooks, put the tomatoes in the bowl of a food processor and process the sauce to a textured puree. Heat the olive oil in a medium nonreactive saucepan. Stir in the onion and sauté over medium-high heat for about 7 minutes, until the onion is translucent. Stir in the garlic, sauté about 15 seconds, then stir in the pureed tomatoes. Stir in 2 or 3 tablespoons of water, the basil, and balsamic vinegar if you are using it; add it about ¹/₂ teaspoon at a time because you don't want to overwhelm the sauce. Heat the sauce through, adding a few more tablespoons water if necessary. The sauce should stay pretty thick, but it should be moist enough to coat the pasta.

Once the fusilli is done, drain and transfer to a large bowl. Toss the pasta with a little olive oil, then scrape the sauce over the top and toss again. Serve right away, with Parmesan cheese on the side.

Rigatoni with Tomato, Lentils, Eggplant, and Spinach

MAKES 6 TO 8 SERVINGS

Rigatoni is fun to eat. The kids like the tubes and they're effective for catching the many elements of this thick, hearty sauce. Lentils give the sauce a meaty quality and boost the nutritional profile of this dish, while the eggplant cooks to a melt-in-your-mouth softness. Filling, healthy, low-fat, and delicious, this is an altogether excellent pasta.

$1/2$ cup lentils

salt

3 tablespoons olive oil

2 medium onions, chopped

1 large green bell pepper, chopped

2 garlic cloves, minced

1 medium eggplant, cubed

1 bay leaf

freshly ground pepper

3 large tomatoes, cored, seeded, and coarsely chopped, or 1 28-ounce can crushed tomatoes in puree

$3/4$ pound fresh spinach leaves, rinsed, or 1 10-ounce package frozen chopped spinach

2 teaspoons dried basil or 2 tablespoons fresh

$1/2$ teaspoon crushed dried rosemary or 1 teaspoon minced fresh

a little balsamic or red wine vinegar

$3/4$ pound rigatoni

2 to 3 tablespoons minced fresh parsley

freshly grated Parmesan cheese or crumbled feta cheese, for garnish

*R*inse the lentils and put them in a small saucepan covered with about 3 inches of water. Bring to a boil, then reduce to a simmer and cook the lentils, partially covered, for about 20 minutes. Salt the lentils lightly and cook about 5 to 10 more minutes, just until tender. Drain, reserving the cooking water.

Heat the olive oil in a large, enameled covered casserole. Add the onions and pepper and sauté over medium-high heat for 7 minutes, stirring occasionally. Stir in the garlic, sauté 30 seconds more, then stir in the eggplant, bay leaf, and salt and pepper to taste. Sauté for 2 minutes, then reduce the heat slightly and cover. Cook the vegetables for about 8 to 10 minutes, until the eggplant is tender, then stir in the tomatoes. Re-cover the casserole and cook for 5 minutes, then add the spinach; if you are using frozen, cut the block into 7 or 8 pieces and scatter them around the pan. Cover the pan and continue to cook for an additional 5 minutes, until the spinach is tender. Add the lentils and a little of their cooking liquid. Stir in the basil, rosemary, and a tablespoon or two of vinegar. The sauce should be thick but loose enough so it will cover the pasta nicely; use more lentil water if necessary. Check the seasonings, then cover and hold the sauce over low heat.

Meanwhile, bring a pot of salted water to a boil. Cook the rigatoni just until tender, then drain and toss it with the sauce and parsley. Serve at once, passing the cheese at the table.

Greens Linguine

MAKES 4 TO 5 SERVINGS

Here is a good way to serve greens to kids who say they don't like greens. It is also a good way to serve greens to kids who do like greens; one young member of this family, with no prodding whatsoever, offered that this dish was "obsooltlee ghwrat," or "absolutely great" with your mouth full (ever notice how the best compliments kids give are the ones that simply can't wait?). Anyway, I realized at some point that what stands between many kids and greens are their texture: too big, too chewy, and texturally suspect, the same way I felt about most of the food I was served in the navy. And then I realized that if you just ran cooked greens through the food processor, it would eliminate all of those problems and leave you with a sort of greens pesto you could toss with pasta. I tried it and it worked better than I imagined. The bits of greens cling to the linguine like flecks of confetti, so it looks fun to eat, too. For the adults in the family you can put out a little bowl of chopped olives and another of freshly grated Parmesan for anybody who wants it.

1 big bunch (about 1¹/₂ pounds) fresh kale

10 to 12 ounces (about 10 cups loosely packed) fresh spinach

¹/₂ cup olive oil

2 garlic cloves, minced

salt and freshly ground pepper

juice of ¹/₂ lemon

³/₄ to 1 pound dried linguine

freshly grated Parmesan cheese, for garnish (optional)

chopped pitted olives, for garnish (optional)

*S*trip the kale leaves from their central stems. Put the leaves in a very large bowl of cool water and agitate them vigorously to wash out the sand and grit. Put the leaves in a large covered enameled pot with about ¹/₂ inch of water. Cover and turn the heat up. As the kale begins to steam, remove the stems from the spinach and rinse it as you did the kale. Add the spinach to the pot and re-cover. Steam the greens until they are tender, a total of about 12 minutes from the time you start the kale. Check the water level in the pot periodically; you don't want it to boil off completely. Drain the greens, pressing on them with a wooden spoon to express some of the excess moisture. Transfer the greens to a food processor, chop them finely, and set aside. Meanwhile, bring a large pot of salted water to a boil for the linguine.

Warm the olive oil over low heat in a medium skillet. Stir in the garlic and continue to heat the oil for another minute; don't let the garlic color. Stir the chopped greens into the oil and let the mixture heat for 1 minute more. Remove from the heat and season to taste with salt and pepper. Stir in the lemon juice.

Cook the pasta. When it is done, transfer it to a large bowl and scrape the greens mixture over it. Toss well and serve at once, garnished with Parmesan and olives if you like.

> ## 🌿 *Food for Thought* 🌿
> ### GREENS ON GRAINS AND MORE . . .
>
> Those greens we just tossed with pasta? If they're a hit with your kids, you've got a real opening to give them their greens in a variety of ways. You can toss them with cooked brown rice, couscous, or any other grain they like. Or you can spread them on a pizza, toss them with roasted or boiled potatoes for dinner, or even spread them over toast, bruschetta style. I love the stuff plain myself, but the flavor may be too intense for young children. In any case, use your imagination, team them up with foods they already approve of, and you're in business.

Spaghetti with Great Northern Beans and Asparagus

MAKES 5 TO 6 SERVINGS

I like to cook beans for pasta—as I've done here—and use some of the flavorful cooking liquid for the sauce; if you use just a little water to cook the beans in, the flavors condense into a rich-tasting, stewlike stock. The trick is in the timing: You want to end up with just enough intensely flavored broth to douse the pasta; too much and it will likely lack flavor, too little and there won't be enough to go around.

1 cup dried Great Northern beans or other white beans

1 pound thickish asparagus stalks

2$^{1}/_{2}$ tablespoons olive oil

1 large onion, finely chopped

3 garlic cloves, minced

1 small bay leaf

1 vegetable bouillon cube (optional)

1 large carrot, peeled and finely diced

$^{1}/_{2}$ teaspoon salt, plus more to taste

1$^{1}/_{4}$ pounds dried spaghetti

2 tablespoons chopped fresh parsley

freshly ground pepper to taste

juice of $^1/_2$ lemon

freshly grated Parmesan cheese, for garnish

*P*ick the beans over, rinse, then put them in a saucepan with 1 quart of water. Bring the beans to a boil, then boil for 2 minutes. Cover, remove from the heat, and set aside for 1 hour.

Peel the lower half of the asparagus spears with a vegetable peeler, then cut the stalks on the bias into pieces about $1^1/_2$ inches long. Set aside.

Heat the olive oil in a large nonreactive covered skillet or Dutch oven. Add the onion and sauté over medium-high heat for 6 or 7 minutes. Stir in the garlic, sauté 15 more seconds, then stir in the bay leaf. Drain the beans and add them to the pan with enough fresh water to cover by about 1 inch, perhaps a little more. Add the bouillon cube and bring the water to a boil. If you haven't already, put a big pot of water on for the spaghetti.

Lower the beans to a gentle boil, cover the pan, and cook the beans for about 45 minutes, until the beans are almost tender. Stir in the carrot and salt, cover again, and simmer for 15 more minutes. When you add the carrot, there should be enough liquid in the pan to cover the beans by about $^1/_2$ inch. Add a little if necessary, or take the lid off if there seems to be a bit much so the liquid can evaporate.

After 15 minutes, start cooking the pasta, then add the asparagus, parsley, and pepper to the beans. Cover, then simmer about 5 to 6 more minutes, until the asparagus is tender. Remove from the heat and pour the lemon juice over the vegetables.

When the spaghetti is done, drain and transfer to a large shallow pasta bowl. Pour the beans and vegetables over the top and bring it to the table like that. Toss everything together just before serving; use a spoon to serve some of the broth with each portion. Pass the Parmesan cheese at the table.

Spaghetti with Tempeh Tomato Sauce

MAKES 4 TO 5 SERVINGS

Here's a hearty spaghetti dish for anyone who loves a good sauce, but it's one I think will especially appeal to transitional vegetarians who might miss a thick meaty sauce on their pasta. Though it would be a stretch to say that tempeh tastes like meat—some have compared the flavor to cheese—it does have a meaty texture. And when you crumble it up like I do here the texture is amazingly close to ground beef. I even "brown" the tempeh by first simmering it in water and a little tamari; as the water evaporates, both the color and the flavor of the tempeh deepen even further to a meatlike credibility. If your kids are meat sauce fans, try this out. My son Ben is a big-time fan.

1 8-ounce cake tempeh

2 tablespoons olive oil

1 medium onion, finely chopped

2 garlic cloves, minced

1 cup water

1 tablespoon tamari or soy sauce

1 28-ounce can crushed tomatoes in puree

1 cup tomato puree

2 tablespoons chopped fresh basil or 2 teaspoons dried

2 tablespoons chopped fresh parsley

2 teaspoons dried oregano

$^{1}/_{2}$ teaspoon thyme

1 small bay leaf

salt and freshly ground pepper to taste

1 pound dried spaghetti

*U*sing your hands, crumble the tempeh into a bowl until it is broken into fine pieces. Set aside. Heat the oil in a large nonreactive saucepan or skillet. Stir in the onion and sauté over medium-high heat for 7 minutes, stirring often. Stir in the garlic, sauté 15 more seconds, then stir in the tempeh, water, and tamari. Bring the water to a boil, cover, and reduce the heat slightly. Simmer the tempeh for 5 minutes, then remove the cover and let the water boil off to the point that you can hear the tempeh sizzling in the pan.

Stir the remaining ingredients except the spaghetti into the tempeh. Cover and simmer the sauce for 10 minutes, correcting the seasoning as it simmers. Meanwhile, bring a large pot of salted water to a boil. Cook the spaghetti just until tender, then drain and serve with the hot sauce.

Sesame Peanut Noodles

MAKES 4 TO 6 SERVINGS

We've all seen variations on this theme at salad bars and Chinese restaurants, but the homemade version is the best ever. The flavor of these noodles is exotic, but it is accomplished with only a minimum of exotic ingredients, all of which you should be able to find at local supermarkets.

$^3/_4$ pound thin spaghetti

$2^1/_2$ tablespoons sesame oil

$^1/_3$ cup roasted salted peanuts

PEANUT SAUCE AND ASSEMBLY

$^1/_3$ cup plus 1 tablespoon natural smooth peanut butter

2 tablespoons tamari or soy sauce

2 tablespoons rice vinegar

$2^1/_2$ teaspoons honey

$^1/_2$ teaspoon molasses

1 tablespoon minced fresh ginger

1 garlic clove, minced

1 teaspoon red pepper flakes

3 tablespoons chopped fresh parsley or coriander

1 medium carrot, peeled and grated

lemon wedges

*B*ring a large pot of salted water to a boil. Add the spaghetti and cook until just tender. Drain and toss with the sesame oil in a large shallow bowl. Set aside. Put the peanuts in the bowl of a food processor and chop them finely. Set aside.

Make the sauce. Combine the peanut butter, tamari, vinegar, honey, molasses, ginger, garlic, and pepper flakes in the bowl of a food processor. Pulsing the machine, process the sauce to a smooth texture, gradually adding up to 3 or 4 tablespoons of water; the finished sauce should have the approximate consistency of thin yogurt.

Pour the sauce over the noodles and toss to coat well. This is easier said than done because the sauce tends to clump here and there rather than spread evenly. Just take your time and use your hands if necessary. Toss in the parsley or coriander and grated carrot. Cover with plastic wrap and refrigerate for at least 30 minutes.

Just before serving, toss the pasta with the finely chopped peanuts. Pass the lemon wedges separately; anyone who likes can squeeze some juice on their pasta at the table.

❧ *Food for Thought* ❧

A FIELD GUIDE TO EATING OUT MEATLESSLY

I love my adopted state of New Hampshire, but I have to admit—somewhat sadly—that our restaurant scene is not exactly on the cutting edge of innovative vegetarian cooking. In fact, the one totally vegetarian restaurant in the state just went out of business. Perhaps it is better where you live?

This is not to say that we haven't discovered some very good non-vegetarian restaurants in the state that cater to the vegetarian crowd. Mind you, finding the ones who do a good job with vegetarian food hasn't been a piece of cake. And when we do venture from our regular stable, more often than not the opening scene goes like this:

Hi, I'm Jenny and I'll be your waitperson tonight. Can I tell you about our specials?

Sure. Are any of them vegetarian?

Certainly. Our appetizer is the chef's special version of surf and turf, served with . . .

Excuse me, I have this terrible habit of mumbling in restaurants so perhaps I didn't make myself clear. We don't eat any seafood or meat.

Oh, I get it. Sorry. Our other special is coq au vin made with free-range chicken . . .

Sorry, but we don't eat chicken either, free range or otherwise.

But the portion is very modest . . .

Frankly, I don't care if the portion is very modest, and it wouldn't matter if the chicken died of natural causes and the Pope himself was there to administer the last rites . . .

Actually, I'm not really a wise guy, at least not publicly, so I really wouldn't say that last part. But I would bring my kids the next time and let them say it.

In all fairness to the waitstaffs of the world, part of the confusion around ordering vegetarian food in restaurants can be blamed on the fact that there really isn't one definition of vegetarian. Compounding the problem is the new crop of *quasi*-vegetarians, the *sometimes* and *practically* vegetarians. There are *vegans*, *lacto-*, and *lacto-ovo* vegetarians, too. All of which, for those of you who are liable to find yourself in the same predicament, leads us to Rule #1: **When you speak to restaurant people, be explicit about your dietary guidelines.** Don't say: *I'm a vegetarian.* Say: *I'm a vegetarian. I don't eat meat or seafood but I do eat eggs and dairy products.* Or: *I don't eat meat or fish, but I will eat just about anything else except the stuff the fellow at the next table just sent back.* Get it? This initial introduction will help narrow down the field and quickly attune your waitress to your preferences so she can help you out. If it doesn't, finish your drink and leave.

Rule #2: **Always call ahead before trying a new restaurant.** Or at least try to. You can tell a lot about a restaurant's receptivity to vegetarians by the way they handle you on the phone. Call between meals and ask to speak to the chef or kitchen manager. He or she should be willing and able to talk to you intelligently about the sort of food you would like. And you should get the distinct impression that the chef knows something about meatless cuisine and looks at feeding you as a creative challenge, not as a pain in the patootie. If the chef mumbles something about a baked potato and the salad bar, this is not a good sign. It is clearly in the chef's best interest to accommodate you and if he can't figure that out, don't bother. Our favorite restaurant is Italian, not vegetarian, but the chef literally knocks himself out for us whenever we go there; consequently, we go there very often.

Finally, Rule #3: **If you do get a good meatless meal, let the chef know.** Chefs are not known for their small egos, and the more you can express your gratitude for a job well done, the better the kitchen is going to take care of you. Tell them you appreciate their efforts. If you do, tell them you feel strongly about supporting places that cater to vegetarians; then tell your friends. Don't be afraid to drop specific hints about the sort of vegetarian foods you like and would *love to try* if the chef ever made anything like that. Most good chefs like a challenge and they'll do everything they can to keep you happy.

Mainly Grains and a Few Bean Dishes

Grains and beans have played a large role in our family diet for as long as I can remember. Without exception, all of the kids like them in a very reassuring kind of way. My kids feel about grains and beans the way they do about me: reliable, if not exactly charismatic. That's good enough. (We can't all be Bruce Willis.)

Grain covers a lot of ground, but in our family the word is almost synonymous with rice. Which explains why so many of the recipes here are rice-based dishes: There's just no question that all the kids will eat it. I don't have too many complaints about that because it makes life easier for the cook-shopper in the house when you're only buying one or two kinds of rice instead of eight different grains.

Along with the rice recipes we love most, this section also includes another form of grain we eat a lot of, polenta. Even if your kids have rejected polenta in the past, you might want to try them again with this recipe. It's a softer, less coarse version than most, the result of substituting some Cream of Wheat cereal for part of the cornmeal. It's less than authentic, perhaps, but the kids are crazy about it.

Beans, like rice and other grains, are most enthusiastically received by kids when they aren't served too plainly. Plain beans can be pretty boring. Toward the end of this chapter you'll find two bean dishes that are anything but: Maple Baked Beans and a spicy black bean chili. The chili can be served with the optional cornmeal dumplings if you like. You simmer the dumplings directly in the chili, then scoop one or two of them over each portion. And that's one pretty fine meal.

Creamy Broccoli-Rice Casserole

✧

MAKES 6 SERVINGS

This recipe started out in life as a dish Karen used to make when she first started cooking on her own with, of all things, Campbell's cream of broccoli soup. Eventually Campbell's dropped out of her life—these things happen, you know—as did the thing she used to serve this with, that being chicken. But some taste memories never go away and when we started having kids she started toying around with her beloved casserole of yore, replacing the soup with cream cheese or, more recently, Neufchâtel cheese.

2 cups long-grain brown rice

5 cups water

$^3/_4$ teaspoon salt

3 tablespoons olive oil

1 cup finely chopped celery

1 cup finely chopped onions

4 cups broccoli (flowerets and peeled chopped stalks)

4 ounces Neufchâtel cheese or low-fat cream cheese

freshly ground pepper to taste

1 teaspoon dried basil (optional)

Bring the rice, 4 cups of water, and $^1/_4$ teaspoon salt to a boil in a medium saucepan. Lower the heat, cover, and simmer the rice for about 40 minutes, until the water is absorbed and the rice is just barely tender. Transfer the rice to a large bowl and set aside. Preheat the oven to 350° and lightly oil a large shallow casserole dish.

Heat the olive oil in a large nonreactive skillet and stir in the celery and onions. Sauté the vegetables for about 7 minutes, until the onions are translucent. Add the broccoli, $^1/_2$ teaspoon salt, and 1 cup of water and bring to a boil. Steam the broccoli for about 3 minutes, until not quite tender. Break up the cheese and add it to the skillet, stirring it in to make a thickish creamy gravy that coats the vegetables. Season to taste with pepper.

Scrape the vegetable-sauce mixture into the bowl with the rice and toss well, adding the basil if you like. Transfer the mixture to an oiled casserole dish, cover with foil, and bake for 30 to 35 minutes, until heated through. Serve hot.

Bulgur and Veggies

MAKES 5 TO 6 SERVINGS

One of the advantages of this grain dish over others is the shorter cooking time bulgur requires. Carrots and broccoli are our standard veggies for this dish. However, there have been many times when we only used onions and mushrooms. Now we almost always use fresh firm portobello mushrooms because we've found that the kids will eat them (or at least some of them will) even when they won't eat the regular white button mushrooms. You'll get the best results—more separate grains—if you can cook the bulgur ahead and let it cool thoroughly. But even if you can't, don't let that stop you from enjoying this.

1 1/2 cups bulgur

3 cups water

1/2 teaspoon salt, plus more to taste

2 tablespoons olive oil

1 large onion, chopped

1 large carrot, peeled, quartered lengthwise, and sliced

2 or 3 good-size portobello mushroom caps, thickly diced

5 cups broccoli flowerets

1 garlic clove, minced

1 teaspoon dried basil

1/4 to 1/2 teaspoon red pepper flakes (optional)

tamari to taste

Bring the bulgur and water to a boil in a medium saucepan. Stir in the salt, cover, and cook the bulgur over very low heat for 20 to 23 minutes, until all of the water is absorbed. Remove from the heat and set aside, covered, for 15 minutes. Remove the lid, fluff the grain with a fork, and turn it out onto a cookie sheet to cool.

While the bulgur cools, heat the olive oil in a large skillet. Add the onion and carrot and sauté over medium-high heat for about 7 minutes, until translucent. Stir in the mushrooms and broccoli, salt them lightly, and sauté about 4 minutes more. When the broccoli is almost tender, stir in the garlic and sauté for 15 seconds.

Stir the bulgur, basil, and red pepper flakes into the vegetables. Heat, stirring, just until the bulgur is hot, then stir in the tamari.

Pumpkin and Red Pepper Risotto

MAKES 6 SERVINGS

The popularity of risotto in this country had peaked long before I took any notice of it, mainly, I think, because all of the recipes I saw seemed to be based on meat, fish, or chicken broth. Once I figured out that you could simply substitute a good, flavorful meatless broth, I began making them on a regular basis, this being one of my first and favorite variations. Before I get underway, I partially precook the cubes of pumpkin and red pepper in a little of the broth, until the pumpkin is almost tender; if pumpkin season has passed, use any good winter squash. Then I add the vegetables back to the rice a few minutes before the dish comes off the burner to reheat them and finish the cooking. All you will need on the side is a salad, cold applesauce, or cold pickled beets.

1 recipe Quick Mushroom Broth (page 49)

RISOTTO
2 tablespoons olive oil
1 medium-small red bell pepper, chopped
2 cups peeled fresh pumpkin or winter squash, cut into $^1/_2$-inch cubes
salt
1 small onion, finely chopped
$1^1/_4$ cups arborio rice
2 garlic cloves, minced
freshly ground pepper
chopped fresh parsley, for garnish
freshly grated Parmesan cheese, for garnish (optional)

Make the broth if you haven't already and have it on a nearby burner, holding at a near simmer. Meanwhile, heat 1 tablespoon of the olive oil in a medium skillet. Add the pepper and pumpkin and sauté over medium-high heat for 1 minute, stirring occasionally. Carefully—it may splatter—pour in about $^1/_2$ cup of the hot broth; add a pinch of salt. Cover and simmer the vegetables for 4 to 5 minutes, until the pumpkin is almost tender. Remove the saucepan from the heat and set aside.

Heat the remaining tablespoon of oil in a medium enameled pot. Stir in the onion and sauté over medium heat for about 5 minutes, stirring often. Stir in the rice and garlic and sauté 30 seconds more, stirring. Ladle about 1 cup of the hot broth into the rice.

Cook the rice over low heat, stirring very often, for about 3 to 5 minutes; the rice should absorb most of the liquid in that time and it will start to feel like it is sticking to the pan. At that point ladle another $^1/_2$ cup of hot broth over the rice. Cook 3 to 4 more minutes, until the liquid is absorbed, then ladle in more broth. Continue in this fashion—stirring, adding broth, and letting it absorb—for about 20 to 25 minutes, until the rice is tender on the outside but still has a bit of a bite. By now you will have used up most of the broth. Season the dish with salt and pepper to taste. At that point, stir in a little more broth and the reserved vegetables. Stir and heat the vegetables for about 5 minutes more. When the rice is done it will be moist and creamy. Serve right away, garnished with the chopped parsley and Parmesan cheese.

Bulgur and Potato Hash

MAKES 6 SERVINGS

This is the hash we eat most often for both breakfast and dinner. It is loved by vegetarians and meat eaters alike. In traditional style, I sometimes like a poached egg over my portion, but more often than not the only extra any of us adds is ketchup. Salsa is also good, with a little bowl of chopped pickled jalapeño peppers served on the side. For dinner, serve with a simple steamed vegetable, such as Garlic-Braised Asparagus (page 110), or a salad.

$2^1/_4$ cups water

1 cup bulgur

$^1/_2$ teaspoon salt, plus more to taste

5 medium all-purpose potatoes, peeled and cut into $^1/_2$-inch dice

$2^1/_2$ tablespoons olive oil

1 large onion, chopped

1 garlic clove, minced

$1^1/_2$ teaspoons paprika

$1^1/_2$ tablespoons tamari

freshly ground pepper

Combine the water, bulgur, and salt in a small saucepan. Bring to a boil, then cover and reduce the heat. Cook the bulgur over very low heat for about 20 minutes; all of the water should be absorbed, but the bulgur may still seem a little wet. That's fine. Remove the bulgur from the heat and let it stand, covered and undisturbed, for 15 minutes. Fluff the bulgur with a fork and let it cool, uncovered.

While the bulgur cooks, cover the potatoes with salted water and bring to a boil in a large saucepan. Boil the potatoes for about 9 to 10 minutes, just until tender. Drain, reserving the broth for soup; you may need a little in the hash, too. Transfer the potatoes to a platter to cool down.

Heat the oil in a large cast-iron skillet and stir in the onion. Sauté over medium-high heat for 7 minutes, then stir in the garlic and paprika. Sauté for 30 seconds more, then stir in the potatoes and bulgur. Sprinkle the tamari over the hash and continue to heat the hash, stirring occasionally, for 2 to 3 minutes, until heated through. Season to taste with salt, if any additional is needed, and pepper.

At this point, if you would like to moisten the hash, you may drizzle spoonfuls of the potato water over the hash and stir it in. Serve hot.

Red Rice

MAKES 6 TO 8 SERVINGS

This recipe makes a good all-purpose Mexican rice for all your south-of-the-border meals. It's easy to prepare, an attractive chili red, and the rice emerges from the skillet in fluffy, individual kernels. An excellent side dish, you can turn this into a more substantial main dish if you stir in some black beans—either dried and cooked or drained and rinsed canned—when you add the tomatoes.

3 tablespoons olive oil or flavorless vegetable oil

1 large onion, chopped

2 cups long-grain brown rice

2 garlic cloves, minced

2 teaspoons chili powder

$1^{1}/_{2}$ teaspoons ground cumin

$1^{1}/_{2}$ teaspoons ground coriander

$^{1}/_{2}$ teaspoon paprika

$3^{3}/_{4}$ cups water

1 vegetable boullion cube (optional)

1 cup crushed canned tomatoes in puree

$^{1}/_{2}$ cup finely chopped fresh parsley

1 cup grated sharp Cheddar or Monterey Jack cheese (optional)

*H*eat the oil in a large, heavy nonreactive skillet. Add the onion and sauté over medium heat for about 7 minutes, until translucent. Stir in the rice and sauté, stirring occasionally, for 2 minutes. Stir in the garlic and spices and sauté another 1¹/₂ to 2 minutes, stirring often. Stir in the water and boullion cube, broken or cut into pieces, if you're using it. Bring the rice to a boil, cover, then reduce the heat and simmer the rice gently, without removing the lid, for about 35 minutes. Remove the lid and stir in the tomatoes and parsley. Cook the rice for another 10 minutes, again without removing the lid. Remove from the heat and let stand for 10 minutes with the lid on before serving. If you're using the cheese, remove the lid after 5 minutes, sprinkle on the cheese, and cover for 5 more minutes.

Indian-Spiced Rice and Peas

MAKES 6 TO 8 SERVINGS

This is a colorful, mildly spiced rice that feeds a crowd and disappears quickly. It is common in dishes such as this to use whole spices, such as cardamom pods. However, I often don't have whole spices around so I find it easier just to use ground. If eggplant isn't a family favorite, you can leave it out or substitute 1 cup rinsed and drained canned chickpeas. In summer, this dish benefits from garden fresh vegetables and herbs, but it is no less satisfying in the colder months. Serve with a light fruit dessert.

2 tablespoons flavorless vegetable oil

1 medium onion, chopped

1 red or green bell pepper, chopped

1 small eggplant, cut into ³/₄-inch dice

1 garlic clove, minced

1 tablespoon finely chopped fresh ginger

¹/₂ teaspoon turmeric

¹/₂ teaspoon ground cloves

¹/₂ teaspoon ground cinnamon

¹/₂ teaspoon paprika

¹/₄ teaspoon ground cardamom

3 cups water or vegetable stock

2 carrots, finely chopped

1 large tomato, cored and coarsely chopped, or 1 cup chopped canned
    tomatoes

1 cup small fresh or frozen green peas

1 1/2 cups basmati rice

1 teaspoon salt

chopped fresh parsley or cilantro, for garnish

*H*eat the oil in a large nonreactive skillet or Dutch oven with a tight-
fitting lid. Add the onion and sauté over medium heat, stirring often, for 7 minutes. Stir in the pepper and eggplant. Cover and let
the vegetables sweat for 3 to 4 minutes, stirring occasionally. Stir in the garlic
and ginger and sauté 1 minute more.

Combine the spices in a small bowl, then stir them into the vegetables.
Cook the mixture, stirring, over moderate heat for 1 minute, then stir in the remaining ingredients except for the parsley or cilantro. Increase the heat, bring
the mixture to a boil, then cover. Reduce the heat to low, then simmer the rice
for 20 minutes. Turn off the heat and leave the cover on for an additional 10
minutes; no peeking! Serve.

Pinto Beans, Spinach, and Rice

MAKES 6 TO 8 SERVINGS

A good, basic combination everyone will like—what more could you ask from
a healthy main dish? In fact, my youngest son, Sam, likes this so much he has
requested it for his birthday meal. Serve with diced avocados dressed with
lemon juice, warm tortillas, and—if they're in season—chunks of fresh ripe
tomato. Use canned beans if you like, drained and well rinsed; you'll need 1 19-
ounce can (see Note). If you're using dried beans, cook them and the rice simultaneously while you work on the rest of the dish.

1/2 cup dried pinto beans, picked over and rinsed

1 1/2 cups long-grain brown rice

3 cups water

3/4 teaspoon salt

1 unsalted vegetable bouillon cube

1 medium carrot, finely chopped

2 tablespoons olive oil

1 cup chopped onion

2 garlic cloves, minced

1^1/$_2$ teaspoons mild chili powder

1 10-ounce package chopped frozen spinach, thawed

*P*ut the dried beans into a saucepan with enough water to cover by about 2 inches. Bring to a boil, then boil for 2 minutes. Cover and set the beans aside for 1 hour. After an hour, drain the beans and cover generously with fresh water. Bring the beans to a boil, reduce the heat slightly, then boil gently, partially covered, for about 1 hour, until tender. Drain, reserving the bean water.

While the beans cook, prepare the rice. Combine the rice, 3 cups of water, and ^{1}/$_2$ teaspoon of salt in a medium saucepan. Crumble up half of the bouillon cube and add it to the rice along with the carrot. Bring to a boil, then cover the saucepan and cook over very low heat for about 35 minutes, until the water is absorbed and the rice is tender. Remove from the heat and set aside.

Heat the olive oil in a large, heavy nonreactive skillet. Stir in the onion and sauté over medium heat for 7 minutes, until translucent. Stir in the garlic and chili powder, sauté for 30 seconds more, then stir in the spinach. Crumble the remaining half bouillon cube into ^{1}/$_2$ cup of the reserved bean water, whisking well to dissolve. Add the water to the pan with an additional ^{1}/$_4$ teaspoon salt and gently simmer the spinach for 5 minutes, until much of the excess water has evaporated.

Stir the cooked rice and beans into the spinach and heat the dish, stirring, for 5 minutes, until hot.

N O T E : If you are using canned beans, drain and rinse them well. Stir them into the spinach mixture until heated, then stir in the rice. Instead of using the bean cooking water, simmer the spinach in fresh boiled tap water mixed with half of the bouillon cube.

Black and Red Bean Chili with Cornmeal Dumplings

ॐ

MAKES ABOUT 1 GALLON,
ENOUGH TO FEED A CROWD

A good meatless chili is a great equalizer, something that shrinks dietary borders and prejudices. I mean, a true Texan might blanch at the idea of a chili without the meat, but who can argue with good taste? Though it is possible to make an edible chili in a couple of hours, it is far better if it can simmer slowly, take some time away from the heat, then be reheated. Time is what gives chili its complexity, smooths its rough edges, and there's really no substitute for it. In these days of streamlined recipes, the following list of ingredients may seem excessive; everything's here but the kitchen sink. But it works. The dumplings are optional, but they accomplish a couple of things: They help thicken the broth and they eliminate the need for a separate serving of bread, corn bread, or rice on the side.

^{1}/2 pound dried black beans, picked over and rinsed

^{1}/2 pound dried kidney beans, picked over and rinsed

2 tablespoons ground cumin

1^1/2 tablespoons mild chili powder

1 tablespoon ground coriander

^{1}/4 teaspoon cayenne

2 teaspoons unsweetened cocoa powder

^{1}/3 cup olive oil

2 large onions, chopped

1 large green bell pepper, chopped

3 garlic cloves, minced

1 28-ounce can crushed tomatoes in puree

1 teaspoon salt, plus more to taste

^{1}/2 to 1 cup fresh or canned chopped mild green chilies

2 tablespoons tomato paste

1 tablespoon dried oregano, crumbled

2 teaspoons dried basil

2 teaspoons sugar or honey

2 tablespoons barbecue sauce (optional)

Cornmeal dumpling dough (below)

handful of chopped fresh parsley for garnish

*P*ut the black and kidney beans into a large pot and cover with plenty of water. Bring to a boil, uncovered, then boil for 2 minutes. Turn the heat off, cover, and let sit for 1 hour. Drain the beans and put them back in the pot with 3 quarts of fresh hot water. Bring to a boil, then cook at a low boil, partially covered, for about 45 to 60 minutes, until tender. Remove from the heat but don't drain.

Mix the cumin, chili powder, coriander, cayenne, and cocoa powder in a small bowl; set aside. Heat about half of the olive oil in a very large skillet. Add the onions and pepper and sauté over medium heat, stirring, for about 7 minutes. Add the rest of the oil to the pot, then stir in the garlic and spice mixture. Lower the heat slightly and stir the onion-spice mixture for 2 minutes; it will be dry, but just keep stirring. Turn off the heat.

Ladle a cup or so of the bean water into the spice pan, then scrape the contents of the skillet back into the beans. Stir in the remaining ingredients, except for the dumplings and the parsley, and bring to a simmer. Gently simmer the chili, partially covered, for 30 minutes, stirring occasionally; taste as it simmers, adding more salt if necessary. Remove from the heat and let the chili stand for at least 1 hour. Meanwhile, prepare the cornmeal dumpling dough, but don't combine the wet and dry ingredients until you're ready to cook them.

About 15 minutes before you eat, bring the chili back to a simmer. Mix the dumpling dough, then spoon it over the surface; it will make about 6 large or as many as 10 smaller dumplings. Gently simmer the chili, covered, for 10 minutes; don't uncover it to check on the dumplings. Serve the chili and dumplings in bowls, garnished with the fresh parsley.

Cornmeal Dumplings

MAKES 8 TO 9 DUMPLINGS

These are a favorite dumpling we use in soups and stews; I particularly like them in the black and kidney bean chili (above). A dumpling—this sort of dumpling, at least—is essentially made from biscuit dough with a bit less liquid; dumplings need less liquid because they absorb quite a bit as they simmer. Set the heat at a bare simmer, a sort of burble, before the dumplings go in.

Then leave the lid in place as they simmer so the steam cooks them from above. The cheese can be omitted if you like.

1 cup unbleached all-purpose flour

1 cup fine yellow cornmeal

2 teaspoons baking powder

$^1/_2$ teaspoon salt

3 tablespoons cold unsalted butter, cut into 5 or 6 pieces

1 cup grated sharp Cheddar cheese

$^2/_3$ cup milk

*D*o not mix the dumplings until your soup, stew, or chili is ready. At that point, sift all of the dry ingredients into a large bowl. Add the butter and rub it in with your fingers until the mixture resembles a coarse meal and the butter is broken into tiny bits. Mix in the grated cheese. Make a well in the dry ingredients and add the milk. Stir just until the batter coheres in a uniform mass. Let the dough rest for 2 to 3 minutes.

Divide the batter into 8 or 9 roughly even lumps and gently spoon them into the simmering liquid; leave as much room between them as possible. Cover and simmer the dumplings for 10 minutes without disturbing or peeking. Serve each portion of the soup or stew with 1 or 2 dumplings, 2 if you're using wide, shallow bowls.

Maple Baked Beans

MAKES 6 TO 8 SERVINGS

Is there anybody who doesn't like baked beans? I doubt it. In this part of the country baked beans are almost a religion, like chili is in Texas. And like any religion, it is easy to find proselytizers for such personal beliefs as the correct bean to use, how to sweeten them, which seasonings are allowable and which are not, even how to eat the leftovers. My friend Dick Doucet, a New Hampshire native, schooled me in one of the most, er, *unique* approaches to eating cold leftover baked beans I've ever seen—in a sandwich. You just take sturdy bread, pile it with the beans, ketchup, mustard, and some other stuff—I wasn't exactly running for my notebook at this point, so some of the details are sketchy—and you eat it. Dick says all the old-timers know about this.

1 pound dried Great Northern beans

$^1/_4$ cup flavorless vegetable or safflower oil

1 cup chopped onions

1 green bell pepper, finely chopped

1 celery rib, finely chopped

2 garlic cloves, minced

$^1/_2$ cup maple syrup

$^1/_2$ cup canned tomato puree

3 tablespoons apple cider vinegar

2 tablespoons blackstrap molasses

2 tablespoons Dijon mustard

$1^1/_4$ teaspoons salt

1 bay leaf

$^1/_4$ cup chopped fresh parsley

freshly ground pepper to taste

*P*ick the beans over and rinse them well. Put the beans in a large pot and cover with about 3 inches of water. Bring to a boil, then boil uncovered for 2 minutes. Remove from the heat and cover. Let the beans soak for 1 hour, then drain.

Cover the beans generously with fresh water and bring to a boil. Gently boil the beans, partially covered, for 1 to $1^1/_2$ hours, until the beans are tender but not mushy. Make sure they are tender because the acidity of the liquid they'll cook in will essentially prevent the beans from getting any softer. Drain the beans, but this time don't discard the cooking water.

While the beans cook, heat the oil in a large skillet. Add the onions, pepper, and celery and sauté over medium-high heat for about 6 minutes. Stir in the garlic, sauté 15 seconds more, then remove the skillet from the heat. Preheat the oven to 325° and get out a large shallow casserole.

Whisk together the remaining ingredients, adding $1^1/_2$ cups of the bean cooking water. Transfer the beans, sautéed vegetables, and tomato liquid to the casserole and stir gently to blend. Cover the casserole tightly with foil and bake the beans for 2 to 3 hours. Check the progress of the beans every hour, stirring them and checking on the level of the liquid; if it is getting too low, stir in a bit more bean water. When the beans are done, the liquid should be fairly thick and saucey. Serve hot.

Polenta and Potato Dumplings

MAKES ABOUT 6 SERVINGS

Dumplings are one of the world's great foods, if you ask me. Think about it: A few simple starches are combined with a few simple seasonings to make a filling, satisfying dish that tastes like a million bucks with little more than a dusting of cheese or marinara sauce, which happens to be my preferred way of serving these; my son Ben simply can't get enough of these when I serve them thus. Serve with marinated vegetables, steamed broccoli, or a garden salad.

DUMPLINGS
4 medium-large russet baking potatoes

1$^{1}/_{2}$ cups cold water

$^{1}/_{2}$ cup yellow stone-ground cornmeal

1 tablespoon unsalted butter, cut into several small pieces

$^{1}/_{2}$ cup freshly grated Parmesan cheese

1 large egg, lightly beaten

2 teaspoons dried basil

salt and freshly ground black pepper

$^{2}/_{3}$ cup unbleached all-purpose flour

FINAL COOKING AND SERVING
1$^{1}/_{2}$ tablespoons unsalted butter or olive oil

1 quart homemade or good store-bought marinara sauce, heated

freshly grated Parmesan cheese, for garnish

finely chopped fresh parsley, for garnish

Bake the potatoes in a 450° oven for about 50 to 60 minutes, until they're quite tender when pierced with a sharp knife. Remove from the oven and let them start cooling.

When you take out the potatoes, begin making the polenta. Put the cold water into a medium saucepan and whisk in the cornmeal. Continue to whisk the mixture over medium heat until it starts to thicken. Switch to a wooden spoon—and turn down the heat just a hair if the mixture bubbles wildly—and stir the polenta almost continuously for 10 minutes; it will become pretty thick. Scrape the polenta into a large mixing bowl.

Halve the potatoes and scoop the flesh into the bowl with the polenta. Add the butter, then, using a potato masher, mash the mixture until it is well mixed and smooth, like mashed potatoes. Mix in the Parmesan cheese, egg, basil, and salt and pepper to taste. Let the mixture cool for 5 minutes, then stir in the flour. Bring a large pot of water to a boil.

Working with about one-third of the dough at a time, roll it into a thickish (1¼-inch diameter) rope on floured surface. Cut the dough into 1-inch segments. When the water comes to a boil, gently drop the dumplings into the boiling water. When the water returns to a boil (about the time the dumplings rise to the surface), gently boil them for 7 minutes. Using a slotted spoon, transfer the dumplings to a large platter and cool. Repeat for the rest of the dumplings. Cool to room temperature, then cover and refrigerate for at least 2 hours or up to 48 hours.

When you are ready to serve them, heat the butter or oil in a large skillet. Add as many dumplings as the pan can hold without crowding them and sauté over medium-high heat for 4 to 5 minutes, browning the surfaces lightly; hold them in a warm oven if you need to sauté the rest of the dumplings. Serve the dumplings hot, lightly sauced with the marinara and dusted with Parmesan cheese and parsley.

Kid-Soft Polenta

MAKES 8 OR MORE SERVINGS

I don't remember how I first came up with the idea of putting Cream of Wheat cereal in polenta, a potential heresy that's liable to disqualify me from winning any prestigious cooking awards the Italian government bestows on foreign food journalists. Nonetheless, in this version I use two parts cornmeal, one part Cream of Wheat, a mixture that softens both the flavor of the polenta as well as its presence in the stomach. Some people, I've noticed—kids in particular—simply find it difficult to digest cornmeal full strength and others don't care for the intense corn flavor, which makes this a kid-friendly polenta, thus the name. Polenta needs your nearly undivided attention for about 15 to 20 minutes, during which time it should be stirred regularly; one of those flame tamers over the burner helps prevent scorching. The polenta can be eaten warm, in combination with sweet or savory foods, or it can be transferred to a loaf pan, cooled, then chilled overnight before slicing (see index for a number of polenta ideas).

4½ cups cold water

1 scant teaspoon salt

1 cup fine yellow cornmeal

$^1/_2$ cup Cream of Wheat cereal (the 10-minute cooking type)

1 tablespoon unsalted butter or olive oil

*B*utter a large loaf pan and set it aside. Put the water and salt in a large saucepan. Whisk in the cornmeal and Cream of Wheat. Begin to cook the polenta over medium heat, whisking often. When it reaches a boil, reduce the heat slightly and continue to cook the polenta, stirring often with a wooden spoon, for about 10 minutes. If it becomes almost too thick to stir, add a little extra water a tablespoon or so at a time.

After the 10 minutes, when it is quite thick, stir the butter or oil into the polenta, then scrape the polenta into the loaf pan. Cool on a rack to room temperature, then cover and refrigerate overnight. When the polenta is thoroughly chilled, run a knife around the edge, then invert the polenta onto a cutting board. Slice as needed.

Hearty Casseroles, Gratins, and a Couple of Enchiladas

Here is a selection of more ambitious dishes, for those occasions when you want a clearly defined and substantial focal point for a meal. These are dishes that, for the most part, combine a large variety of elements. They're inclusive, they tend to have complex flavors, and they generally take longer to make than the recipes in the previous sections. Though you certainly don't need a party to serve one of these, you wouldn't be incorrect to think of them as party or special occasion recipes.

Even an ambitious dish, however, can be broken down into small, doable steps. You don't have to make a recipe from start to finish in one session; in fact, there are often advantages—even if they're just psychological ones—to spreading the preparation out over the course of a casual weekend day. Not feeling rushed, you'll enjoy the process more. You can take the time to clean up as you go; that always helps. And there's a better chance someone will come along to help you chop onions, mince garlic, or whatever. Most of us could probably use a little more communal cooking in our lives.

One of the tricky aspects of serving a special dish like the ones here is deciding what to serve with it—tricky because you don't want to duplicate the ingredients you're already using. And also because you want to avoid foods with similar textures. The idea of serving a salad isn't terribly inventive, but it is probably the best start to almost all of these dishes. These casseroles and gratins tend to be soft, hot, muted in color; a good salad is fresh, crisp, cool, and bright—a perfect contrast. Besides, salads can be quite inventive if you avoid getting into a rut. If you normally use one type of lettuce, add interest with mixed baby greens, very thinly sliced red cabbage, grated carrots—anything to liven it up.

I love good crusty bread with a special entrée, but think about whom you're serving and how much they like to eat. Dessert might be a better choice. Few people can resist a wonderful dessert, be it something light and refreshing or plainly decadent. My feeling is that the dessert shouldn't upstage the main course, but it's okay if it comes pretty darn close.

Couscous Paella

MAKES 6 TO 8 SERVINGS

Paella is pilaf from heaven, traditionally made with shellfish, sausage, and rice. Though this is made with none of the above, it is still quite heavenly, and I believe I borrowed enough inspiration from the classic version to justify the adoptive name. This has to be one of the best quick vegetarian crowd pleasers you could make for a party; it's colorful, festive, and downright delicious. And because couscous cooks up in just a few minutes, you can do most of the preparation ahead, then simply add the vegetable stock and couscous about 5 to 10 minutes before you plan to eat. Saffron is the traditional paella spice and it gives the dish a gorgeous golden color. It is also expensive and I can't honestly say I use it very often. You can approximate the color, though not the flavor, by adding 1/4 teaspoon each of paprika and turmeric to the sautéing vegetables, if you like. Try this; you'll like it.

3 tablespoons olive oil

2 medium onions, chopped

1 large green bell pepper, chopped

1 large red bell pepper, chopped

2 or 3 garlic cloves, minced

2 large tomatoes, cored, seeded, and coarsely chopped

1 cup frozen peas

1 19-ounce can chickpeas, drained and well rinsed

3 cups water

1 unsalted vegetable bouillon cube

1 scant teaspoon salt

$^1/_2$ teaspoon saffron threads

freshly ground pepper to taste

2 cups couscous

1 8-ounce jar artichoke hearts packed in water, quartered

1 lemon, cut into 8 wedges

small handful of pitted black or stuffed green olives, quartered

2 tablespoons chopped fresh parsley

*H*eat the oil in a very large, covered nonreactive skillet. Add the onions and peppers and sauté over medium-high heat, stirring occasionally, for about 7 to 8 minutes, until the onions are translucent. Stir in the garlic and tomatoes and sauté another 2 minutes. Add the peas and chickpeas, cover, and reduce the heat to low.

Meanwhile, bring the water and bouillon cube to a simmer in a small saucepan. When the cube dissolves, pour the water over the vegetables. Increase the heat and bring the water to a boil. Stir in the salt, saffron, pepper, and couscous. Stir, quickly returning the water to a boil. Cover, reduce the heat to low, and cook—without lifting the lid—for 1 minute. Remove from the heat but leave the cover on for 5 minutes. Just before serving, gently fluff the paella with a fork; couscous tends to clump up as it cooks. Arrange the artichoke hearts in a circle around the paella and the lemon wedges in a smaller circle inside the first. Garnish with the olives and parsley and serve at once.

Sort of Moussaka

MAKES 8 TO 10 SERVINGS

This is our family's version of the traditional Greek moussaka, though we've clearly taken liberties with the original. For one, there's no lamb or custard sauce, so I hesitate to call it authentic. Authentic or not, you won't want to miss this casserole; next to lasagne, it has to rank right up near the top of our list of favorite dishes.

RICE-LENTIL LAYER
1 cup long-grain brown rice
1 cup dried lentils

4 cups water

$^1/_4$ teaspoon salt

$^1/_4$ cup packed chopped parsley

3 tablespoons lemon juice

EGGPLANT-MUSHROOM LAYER
2 tablespoons olive oil

1 cup finely chopped onions

2 garlic cloves, minced

2 medium-large eggplant (8 to 9 cups), peeled and cut into small dice
salt

12 ounces mushrooms, cleaned and finely chopped in a food processor

$^1/_4$ teaspoon cinnamon

freshly ground pepper

3 cups Everyday Quick Tomato Sauce (page 193) or other tomato sauce

*M*ake the rice-lentil layer. Put the rice and lentils in a saucepan with the water and salt. Bring to a boil, reduce the heat, and cover. Simmer the mixture over low heat for approximately 30 to 35 minutes, until the water is absorbed and the rice is done; if it is still a bit chewy, that's fine. Let the mixture remain in the pan, covered, for 30 minutes, then transfer to a bowl and toss with the parsley and lemon juice. Set aside.

Make the eggplant-mushroom layer. Heat the oil in a large skillet and stir in the onions. Sauté the onions over medium-high heat for about 7 minutes, then stir in the garlic and eggplant. Add salt to taste. Sauté the eggplant for 1 or 2 minutes, then stir in the mushrooms. Cover the skillet and let the vegetables steam-cook for about 5 minutes over medium heat, stirring once or twice. Uncover the skillet and continue to cook the vegetables until most of the excess liquid has cooked off and the eggplant is quite soft. Stir in the cinnamon and pepper to taste, then remove from the heat. Preheat the oven to 400° and lightly oil a 9 × 13-inch baking dish.

To assemble the dish, spoon about 1 cup of the tomato sauce into the pan. Cover with one-half of the rice-lentil mixture, flattening it with the back of a spatula; pepper the layer to taste. Spread one-half of the eggplant-mushroom layer over the rice, followed by another cup of the tomato sauce. Repeat the layering, alternating the 2 mixtures in even layers, and finish with the sauce.

Cover the casserole with foil and bake for about 45 to 50 minutes, until heated through. After 30 minutes, check the casserole and if it seems a bit too moist, finish baking it without the foil. Let the casserole cool for 5 minutes, then serve.

VARIATION: Some of us occasionally like this with a layer of cheese, and you can easily cheese half of it and not the other. To do just that, use $^1\!/_2$ pound grated sharp Cheddar or Monterey Jack cheese, sprinkling half of it on top of each eggplant layer.

Gratin of Couscous, Sweet Potatoes, and Neufchâtel Cheese

⌇

MAKES 6 SERVINGS

I love casseroles and gratins; they're fun to improvise and you can come up with all sorts of wonderful combinations of grains, vegetables, cheeses, and other ingredients. Here is one I think you and yours will enjoy as much as my family has. It makes a hearty main dish and tastes great with Ginger-Honey Spiced Applesauce (page 268) on the side.

5 medium-large sweet potatoes (about $2^1\!/_2$ pounds)

COUSCOUS
2 cups water
$^1\!/_2$ bouillon cube (optional)
$^1\!/_4$ teaspoon salt
1 cup couscous

CHEESE LAYER
8 ounces Neufchâtel cheese, at room temperature
$^1\!/_3$ cup freshly grated Parmesan cheese
2 tablespoons chopped fresh basil or 2 teaspoons dried
1 teaspoon Dijon mustard
salt and freshly ground pepper

SWEET POTATO LAYER
$^1\!/_2$ cup hot milk
1 tablespoon unsalted butter
salt and freshly ground pepper
additional grated Parmesan, to dust the top (optional)

*P*reheat the oven to 450°. Place the sweet potatoes on a baking sheet and pierce each of them several times with a fork. Bake for about 45 to 55 minutes, until quite tender at the center. Set aside. Reset the oven to 400°. Lightly oil or butter a medium-large oval gratin dish or a medium shallow casserole dish.

Prepare the couscous. Bring the water to a boil in a small saucepan, adding the bouillon cube in small pieces if you are using it. Stir in the salt and couscous. When the couscous comes back to a boil, reduce the heat to low, cover, and cook for 2 minutes. Remove the couscous from the heat, leaving the lid on. After 10 minutes, remove the lid and gently fluff the couscous with a fork to keep it from getting too lumpy. Set aside.

Make the cheese layer. Combine the Neufchâtel cheese, Parmesan, basil, and mustard in a mixing bowl. Add the flesh of one of the hot sweet potatoes and whip the mixture with an electric mixer. Season with a little salt and a generous amount of pepper. Set aside.

Make the sweet potato layer. Scoop the flesh from the remaining potatoes into a mixing bowl. Begin whipping the potatoes with the mixer, gradually adding the hot milk and butter until softly whipped. Season to taste with salt and pepper.

To assemble the gratin, turn the couscous into the gratin or casserole dish and even it with a fork, packing gently. Spread the cheese mixture evenly over the couscous, then spread the sweet potato layer evenly over that. If you like, dust the top of the casserole with a little additional Parmesan cheese. Bake the gratin for 35 minutes, until heated through. Serve hot.

Grilled Eggplant Roll-Ups with Herb Couscous Filling

MAKES 6 SERVINGS

These are like crepes, by inspiration, slices of grilled eggplant used as wrappers for a couscous filling seasoned with fresh basil and parsley, chopped mushrooms, and cheese, if you like. The roll-ups are baked in your favorite tomato sauce—homemade or otherwise—and served with salad and fresh hot bread. If you are serving a dessert and several other courses with the meal, one roll-up per person will be enough. But you should probably double the recipe if you're only serving a salad with the meal. Be careful not to overcook the eggplant or it will tend to fall apart when you assemble the dish; a few little cracks in the eggplant are inevitable. On the other hand, if you undercook it, the eggplant won't be supple enough to roll. And if you can't fire up the grill, just brush the slices with oil and bake them in a 400° oven for about 25 to 30 minutes, until tender. My kids think these are great.

2 large eggplants

1 cup water

3/4 cup couscous

salt

2 tablespoons olive oil

1 small onion, minced

1 garlic clove, minced

8 ounces mushrooms, sliced

small handful of fresh basil leaves

small handful of fresh parsley

1/2 cup freshly grated Parmesan cheese

1/2 cup grated mozzarella cheese

freshly ground pepper

1 quart tomato sauce, homemade or store-bought

Trim the stem end off the eggplants. Starting at the center of the eggplant, cut 3 lengthwise slices from each one, each about 3/4 inch thick. (Reserve the rest of the eggplant for another use.) Grill the slices until tender or bake until tender; see headnote. Set them aside to cool. Preheat the oven to 400°.

Bring the water to a boil in a small saucepan. Stir in the couscous and a large pinch of salt. Bring the water back to a boil, cover, and cook for 30 seconds. Remove from the heat and set aside, covered, for 10 minutes. After 10 minutes, uncover the couscous and fluff it with a fork.

Heat the oil in a medium skillet. Add the onion and sauté, stirring often, over medium heat for about 5 minutes. Stir in the garlic and mushrooms. Cover and cook for 2 to 3 minutes, until the mushrooms release much of their liquid, then uncover and cook until the pan is almost dry. Set aside to cool. Meanwhile, put the basil, parsley, and Parmesan cheese in the bowl of a food processor and process until finely chopped. Transfer the mixture to a medium mixing bowl. Stir in the couscous. Transfer the mushroom sauté to the food processor. Chop well, then add it to the couscous also. Stir in the mozzarella cheese. Taste the filling, adding salt and pepper if needed.

Heat the tomato sauce and pour it into a medium-large baking dish. Working with 1 piece of eggplant at a time, place a mound of the filling on the slice and pack it down over the entire surface. Carefully roll the filling up inside the slice, then place the eggplant, seam side down, in the sauce. Repeat for the remaining slices. Cover the dish with foil, then bake the eggplant rolls for about 30 to 40 minutes, until heated through. Cool for about 5 to 10 minutes before serving.

VARIATION: To make a vegan version, omit the cheese. Use a squeeze of lemon juice to season the filling and add chopped olives, if your crowd likes them. Some of my kids do, some don't.

Squash Shepherd's Pie

MAKES 8 GENEROUS SERVINGS

This is pretty, filling, and delicious, one of Karen's pet recipes she's been tinkering and toying with for years. In this, our best and latest version, she uses a mashed squash topping, which gives this old favorite a new twist. It's a near across-the-board hit, though my youngest son, Sam, still swears by the spuds. The assembly is not complicated, but it involves several components you'll need to make ahead, namely the crust, gravy, and the squash topping. On the side, we like our favorite cranberry sauce (page 189) or cold applesauce and a salad.

> 1 10-inch pie shell; we use the Whole Wheat Press-In Oil Pastry (page 281)
>
> 2 cups Great Gravy (page 197)
>
> 4 cups Garlic-Baked Squash (page 103)

FILLING

> 2 tablespoons olive oil
>
> 1 cup chopped onions
>
> 2 celery ribs, finely chopped
>
> 2 large carrots, peeled and thinly sliced (halved first if they're very thick)
>
> $2^1/2$ cups broccoli flowerets, cut into bite-size pieces
>
> $1^1/2$ cups frozen corn
>
> 1 cup frozen petite peas

$^{1}/_{2}$ teaspoon salt

1 teaspoon dried thyme

freshly ground black pepper

*P*repare and partially prebake the pastry; if you are using the whole wheat pastry on page 281, prebake it for the prescribed 7 minutes. Otherwise, bake according to your recipe's instructions. Set aside. Prepare the gravy and the squash and set them both aside. Karen prefers to whip the squash when she is making this for a smooth texture; see the instructions with the recipe. Preheat the oven to 400°.

Make the filling. Heat the oil in a very large skillet. Add the onions and celery and sauté over medium-high heat for 4 minutes. Stir in the carrots, sauté 4 minutes more, then stir in the broccoli, corn, peas, and salt. Cover the mixture, reduce the heat slightly, and cook, stirring occasionally, for about 6 to 8 minutes, until the broccoli is almost tender and the frozen vegetables are heated through. Stir the 2 cups of gravy and the thyme into the vegetables and heat for several minutes. Season the filling to taste with pepper. Turn the filling into the crust and set aside. Spoon the squash over the pie and shape it into a low mound with the back of a spoon. Bake the pie for about 35 to 40 minutes. Serve hot, sliced into big wedges.

Neoclassical Polenta Lasagne

MAKES 8 TO 10 SERVINGS

Lasagne used to mean just one thing, but nowadays the word is being used to describe just about every layered dish under the sun. Here are delicious soft layers that meld together beautifully in the oven, thinly sliced polenta instead of the noodles, and both a red sauce and white sauce layer. Finally, there's a single layer of cooked kale and another of Delicious Disguised Mushrooms; my kids, who like the texture of sliced cooked mushrooms about as much as they do housework, don't make a peep about the mushrooms in here because they're food processed and therefore unrecognizable. I highly recommend this dish for a party, or visiting vegetarian family. Note that the polenta must be made one day ahead of when you plan to prepare this.

1 recipe Kid-Soft Polenta (page 167)

1 recipe Delicious Disguised Mushrooms (page 115)

$1^{1}/_{2}$ pounds kale

salt

3 cups good marinara sauce, homemade or store-bought

COTTAGE CHEESE LAYER
$^1/_4$ cup coarsely chopped fresh parsley

1 pound low-fat cottage cheese

1 cup finely grated Parmesan cheese

1 large egg

1 teaspoon dried basil or 1 tablespoon fresh

pinch of salt

freshly ground pepper to taste

The day before, prepare and refrigerate the polenta. Prepare the mushrooms and set them aside in a bowl; cover and refrigerate if you are holding them much more than 1 hour. Meanwhile, prepare the kale. Strip the leaves from the stems and place the leaves in a large bowl. Fill the bowl with cool water and agitate the leaves vigorously to clean them. Place the wet leaves and about $^1/_2$ inch of water in a large nonreactive pot, cover, and steam the leaves for about 10 minutes, until tender. Transfer the kale to a colander and let cool. Squeeze out some but not all of the liquid, then chop the leaves well and salt them lightly. Set aside.

When you are ready to assemble the dish, lightly oil a 9×13-inch glass or enameled baking dish or other large gratin dish. Heat the marinara sauce, then place it in your prep area. Prepare the creamy sauce by putting all of the cottage cheese layer ingredients in a food processor and processing to a smooth puree. Preheat the oven to 400°.

To assemble the lasagne, cut the polenta crosswise into twenty-four $^1/_4$-inch-thick slices. Spoon half of the marinara sauce over the bottom of the pan and cover with 12 of the polenta slices; they'll fit snugly. Using about half of the cottage cheese puree, place a large spoonful on top of each piece of polenta, then smooth the layer out with the back of the spoon. Cover the creamy layer evenly with the chopped kale, then dot the surface with the mushrooms. Pat the surface gently with a spatula to even things out, then ladle the remaining sauce evenly over the surface. Arrange the remaining 12 slices of polenta over the sauce, then, as before, spoon the rest of the cottage cheese mixture over the polenta and smooth it. Bake the lasagne for about 40 minutes, until hot and bubbly. Serve at once.

Barley, Mushroom, and Spinach Tian

MAKES 6 SERVINGS

Barley, one of the most underappreciated of the commonly known grains, is most often relegated to the soup pot. I think one of the problems is that many cooks prepare it incorrectly (see *Food for Thought*), according to misguided tradition. But a well-made pot of barley is great food, adaptable to many dishes beyond soup. Here we mix it with spinach and finely chopped mushrooms to make a substantial casserole. It is delicately seasoned with basil and a pinch of nutmeg and finished with a layer of olive oiled bread crumbs. As long as it is thoughtfully prepared, my experience is that kids really like barley; I've served this dish not only to my own kids but also their friends and it has been a real winner. We like this with cold Spiced Applesauce (page 268) and a green salad.

3 cups water

1 unsalted vegetable bouillon cube (optional)

1$^1/_2$ cups pearled barley

$^1/_2$ teaspoon salt, plus more to taste

1 bay leaf

2 tablespoons olive oil, plus a little extra to drizzle on top

1 large onion, finely chopped

2 garlic cloves, minced

8 ounces very finely chopped mushrooms

1 10-ounce package chopped frozen spinach, thawed

1 tablespoon balsamic or red wine vinegar

1 teaspoon dried basil

big pinch of grated nutmeg

freshly ground pepper to taste

1 cup fine dry bread crumbs or $^1/_2$ cup bread crumbs plus $^1/_2$ cup freshly grated Parmesan cheese

Bring the water to a boil in a small saucepan. If you're using the bouillon cube, break it into several small pieces and stir it into the water along with the barley, salt, and bay leaf. Once the water has boiled, cover the pan and cook over very low heat for about 35 minutes, until all of the water is absorbed. Remove from the heat and let stand, covered, for 20 minutes. Fluff the grain with a fork to break up the clumps and set it aside. Preheat the oven to 425° and lightly oil a large oval gratin dish or medium-large shallow casserole.

Heat the oil in a large skillet. Stir in the onion and sauté over medium-high heat for 7 minutes, until translucent. Stir in the garlic and sauté about 15 seconds more, then stir in the mushrooms. Salt the mushrooms lightly, then cover the skillet and steam them over medium heat for 2 minutes. Mix in the spinach and vinegar. (If you haven't had a chance to thaw the spinach, don't worry. Just throw it in frozen, turn down the heat, and within about 8 minutes it will soften.) When the spinach is heated through, stir in the basil, nutmeg, and pepper.

Toss the spinach mixture with the barley, then turn the grain into the prepared dish, tamping it lightly with a spatula. Sprinkle with the bread crumbs, or mix together the crumbs and cheese and sprinkle them over the top. Drizzle the topping with olive oil to dampen the crumbs, then bake for 25 to 30 minutes, until heated through. Serve hot.

❧ *Food for Thought* ❧
BARLEY RECONSIDERED

Most of my basic kitchen references tell me I should cook pearled barley 3 to 1 (3 cups of water to 1 cup of grain). I've tried this, and—much as I'd rather not fly in the face of tradition—I don't like the results. Thus cooked, the barley gets way too gummy and soft, like oatmeal, and loses all of its individual charm. I think you get much better results with a lower ratio of water to grain. So I've developed my own rules for cooking barley, which I call Haedrich's Own Rules for Cooking Barley. They go like this: For slightly chewy barley and especially any barley you plan to add to soup, use 2 to 1 proportions. Slightly chewy barley makes an excellent grain salad, too. For relatively soft barley, use 2^1/$_2$ cups water to 1 cup grain. In either case, the total cooking time should not exceed 35 minutes. If there is unabsorbed water left in the pan when the time is up, remove from the heat and let the grain sit, covered, for 15 to 30 minutes, until the water is absorbed. It is important that you use a pan with a tight-fitting lid so the water cooks into the grain instead of evaporating.

Tempeh, Onion, and Cheese Enchiladas

MAKES ABOUT 12 ENCHILADAS (6 SERVINGS)

Here's a good "meaty" enchilada for anyone who might miss the real thing in their enchiladas. Tempeh is lightly sautéed, then softened by boiling it in water. I add some tamari to season and brown the tempeh for a more authentic look and flavor. The tempeh is then rolled in the enchiladas with peppers, onions, and either Monterey Jack or Cheddar cheese. This makes an excellent dinner with corn chips and guacamole.

Red Chili Sauce (page 196)

1 8-ounce package tempeh

1 tablespoon flavorless vegetable oil

1 tablespoon tamari or soy sauce

2 garlic cloves, minced

salt and freshly ground pepper

1 small onion, finely chopped

1 medium green bell pepper, finely chopped

2 tablespoons chopped fresh parsley or cilantro

1/2 teaspoon dried oregano

12 corn tortillas (6-inch-diameter size)

6 ounces grated Cheddar or Monterey Jack cheese

If you have not already done so, prepare the chili sauce; keep it in the pan so you can reheat it. Preheat the oven to 400°.

Using your hands, crumble the tempeh into very small pieces; set aside. Heat the oil in a large skillet and add the tempeh. Sauté over medium-high heat for about 2 minutes. Add enough water to not quite cover the tempeh, then stir in the tamari. Bring to a boil, then boil until all of the water evaporates and you can hear the dry sizzle of the tempeh; stir in the garlic, sauté briefly, then remove from the heat. Season to taste with a little salt, if necessary, and pepper. Transfer the tempeh to a mixing bowl and stir in the onion, green pepper, parsley, and oregano.

Heat the chili sauce, then spread a little more than half of it in a large shallow casserole. Working with one tortilla at a time, soften them using one of the methods outlined on page 183. Spoon a generous row of tempeh mixture across the center of the softened tortilla. Top that with grated cheese, then roll up the enchilada. Place, seam side down, in the pan. Repeat for the remaining tortillas, placing them close together in the pan. Spoon and spread the remaining sauce over the top of the tortillas.

Bake for about 20 minutes, until heated through. Serve at once.

Enchiladas with Corn and Fresh Vegetables
◆
MAKES 6 SERVINGS (2 EACH)

The chief wow factor with good enchiladas is the sauce you cook them in; at least that's my experience. Not that you can or should skimp on the filling, but a good sauce lets you keep the filling simple. So it is that we love these enchiladas stuffed with a salsalike assortment of fresh vegetables and baked in our reliable Red Chili Sauce. Using raw vegetables adds some texture to an ordinarily soft dish and an appetizing fresh flavor. My kids wolf these down like you can't believe. Figure 2 per serving or at least 3 if you don't plan to flesh out the meal with Red Rice (page 158), chips, and guacamole. The traditional method of softening tortillas before rolling them is in hot oil; I discuss some alternative methods below (see *Food for Thought*) if you'd rather not use the oil.

1 cup thawed frozen or freshly cut corn kernels

1 medium red onion, finely chopped

1 small green bell pepper, finely chopped

2 smallish inner celery ribs, finely chopped

3 tablespoons finely chopped cilantro or parsley

6 ounces grated sharp Cheddar or Monterey Jack cheese

Red Chili Sauce (page 196)

12 small (8″ diameter) corn tortillas

oil for softening the tortillas (optional; see *Food for Thought*)

*C*ombine the corn, onion, pepper, celery, and cilantro in a small bowl and set aside. Put the cheese on a plate and set aside. Preheat the oven to 425° and get out a large shallow casserole dish. Spread about half of the chili sauce in the casserole and put the casserole in your work area.

Prepare the tortillas. Over medium heat, heat about ¹/₂ inch of oil in a smallish skillet, one large enough to accommodate the tortillas comfortably; have a plate, tongs, and paper towels standing by. Working with one at a time, lower the tortillas into the hot oil and fry them for about 5 seconds on each side; you're just softening them, so take care that the oil is not so hot they start to crisp or they won't roll easily. Remove each tortilla with tongs and place them on the plate with a paper towel between each one to blot the oil.

Spread a little of the cheese and vegetables down the center of each tortilla. Roll them up snugly, placing them seam side down, barely touching, in the sauced casserole. Spoon the rest of the sauce over the enchiladas, spreading so it covers the entire surface. Sprinkle with a little additional cheese, if you like, and bake for about 20 to 25 minutes, until bubbling hot. Serve at once.

❧ *Food for Thought* ❧

SOFTENING TORTILLAS: TWO ALTERNATIVES

Enchilada-bound tortillas are traditionally softened in oil to make them flexible for rolling. Such treatment is perhaps contrary to conventional wisdom about healthy eating, but I've softened dozens of tortillas in the smallest amount of oil, the point being that it seems to add a minuscule quantity of oil to each tortilla. Besides, much of the oil is blotted off by the paper towels. On the other hand, if you'd just as soon not use the oil, you can use another technique that's equally effective but a little sloppier: softening them in the sauce. To do it right, make the chili sauce ahead and keep it on the thin side by using a little extra water. Using your fingers or tongs, lower each tortilla into the hot sauce—it should be turned off so it isn't splattering—and hold it there for 2 seconds. Transfer the tortillas to baking sheets lined with plastic wrap. Cool and use soon.

One other method I've had good luck with is steam-softening, something I've never seen mentioned anywhere, so this might be totally heretical. Nonetheless, I just set up my steamer, get the water boiling, and place one at a time in the pot on the steamer. Then I cover, for no more than about 20 seconds, and remove the tortilla with tongs. So far as I can tell, there's no drawback at all to this method and in fact it is the simplest of the methods mentioned here.

Salsas, Sauces, Relishes, and Gravies

Here is a section devoted to dressing up things other than salads—salsas, sauces, relishes, and gravies you'll no doubt find more uses for than I've suggested. Some of these are cooked sauces, served hot with heavier foods; the rest are raw sauces, good with chips, on burgers, sandwiches, eggs, and that sort of thing. There aren't a lot of recipes in this chapter, but the ones that are here we use quite often.

Summer is the season when I like to prepare fresh salsas, when the ingredients are at their peak. Good, locally grown tomatoes make all the difference in the world. At the height of tomato season, when prices are down and variety is up, add different colored peppers and tomatoes to your salsas. And make lots of it; I'm always amazed how much fresh salsa we can eat in one sitting. There never seems to be enough. Be creative about using any leftovers: Fresh salsas are best when they've had a little time to sit and mingle before you serve them. But the ingredients (especially the tomatoes) can get rather tired after a couple of days.

Corn is another mainstay of summer sauces; we like it in a colorful relish, combined with roasted green peppers (see page 190). We use it on late summer quesadillas, on fresh sliced tomatoes, stirred into scrambled eggs. The nice thing is, once you start keeping fresh salsas and relishes around, you find all sorts of ways to use them. The herb yogurt sauce (page 186) started out as a dressing for sandwiches. Then I found out how good it was on sliced cherry tomatoes, with cold green beans, used like mayonnaise in potato salad, and on and on.

You'll find the hot, cooked sauces in the last part of this chapter: one good red chili sauce for enchiladas, a few tomato-based sauces covering a variety of uses, and our basic gravy for mashed potatoes.

We call it Great Gravy, but we think—and hope you'll agree—that all the recipes in this section are pretty great, too.

Herb Yogurt Sauce with Mustard

MAKES ABOUT 1 CUP

One of the simplest of sauces, this has a friendly versatility in the vegetarian kitchen. It has the sour tang of yogurt, highlighted by fresh herbs, with a depth of flavor provided by the mustard. Though this is a savory sauce, there are times—especially when you are feeding kids—that it benefits from a teaspoon of honey. It works nicely that way as a dressing on cherry tomatoes or tossed with cold cooked green beans in a salad. A little honey goes a long way, so use it judiciously; you don't want to sweeten the sauce so much as tone down the tang. This is also an excellent sauce to perk up plain steamed vegetables or potato patties, to serve with crudités, or to use as the special dressing on your favorite vegetarian burger.

1 cup regular, nonfat, or low-fat plain yogurt

1/4 cup finely chopped fresh parsley

2 tablespoons chopped fresh basil

1 1/2 teaspoons Dijon mustard

1/2 teaspoon fresh thyme or 1/4 teaspoon dried

2 tablespoons finely chopped dill pickles

salt and freshly ground pepper to taste

approximately 1/2 teaspoon honey (optional)

Just whisk everything together in a small bowl; that's it. Cover and refrigerate until using.

Tomatillo and Roasted Pepper Salsa Verde

MAKES ABOUT 1 1/2 CUPS

Most of the time we're content with standard salsa, either the homemade fresh tomato type or off the shelf; there are blessedly a number of good brands on the market. Then there are times when we want something a little different, a salsa with a more complex flavor and touch of exotica. That's when I turn to this recipe. It reminds me of salsas I've eaten in Mexico, on the Yucatán peninsula, where every restaurant seems to have their own excellent version of *salsa verde* (though this is less verde than some, since it has a ripe tomato in it as well). Use it as we do—with chips, on veggie burgers (particularly good with the Pumpkin and Wheat Germ Burgers on page 86), in burritos, and on eggs—but do give it at least a couple of hours to mellow before you serve it; time has a marvelous way of honing the rough edges of separate flavors into a mellow amalgam.

1 large green bell pepper

1 cup canned drained tomatillos

1 small ripe tomato, cored and coarsely chopped

1/2 cup loosely packed parsley or cilantro leaves

1/4 cup chopped red onion

1 tablespoon chopped pickled jalapeño peppers

1 tablespoon lemon juice

2 teaspoons white vinegar

1 small garlic clove, minced (optional)

1 teaspoon sugar

salt to taste

Under a broiler or directly over a gas flame, roast the pepper on all sides until the entire skin is charred. Put the pepper in a small bowl, cover with plastic wrap, and set aside for 30 minutes, until cooled. When cool enough to handle, cut out the stem and ribs, scrape off the skin with a paring knife, and coarsely chop the pepper.

Put the chopped pepper in the bowl of a food processor along with the remaining ingredients. Process to a textured puree, then taste, adding more salt if necessary. Transfer to a bowl, cover, and refrigerate until serving.

Fresh Tomato Salsa
❧
MAKES ABOUT 3¹/₂ CUPS

Fresh salsa is so easy to make—not to mention so much better tasting—that I can't understand why I ever buy the stuff. Oddly enough, even though most of my kids don't like chunks of fresh tomato, they'll eat them in salsa; apparently, the synthesis of the various flavors is sufficient to overcome any objection to the tomatoes. That's the beauty of salsa, that you can take a few basic ingredients and quickly turn them into something so good. This one is like that. There's nothing exotic about any of the ingredients—you don't have to roast anything or make a trip to the store for special spices. Even with pretty mediocre tomatoes this is excellent. Notice that I include tomato puree as an optional ingredient. I mention it because some people, kids and adults, like a slightly thicker salsa and that's what the puree does, thicken it a little.

¹/₂ small green bell pepper

3 large ripe tomatoes, cored and diced

1 small red onion, finely chopped

3 to 4 tablespoons chopped fresh parsley (may be all or part cilantro)

1 to 2 tablespoons finely chopped pickled jalapeño peppers, plus a little of the pickling juice from the jar

juice of 1 lime

1 small garlic clove, minced (optional)

2 to 3 tablespoons tomato puree (optional)

salt

*I*f you have kids who aren't crazy about green peppers, either cut it in large enough pieces that they're easy to spot and remove or small enough that they'll never notice. In any case, combine it with the remaining ingredients, adding salt to taste. Serve right away or cover and refrigerate until serving. It will last 3 to 4 days in the fridge.

Salsa Gold

MAKES ABOUT 2^1/$_2$ CUPS

Occasionally I like to make this pretty salsa in shades of yellow and gold, most often in the summer when I can purchase the ingredients from a local source at a reasonable price; the asking price for yellow tomatoes and peppers can be pretty steep. Not only is it delicious, it really brightens up a mixed platter of your favorite Mexican foods. We love to serve it with chips, guacamole, and enchiladas (pages 181–183) or Salad Burritos (page 85). Children like the color, so I've kept it kid-friendly—relatively mild, with a minimum of scary grown-up stuff. This is great on Veggie Burgers (page 87).

1^1/$_4$ pounds ripe golden or yellow tomatoes, or a combination of both

1 medium yellow bell pepper, finely chopped

1 small red onion, finely chopped

1 4-ounce can chopped mild green chilies

2 tablespoons finely chopped fresh parsley

2 tablespoons lemon juice

1 tablespoon apple cider vinegar, or slightly more to taste

salt and freshly ground pepper

Core the tomatoes and slice them cleanly into bite-size pieces; I say "cleanly" because the salsa looks best if you can see distinct pieces as opposed to appearing as if it got mowed over by a dull chef's knife. Transfer the tomatoes to a bowl and mix in the remaining ingredients, seasoning to taste. Cover and refrigerate if not serving soon.

Cranberry-Apple-Orange Relish

MAKES ABOUT 3 CUPS

The inspiration for this colorful, fruity relish comes from a recipe in *Simple Foods for the Good Life* (Stillpoint, 1985), written by the late Helen Nearing. Helen and her husband Scott were pioneers of the modern back-to-the-land movement, and their writings about their homesteading experiments in Vermont, and then Maine, was fodder for legions of young people who hoped to emulate their lifestyle. This relish, or sauce, was a hit at our house from the very start. I started making it when I cooked full time at a group home for children, and ever since then it has been a cranberry-season tradition. The reason for its popularity, I think, is the other fruit; cranberries are fine, but sometimes their intensity can be overwhelming. The apples and oranges mellow them and add layers of flavor. Everything is dumped right into the pot and simmered to a thickish consistency; that's all there is to it. Eat it warm or cold with just about any savory dish.

1 12-ounce bag fresh cranberries

3 large apples (any kind), peeled, cored, and coarsely chopped

5 oranges

$^1/_2$ cup maple syrup or mild honey, such as clover or orange blossom

$^1/_2$ teaspoon cinnamon

juice of $^1/_2$ lemon

Put the cranberries and apples in a large nonreactive pot. Halve, seed, and section 3 of the oranges, squeezing the sections in with the fruit. Juice the other 2 oranges and add this juice also. Add the maple syrup. Bring the mixture to a simmer over medium heat, stirring occasionally. Cover and simmer gently for 15 to 20 minutes, stirring occasionally. When the relish is done, the apples will be quite soft. If you've used a firmer cooking apple and you want a smoother, rather than a chunkier, consistency, mash the relish with a potato masher.

Transfer the relish to a heatproof bowl and stir in the cinnamon and lemon juice. Serve the relish warm or let cool, cover, and refrigerate before serving. Either way it is wonderful.

Roasted Pepper and Sweet Corn Relish

MAKES ABOUT 2 $^1/_2$ CUPS

My kids love this fresh corn relish in burritos, quesadillas, and all by itself. For a light lunch or snack, Karen and I like it on toast drizzled with olive oil, covered with sliced fresh tomatoes and more relish on top. You'll find plenty of uses for it if you keep a jar on hand. First find the best sweet summer corn, then make this. I've tried fancying it up with spices and other things, but most of it just interfered with the crisp fresh flavor. Back to basics!

2 large green bell peppers, roasted, peeled, and diced

3 good-size ears of corn, shaved

salt

1¹/₂ tablespoons olive oil

1 tablespoon white wine vinegar or red wine vinegar

2 teaspoons lemon juice

2 tablespoons chopped fresh parsley, or a combination of parsley and
cilantro

pinch of freshly ground black pepper

*R*oast and prepare the peppers, if you haven't already. You can do this
under the broiler, on the grill, or right on top of the stove over an open
flame. (I lay the peppers right on the burner grate. In any case, roast
on all sides until the skin is totally blackened and blistered; turn the peppers as
each surface blackens.) Put the peppers in a bowl, cover with plastic wrap, and
let them steam-cool for 30 minutes. Cut out the core, seeds, and ribs and scrape
off the charred skins. Dice the peppers and put them in a mixing bowl.

Put the shaved corn in a medium skillet, adding a pinch or two of salt and
enough water to cover. Bring to a boil and cook at a good boil until the water
has evaporated, about 5 minutes. Scrape the corn into the mixing bowl with
the diced peppers and cool slightly. Toss with the remaining ingredients, tasting to correct the seasoning; if it seems to need a bit more of this or that, add it.
Transfer the mixture to a widemouthed jar or storage container and refrigerate
until needed.

VARIATIONS: Even though I just said I liked this best plain, you could
always fancy this up with a cupful of tender-cooked black beans, a teaspoon or
two of chopped chipotle peppers (*hot!;* definitely not for the kids), or halved
cherry tomatoes added just before serving.

Parsley-Lemon Sauce

MAKES ABOUT 1 CUP

Most of us take parsley for granted, but I think you'll have a whole new appre-
ciation for it once you've tried this perky sauce. So even if you aren't the sauce-
making type, do try it; you'll be surprised at how little effort it requires, not to
mention how many uses you will find for it. We use it on fried polenta slices,
plain steamed new potatoes and other steamed vegetables, omelets and egg
dishes, toast and bruschette, sandwiches, or stirred into brothy soups just before serving. I could go on. Use Italian flat-leaf parsley instead of the curly

sort; you end up with a smoother texture. The sauce can be served at any temperature.

1^1/$_2$ tablespoons olive oil

^{1}/$_4$ cup minced onion

1 cup water

^{1}/$_2$ vegetable bouillon cube

^{1}/$_4$ cup peeled, finely diced all-purpose potato

salt

1 cup loosely packed flat-leaf parsley leaves

juice of ^{1}/$_2$ lemon

freshly ground pepper

*H*eat the olive oil in a small saucepan. Stir in the onion and sauté over medium heat for 5 minutes, stirring often. Add the water, bouillon cube, potato, and a big pinch of salt, then bring to a boil. Cover and gently boil the potato pieces until very tender.

Transfer the contents of the saucepan to a blender and add the parsley and some of the lemon juice. Puree the sauce, scraping down the sides if necessary. Taste, adding salt, more lemon juice, and pepper to taste, then process again. Transfer the sauce to a small serving container, then cover and refrigerate until serving.

❧ *Food for Thought* ❧
ATTENTION HERB GARDENERS

If you're an herb gardener-cook, you're probably wondering, If this sauce works with parsley, why wouldn't it work with other herbs as well? Well, it would! Using parsley as your foundation, you can build off this sauce in many other directions. For instance, lovage is one of my favorite springtime herbs, albeit an assertive one. But a few lovage leaves would give this sauce celery-like overtones that would work swell with any of the ideas I mentioned above. Do you grow lemon thyme? A little bit will accentuate the lemon tones of the sauce and add a fragrant touch. Basil leaves naturally would make a good dressing for fresh tomatoes or a garnish for a cold tomato soup. And steamed potatoes would love to see fresh dill weed. In general, use a light touch with the accompanying herb: You want to accent the parsley, not overwhelm it. And keep the mix simple because if you use too many different herbs you create too much competition, which spoils the sauce.

Everyday Quick Tomato Sauce

MAKES ABOUT 1 1/2 QUARTS

Some may not agree, but I think tomato sauce is a fascinating subject, and the most fascinating aspect is how someone can take the same basic ingredients—tomatoes, oil, onions, garlic, herbs—and come up with a sauce that's so vastly different from one made with virtually the same ingredients. The quantity and kind of oil, the size of the chopped onions, brand and type of tomatoes—the accretion of these variables accounts for some big differences. For what it is worth, then, here is the way I make basic tomato sauce for spaghetti, lasagne, pizza, what have you. Two important ingredients in homemade sauce are salt and sugar; most homemade sauces will benefit from both, though they should be used discreetly and in balance. Keep tomato paste at the ready and use it to thicken the sauce if necessary.

3 tablespoons olive oil

1 medium onion, finely chopped

1 medium green bell pepper, finely chopped

1 or 2 garlic cloves, minced

1 28-ounce can crushed tomatoes in puree

1 28-ounce can tomato puree

2 teaspoons dried basil

1 teaspoon dried oregano

1/2 teaspoon salt, plus more to taste

freshly ground pepper to taste

about 1/2 teaspoon sugar or honey

tomato paste to thicken the sauce (optional)

Heat the olive oil in a heavy, medium saucepan. Add the onion and pepper and sauté, stirring occasionally, for 7 to 8 minutes. Add the garlic and sauté 30 more seconds. Add the remaining ingredients except for the tomato paste to the pan, then cover and bring the sauce to a simmer. Simmer the sauce, covered, for about 15 minutes, stirring occasionally. After about 10 minutes, correct the seasonings and stir in some tomato paste if the sauce seems too watery. It may need anywhere from 1 to 3 tablespoons. Simmer the sauce a few more minutes, then use as needed.

❧ *Food for Thought* ❧
CANNED TOMATOES

Taste is such a personal thing. Recently, a cooking magazine did a blind tasting of various brands of canned tomatoes, attended by several experts whose thoughts on such matters you would take note of. Problem was, few of the experts could agree upon which of the canned tomatoes tasted the best; one expert's heaven was another's hell. I've tried all of the different brands locally and I still haven't decided which I like best. The local store brand is the cheapest, but they're also the most watery and lacking in flavor. There's an expensive organic brand that's good, but not so good as some of the more familiar mass-market labels. Try them all and see which ones your own family likes. You'll notice that in my sauce recipe here I use a can of puree and another of crushed tomatoes; I think that combination gives the sauce just the right amount of body and kid-friendly texture. If you use all crushed tomatoes, they sometimes don't like it as much. That's something to consider if your kids are used to prepared sauce, which tends to be uniformly smooth and textureless.

Mediterranean Relish

✑

MAKES ABOUT 1 1/2 CUPS

The inspiration, though not the recipe, for this relish came from Cafe Buon Gustaio, a restaurant in Hanover, New Hampshire, that Karen and I just love. It's a crowded, noisy little place where the food is generally right on the mark and the chef will go out of his way to accommodate your whims. On the night I had their Mediterranean relish, it was served with pan-fried polenta slices, but one bite and I immediately realized just how versatile a relish like this could be at home. So I came up with my own version based on the one I remember, a thick concoction full of olives, capers, bits of marinated artichoke hearts, and both crushed and sun-dried tomatoes. The flavor is intense and there's no mistaking the sauce's roots. In addition to serving this with polenta, you could fill or sauce an omelet with it, serve it with slices of frittata, spread it on toast, or dress a pasta dish for two with it. I'm betting this packs more flavor than your kids can handle, but you never know. (Note: If you're using *fresh* basil, rather than dried, stir it in at the last moment.)

2 tablespoons olive oil

1 small onion, finely chopped

2 garlic cloves, minced

3 or 4 oil-packed sun-dried tomatoes, finely chopped

1 cup canned crushed tomatoes in puree

3 or 4 capers, finely chopped (optional)

5 or 6 pitted kalamata or other good olives, finely chopped

3 marinated canned artichoke hearts, chopped

2 tablespoons chopped fresh parsley

freshly ground pepper to taste

1 teaspoon dried basil or 1 tablespoon chopped fresh

2 tablespoons pine nuts or chopped walnuts

In a medium saucepan, gently heat the olive oil and stir in the onion. Sauté the onion over medium-low heat, stirring often, for 3 minutes. Stir in the garlic, sauté 1 minute more, then add the remaining ingredients except for the nuts. Gently simmer the relish for 3 to 4 minutes, until heated through, then stir in the nuts right before serving. This will keep for a week in the fridge in a tightly sealed container.

Kofta Curry Sauce

MAKES ABOUT 1 QUART

This is the sauce for my family's favorite Indian meal, vegetable koftas on brown rice, though it is also excellent on plain noodles. The seasoning is just right to our collective taste: exotic without being overpowering or hot. Since making the koftas is a bit of a production, the sauce can be made a day ahead if you like, then reheated. Our family of six will usually use most or all of this for a kofta meal, but if you have any left over it can be frozen, then reheated with steamed or otherwise cooked vegetables to make a quick veggie curry.

3 tablespoons olive oil

1 cup finely chopped onions

2 small bay leaves

4 teaspoons coriander

1 tablespoon ground cumin

2 to 3 teaspoons minced fresh ginger or 1 teaspoon dried

$^1/_2$ teaspoon ground cardamom

$^1/_2$ teaspoon mild chili powder

$^1/_4$ teaspoon ground cinnamon

pinch or two of cayenne

1 28-ounce can crushed tomatoes in puree

$^1/_2$ teaspoon salt

2 cups plain unsweetened soy milk or plain yogurt

*H*eat the oil in a large nonreactive skillet or medium casserole. Add the onions and bay leaves and sauté over medium-high heat for 7 minutes, stirring often. Stir in all of the spices, reduce the heat slightly, and sauté the mixture another minute or so, stirring continuously. Stir in the crushed tomatoes and salt and simmer for 5 minutes. Blend in the soy milk or yogurt and simmer the sauce until heated through. Serve at once, removing the bay leaves before serving.

Red Chili Sauce

MAKES 2$^1/_2$ TO 3 CUPS

I am not an expert on chilies and chili sauces, a fact that's readily apparent each time a new book on some aspect of Mexican or southwestern cooking crosses my desk. The reason is partly geography—this is New Hampshire, not Santa Fe—but primarily because I find I can get along quite nicely on one quick non-expert-style chili sauce, this one. Rather than custom blending exotic dried chilies, I just use the relatively mild red chili powder I get at the local health food store. Chili powder is not strictly ground chilies; the ground chilies are blended with other herbs, spices, and garlic to yield a sort of all-purpose, somewhat uniform blend for Mexican cooking. What this sauce lacks in refinement it makes up for in ease and congeniality; it can be made in a jiff and it goes great with any Mexican food I've ever used it with.

3 tablespoons flavorless vegetable oil

1 good-size onion, finely chopped

4$^1/_2$ tablespoons chili powder

1 tablespoon ground cumin

1$^1/_2$ teaspoons ground oregano

2 to 3 garlic cloves, minced

1 1/2 cups water

1 1/4 cups canned tomato puree

salt

several good-size pinches of sugar

*H*eat the oil in a large, heavy skillet. Add the onion and sauté over medium heat for 8 or 9 minutes, until lightly golden. Stir in the spices, herbs, and garlic and cook, stirring, for about 1 minute. Stir in the water and bring to a low boil. Simmer for 1 minute, then stir in the tomato puree, about 1/4 teaspoon salt (for starters), and a big pinch of sugar. Simmer gently for 4 to 5 minutes, adding more water as it thickens; it should stay a little on the thin side. Taste the sauce as it simmers, adding more salt and sugar if necessary; it takes a little playing with the salt, sugar, and water at this point to get the sauce just right. Cool the sauce if you're not serving it soon. Transfer to a covered container and refrigerate.

VARIATION: On occasion, just to add some depth of flavor and sweetness, I will add a grilled green pepper to the sauce. To make the sauce this way, broil or grill a medium green bell pepper until all the sides are blackened and blistered. Put the pepper in a plastic bag, close the bag, and let the pepper sweat for 30 minutes. Cut the ribs and seeds out of the pepper, scrape off the blackened skin with a knife, and chop the pepper coarsely. Puree the pepper in a blender with a little of the sauce, then pour back into the sauce.

Great Gravy

MAKES ABOUT 3 CUPS

One of the big challenges of meatless cooking is gravies. Gravies, of course, are usually based upon meat essences; that's what gives them their big, deep flavors. Without the meat, vegetarians need to be creative about putting the flavor in. Here's how we do it. This is the lighter (in both flavor and color) of our two basic gravies; the more robust one follows. This one is based on nutritional yeast and flour, both of which we toast to help bring out the flavor. It is difficult to describe the precise flavor, but—hard-core vegetarians of the world, forgive me—it is almost like a poultry gravy with a hint of cheese. It makes a great all-purpose gravy for potatoes and other vegetables, and it is the essential element in our Vegan Scalloped Spuds (page 125) and Squash Shepherd's Pie (page 176).

1 tablespoon olive oil

1 cup finely chopped onion

1 garlic clove, minced

3 tablespoons nutritional yeast

$^1/_4$ cup unbleached all-purpose flour

3 cups water

$^1/_2$ teaspoon salt

$^1/_2$ teaspoon dried thyme (optional)

freshly ground black pepper

*H*eat the olive oil in a large skillet. Stir in the onion and sauté over medium-high heat for 6 to 7 minutes. Stir in the garlic and sauté a few seconds more. Sprinkle the nutritional yeast over the onions, stirring it for 30 seconds. Sprinkle the flour into the pan and brown it, stirring, for 30 seconds more. Stir in about half of the water, whisking vigorously, then gradually add the rest of the water. Bring the gravy to a boil, stirring in the salt and thyme. Boil the gravy gently for about 5 minutes; if you are using it right away and you would like it thicker, simmer several minutes more. (Don't cook it any more than 5 minutes if you're making the Vegan Scalloped Spuds.) Add pepper to taste and serve hot.

Mushroom Gravy

MAKES ABOUT 3 CUPS

This and the previous Great Gravy are our two nearly all-purpose gravies. We use this on baked and mashed potatoes and sometimes on home fries the next morning, made from leftover baked potatoes. It is also good on Thanksgiving stuffing. Note—if you have kids who don't like mushrooms—that they're first passed through the food processor (the mushrooms, that is, not your kids), making a finely textured gravy without chunks of 'shrooms; most of my kids don't care for pieces of mushroom, but they love this. Use the greater quantity of mushrooms for a deeper flavor.

8 to 12 ounces mushrooms

4 tablespoons olive oil

1¹/₂ cups chopped onions

3 tablespoons unbleached all-purpose flour or whole wheat pastry flour

2¹/₂ cups water

2 teaspoons tamari or soy sauce

1 teaspoon dried thyme

¹/₂ teaspoon salt

freshly ground pepper to taste

*P*ut the mushrooms in the bowl of a food processor and process until they're very finely chopped; you may have to scrape down the sides once or twice. Set them aside.

Heat 2 tablespoons of the oil in a medium skillet. Stir in the onions and sauté over medium heat for 8 to 9 minutes. Add the processed mushrooms and sauté for about 5 minutes, until they've given off almost all of their liquid. Push the mushrooms aside to the edge of the pan, then add the remaining 2 tablespoons of oil and the flour to the center of the pan. Cook the mixture over medium heat, stirring, for 1 minute, then whisk in the remaining ingredients. Bring the gravy to a boil, stirring, then lower the heat and simmer gently for 5 minutes. Taste and correct the seasonings before serving.

Quiche and Other Savory Tarts

A few years ago everyone was hotly debating the big issue of whether or not real men ate quiche. Like most big questions, the more we talked about it the less anybody did about it, and by that I mean actually practicing the art of making good quiche and other savory tarts. So quiche just went away for a while, slipped off the screen of American cooking. That's begun to change, though, and now I notice that quiche is staging a comeback. Home cooks are digging out old recipes, and restaurants are moving quiche back onto menus. It's about time.

Quiche is an easy target for anyone bent on counting eggs, grams of fat, and bad-mouthing butter; it makes no apologies about using any of them. Neither do I. I simply don't share the notion that a healthy diet cannot include the foods we love on an occasional basis, and I really do love quiche. Besides, I don't think eating well is primarily a reductive process: Instead of removing foods from our diet altogether, we should look for more interesting ways to eat a wider variety of healthy foods. End of speech.

Whether I'm eating it in a restaurant, or at some sort of party or social gathering, I always pay close attention when I'm served a slice of quiche, not necessarily because it is generally good—unfortunately it isn't—but because it gives me the opportunity to figure out why it is sometimes so good, and other times so disappointing. And the weak points, I've found, are pretty universal. (Before I leave you with the wrong impression, I'm actually a very gracious guest, and it isn't like I pick and sniff at my quiche like I'm on an archaeological dig or something; I'm very discreet, and truly hope this revelation won't eliminate me from your guest list.)

The first of these weak spots is the crust; soggy crust is one problem, the other is boring crust. Soggy crust is usually the result of not partially prebaking it (a process I've detailed with the crust recipes in the Pantry section). A lot of cooks assume they can cut a few minutes off the preparation time by skipping this step, but it is always a mistake. A soggy crust is a major culinary faux pas, almost as bad as eggshells in the egg salad. As for boring crust, that's pretty much any frozen one you buy in the supermarket. A serious quiche demands a good home-made crust.

Another weak spot is the custard, the egg and cream or milk part. Now, when you bake a sweet custard, it tastes heavenly in large part because of the sugar. A savory tart or quiche has no sugar, obviously, but you do need some serious oomph to make the custard taste like something; it isn't there just to coat the rest of the filling. That wouldn't be fair. You need salt, often more than you think, pepper, herbs, and, more often than not, Dijon mustard. My rule of thumb is to go boldly where quiche custards are concerned.

Other than that, treat all of your main filling ingredients carefully, taking care not to overcook veggies (because they'll cook further as the quiche bakes), sautéing your onions just so, and using good quality cheeses. That's the way to make quiche (take it from a real man).

Asparagus and Havarti Quiche

MAKES 10 TO 12 SERVINGS

This party-size quiche is just the ticket for a springtime gathering of friends and the rustic, earthy wheat germ crust gets an award for best supporting role. This pastry can be used for all of your large pies, sweet or savory.

1 recipe Wheat Germ Cream Cheese Pastry, chilled (page 280)

FILLING AND ASSEMBLY

1 1/4 pounds fresh asparagus

2 tablespoons unsalted butter

2 large onions, halved and thinly sliced

2 garlic cloves, minced

6 to 8 ounces Havarti cheese, half cut into cubes, half grated

5 large eggs

1³/₄ cups milk, half-and-half, or light cream

2 teaspoons Dijon mustard

1 teaspoon dried dill or 1 tablespoon chopped fresh dill

³/₄ teaspoon salt

freshly ground pepper to taste

On a sheet of lightly floured wax paper, roll the dough into a 13-inch circle. Invert the pastry over a 10-inch quiche or pie pan. Peel off the paper, then gently push the pastry into the pan. Turn the overhanging edge under, sculpting it into an upstanding ridge. Cover with plastic wrap and put the pastry in the freezer for 30 minutes.

When you're ready to bake the pastry, preheat the oven to 400°. Line the pastry with aluminum foil and weight it down with dried beans or rice. Bake for 20 minutes, then remove the foil, beans and all. Prick the bottom of the pastry several times with a fork, then bake another 10 minutes. Set aside on a rack. Adjust the oven temperature to 375°.

Choose 12 of the best-looking asparagus spears. Cut off and reserve the top 5 inches of each, discarding the bottoms. Using a vegetable peeler, peel the bottom half of the remaining spears, then cut these peeled spears into 1¹/₂-inch pieces. Put the smaller pieces in the bottom of a steamer pan and lay the longer 5-inch pieces on top. Cover the pan and steam for about 5 minutes, until the asparagus is barely tender. Remove from the heat and reserve.

Melt the butter in a skillet and add the onions. Sauté over medium heat for about 10 minutes, until golden. Stir in the garlic, sauté another 30 seconds, then remove from the heat.

To assemble the quiche, spread the onions in the pastry. Cover with the smaller pieces of asparagus (reserve the longer spears for the top) and the cubes of Havarti. Beat the remaining ingredients with a whisk, then slowly pour this custard into the pastry; top with the grated cheese. Arrange the 5-inch asparagus spears on the top, like the spokes of a bicycle tire. Bake the quiche for 45 to 50 minutes, until golden and set. Cool on a rack and serve at any temperature.

Spinach, Potato, and Monterey Jack Pie

MAKES 8 SERVINGS

Sautéed onions, diced potatoes, and spinach form the bulk of this savory quiche-pie. Some of the cheese goes in the bottom of the shell, the rest on top for a golden finish. Make this early in the day and you can have it for lunch or dinner, with a big salad and a special dessert.

1 9-inch partially baked pie shell; either of the ones on pages 278–283
    would work fine

FILLING

2 tablespoons olive oil

1 large onion, halved and thinly sliced

1 cup peeled and diced red-skinned potatoes

10 ounces fresh spinach, washed, stemmed, and torn into pieces

salt

CUSTARD

3 large eggs

1¼ cups half-and-half or milk

1 teaspoon Dijon mustard

freshly ground pepper to taste

big pinch of grated nutmeg

6 ounces Monterey Jack or pepper Jack cheese, cut into ¾-inch
    cubes

Prepare and prebake the pie shell as directed, but do not prick the shell; set aside to cool. If you've pricked the pastry and there are little holes in the shell, patch them now with a thick flour-and-water paste; just dab a little bit over the holes to seal them (otherwise the custard will leak out). Set the oven temperature to 375°.

Prepare the filling. Heat the olive oil in a large nonreactive skillet. Stir in the onion and sauté over medium-high heat for 7 to 8 minutes. Stir in the potatoes, sauté for 1 minute, then add the spinach. Cover tightly and steam the spinach and potatoes for about 5 minutes, until tender and wilted; the potatoes should not overcook. Salt the vegetables lightly, then transfer to a plate to cool.

To make the custard, whisk the eggs in a bowl until frothy. Whisk in the half-and-half, mustard, pepper, nutmeg, and $1/4$ teaspoon salt. Spread half of the cheese in the pie shell. Cover with the filling, then top with the remaining cheese. Slowly pour the custard over the filling.

Bake the pie for 40 to 45 minutes, until golden and set, then cool on a rack. Serve warm or at room temperature. Cover and refrigerate any leftovers.

Broccoli and Cheddar Polenta Quiche

MAKES 1 9-INCH PIE, 6 TO 8 SERVINGS

Some of my kids aren't crazy about typical quiche because they find it custardy; all of them, however, like this one. The texture is different from the usual quiche; because it is made with a base of polenta it is much firmer, more compact, less jiggly but still light. The filling won't win any awards for originality—it's just broccoli and Cheddar, spiked with a little hot mustard—but it is their favorite formula, so why flirt with anything too fancy? I should mention that this is a far sight leaner than most quiche is. Not only are there fewer eggs, but there's no milk or cream and less cheese. This is excellent hot, warm, or at room temperature, and it makes a nice focal point for a weekend brunch.

1 9-inch pie shell, partially prebaked; I use the Traditional Pastry on page 278

FILLING AND POLENTA
$2^1/2$ cups broccoli flowerets

2 tablespoons olive oil

2 medium onions, finely chopped

salt

$1^1/2$ cups water

$1/3$ cup yellow cornmeal

1 cup loosely packed grated sharp Cheddar cheese

2 large eggs, lightly beaten

1 teaspoon Dijon mustard

1 teaspoon dried basil

$^1/_4$ teaspoon salt

pinch of cayenne

*P*repare and partially prebake the pastry if you haven't already; cool. Steam the broccoli until it is not quite tender and set it aside on a plate. Heat the oil in a medium skillet. Add the onions and sauté over medium-high heat for about 7 minutes, until translucent, salting to taste. Remove from the heat and set aside. Preheat the oven to 375°.

Make the polenta. Combine the water and cornmeal in a small saucepan. Gradually bring to a boil over medium heat, stirring often. Continue to cook for about 10 minutes, stirring; it should become medium thick. Remove it from the heat and stir in the cheese about half at a time. Cool the polenta for 3 to 4 minutes, then whisk in the eggs and seasonings. Fold in the sautéed onions.

To assemble the quiche, arrange the broccoli in the pie shell. Scrape the polenta over the broccoli and wiggle it with your spoon or spatula so it settles down in between the broccoli pieces. Bake the quiche for about 40 to 45 minutes; when it is done the top will have cracks in it and the filling will be solid. You can also probe it with the tip of a sharp knife to make sure it is set in the center. Transfer the quiche to a rack and let it cool for about 10 minutes before slicing.

Caramelized Onion Tart

MAKES 6 SERVINGS

This free-form tart, made with a wonderfully crunchy semolina pastry, would be an excellent choice for a small party or special dinner with friends. (You could also cut it into 8 smaller pieces and serve it as an appetizer.) This is an onion lover's tart, with lots of thinly sliced onions slowly caramelized in olive oil. They're dusted with rosemary and, if you like, either chopped olives or cheese, or both. When tomatoes are in season, consider adding a layer of thin slices over the onions before the tart goes in the oven. And if you're not planning a special occasion meal anytime soon, just go ahead and make this for the family; my kids love it.

1 recipe Semolina Pastry (page 279), chilled

TOPPING
2 tablespoons olive oil
4 cups halved and thinly sliced onions

salt

1 teaspoon chopped fresh rosemary or $^1/_2$ teaspoon crushed dried

freshly ground pepper

$^1/_2$ cup chopped pitted black or green olives (optional)

4 or 5 thin slices of tomato (optional)

1 cup grated Cheddar, provolone, or other melting cheese (optional)

*P*repare and chill the pastry if you haven't already. Heat the olive oil in a large skillet. Add the onions and sauté them slowly over medium heat for about 15 minutes, stirring often. The onions should slowly turn golden without burning, so lower the heat if necessary. Salt the onions to taste as they cook. When they're golden brown, transfer the onions to a plate and cool. Preheat the oven to 425°.

Once the pastry has chilled, roll it into a 12-inch circle on a sheet of wax paper. Invert the pastry over a large cookie sheet and peel off the paper. Pinch the edge of the pastry into an upstanding ridge.

Scrape the onions onto the pastry and spread them evenly up to the edge. Sprinkle the onions with the rosemary and dust with pepper to taste. Layer on any of the remaining optional ingredients—olives, tomato, or cheese— then bake the tart for 20 to 25 minutes. Slide the pastry onto a rack and cool for 5 minutes before slicing. This is excellent hot, warm, or at room temperature.

Rustic Tomato Tart in a Basil Crust

MAKES 6 SERVINGS

A classic summer tart if there ever was one, this has layers of cheese, sautéed onions, and fresh sliced tomatoes baked in an herb pastry. It's a great way to show off those fat juicy tomatoes from your garden.

1 recipe Traditional Pastry (page 278), with 2 teaspoons dried basil added to the dry ingredients, chilled

FILLING

3 tablespoons olive oil

3 cups halved and thinly sliced onions

1 garlic clove, minced

salt

1 tablespoon semolina or fine cornmeal

2 large ripe tomatoes, cored and sliced $^1/_4$ inch thick

freshly ground pepper

1 cup grated provolone or mozzarella cheese

*P*repare the pastry as directed and chill. To make the filling, heat the olive oil in a large, heavy skillet. Add the onions and sauté over low heat for 10 to 12 minutes, stirring occasionally, until golden brown. Add the garlic, salt the onions lightly, and sauté 1 minute more. Scrape the onions onto a plate and cool. Preheat the oven to 375°.

To assemble, roll the pastry into a 13-inch circle on a sheet of lightly floured wax paper. Invert the pastry onto a large cookie sheet and peel off the paper.

Sprinkle the semolina or cornmeal onto the pastry in roughly a 9-inch circle in the center of the tart. Spread the onions over the semolina. Arrange the tomato slices in an overlapping circle over the onions, with several slices in the center. Lightly salt and pepper the tomatoes.

Fold the edges of the dough up over the filling, pleating the dough as you go. Bake on the center rack for 30 minutes. Slide the sheet out and sprinkle with the grated cheese. Bake for 10 to 15 minutes more, until bubbly hot and the cheese is starting to turn golden. Cool the tart on the sheet on a rack for 10 to 15 minutes before slicing.

Pizza

Pardon me if I've said this elsewhere, but pizza is just about my favorite thing in the world to eat. I understand I'm not alone in this either, because last I heard pizza was America's number one fast food, more popular, even, than burgers.

I like going out to pizza parlors, but, as you would imagine, the pizza I like best is the pizza we make at home, from scratch. With the emphasis on *scratch*. There are two keys to excellent pizza, the first being a homemade crust, the second being homemade toppings. If you buy frozen crusts and use prepared sauces, what you get isn't exactly memorable, transcendent pizza, usually not even as good as pizza parlor pizza. (Though I would be lying if I said we don't sometimes do this; it really is the only way the younger kids can prepare pizza, by themselves, in a hurry.)

If you don't already know how, you should really learn to make pizza crust (the bonus being that once you've learned that, you can make almost any bread). Pizza dough is one of the simplest doughs to make: The ingredients are few and simple, the preparation time minimal. Anybody can learn, but if you know someone who is a good bread baker, ask for some tips on kneading; I've taught a lot of people to make bread over the years, and kneading is the thing that throws off a lot of cooks. I go into more detail in the recipe for basic dough (page 210) but it is worth emphasizing the importance of not kneading the dough too roughly, lest it stick to your hands and counter. Use a gentle, rocking motion with the palms of your hands. Don't pinch the dough.

Other cooks often ask me: How do I get a good, crispy crust on my pizza? Everyone seems to want one, and there are all sorts of paraphernalia out there to help: pizza stones, ceramic tiles, round baking sheets with little holes in the bottom, and that sort of thing. Back when I first started baking, I liked playing around with all of them; I was quite curious to see how they worked. And what I eventually found was that while some of these things worked better than others, none of them was really essential to getting a good crisp crust.

Today, I just bake my pizza on two dark, heavy baking sheets; I don't transfer the pizza to oven tiles. The oven should be hot; 450° to 475° is good. I have a gas oven, but I realize many people use electric. If you find, with electric, that your bottom crust gets too dark, consider some way of evening out the heat. You can try putting a dark, heavy baking sheet on an oven rack at the lowest setting, then baking your pizza on the middle rack.

Also, you'll get a crisper crust if the dough has fully doubled in bulk; don't shortchange the rising time. Once the dough is on the sheet, try to give it a little extra rising time before you top and bake.

As for toppings, there's something here for everyone. And if you want a few more ideas, check the box in this section for other possibilities.

All-Purpose Pizza Dough
⇌

MAKES ENOUGH DOUGH FOR 2 LARGE PIZZAS, FLATBREADS, OR CALZONES

This is the dough I make several times a week, year in and year out. I make it almost instinctively when dinner is approaching and I have no other plans: If nothing else, I know I can turn this into a couple of good-size pizzas with nothing more than olive oil smeared over the top—if that's all I have in the larder—and everyone will be happy. More often than not, however, we'll take it a step beyond by adding sautéed onions, mushrooms, or what have you.

If you are not an experienced bread baker, let me say that I've noticed the biggest problem beginners have with this and most bread doughs is in the kneading: The tendency is to push too hard, which breaks the skin of the dough and makes it sticky. The kneader automatically assumes a sticky dough needs more flour, and this starts a cycle of working in too much flour. So remember to rock the dough as you knead, gently at first, so you don't push your hands deep into the dough.

If you have but one bread dough in your repertoire, this is the one. It can be turned into pizza, calzone, bread sticks, French bread, and more. And it can be made the night or morning before you need it and then refrigerated to suit your schedule. It can also be halved if you don't need so much dough; simply halve all of the ingredients.

2¹/₂ cups warm water

1 ¹/₄-ounce package (2 teaspoons) active dry yeast

pinch of sugar

1 cup whole wheat flour

5 cups unbleached all-purpose flour

2 tablespoons olive oil, plus a little extra for the bowl

1 scant tablespoon salt

*P*our the water into a large mixing bowl and sprinkle the yeast over it. Add the sugar, whole wheat flour, and 3 cups of the unbleached flour and stir briskly with a wooden spoon for 100 strokes. Let the mixture rest for 5 minutes.

Stir the olive oil and salt into the dough. Stir in enough of the remaining flour, about ¹/₂ cup at a time, to make a shaggy but kneadable dough; this will require almost 1¹/₂ cups of flour. Turn the dough out onto a lightly floured surface and knead the dough with floured hands for about 8 minutes, until smooth, soft, and springy. Pour about a tablespoon of olive oil into a ceramic bowl and smear it around. Add the dough, rotate it to coat it with oil, and cover the bowl with plastic wrap. Set the dough aside in a warmish, draft-free spot for about 1 to 1¹/₂ hours, until doubled in bulk.

Once the dough has doubled, punch it down and turn the dough out onto a lightly floured surface. Knead the dough for about 1 minute, then divide the dough in half. Knead each half into a ball and sprinkle lightly with flour. Let the balls of dough rest for 10 minutes, then proceed with your recipe.

VARIATIONS: To make a whole-wheatier dough, which gives you a more wholesome though generally less crisp crust, replace up to 3 cups of the unbleached flour with 3 additional cups of whole wheat (a total of 4 cups whole wheat, 2 unbleached). I also like the addition of 2 or 3 tablespoons of semolina, for a crunchier crust, added with the initial 4 cups of flour; you'll need just a tad less flour if you add it.

Wheat Germ Semolina Pizza Dough
ᴏ⌒

MAKES ENOUGH DOUGH FOR 2 LARGE PIZZAS

Even when I make a pizza crust with white flour as opposed to whole wheat, I like to include a little something extra for crunch, texture, and flavor. I do that here with toasted wheat germ and semolina. The wheat germ gives the dough a nutrition boost, a slightly nubby texture and nutty flavor, and the semolina adds a pleasing crunch. This dough is excellent for any pizza; I'm particularly fond of it with the Tomato, Pesto, and Fontina Pizza (page 218), but it is also excellent served plain. Just brush the dough with olive oil, scatter with herbs, and bake as is. Note that there is only 1 teaspoon of yeast here, not the usual 2 or more teaspoons. This will slow the rise and give the crust a better flavor. On the other hand, if you want to accelerate the rise, add an additional teaspoon of yeast.

2 cups lukewarm water

1 teaspoon active dry yeast

big pinch of sugar

$^1/_4$ cup toasted unsweetened wheat germ

2 tablespoons semolina

5 cups unbleached all-purpose flour

2 teaspoons salt

*P*our the water into a large mixing bowl and sprinkle the yeast over it; stir in the sugar. Let the mixture sit for 2 minutes, then stir in the wheat germ, semolina, and 3 cups of the flour. Using a wooden spoon, beat the mixture vigorously for 50 strokes. Let the dough rest for 5 minutes.

Still using your wooden spoon, stir in the salt and enough of the remaining flour to make a soft, kneadable dough. Turn the dough out onto a floured surface and knead for 9 to 10 minutes, kneading in as much of the additional flour as necessary to keep the dough from sticking. You may find the dough most responsive if you knead the dough in 3- to 4-minute sessions, with a 5-minute break between each one; keep the dough covered with plastic wrap, right on your floured counter.

Lightly oil a large ceramic bowl and add the dough, rotating it to coat the entire surface. Cover the bowl with plastic wrap and place a tea towel over the top to trap the warmth. Set the dough aside in a warmish spot, until doubled in bulk; it will take anywhere from $1^1/_2$ to 2 hours.

When the dough has doubled in bulk, punch it down, knead for 1 minute, then divide the dough in half before proceeding with your recipe.

Crisp-Crusted Potato Pizza

MAKES 1 LARGE PIZZA (6–8 SERVINGS)

One day I said to my partner Karen, "What do you think about potato pizzas?" I already knew that she wasn't crazy about the texture of bready pizza dough with potatoes, so it didn't surprise me when she said, "I'm not crazy about the texture of bready pizza dough with potatoes." But what if, I countered, we made a thin, crisp-crusted potato pizza? Would the contrasting textures make a difference? We thought that it would, so to test out our hunch I quickly made up a batch of dough and once it had risen I rolled some of it extra thin. And it made a *big* difference. We all loved it. So that's our secret for a good potato pizza: a thin, crisp crust. This is excellent with or without the cheese. Instead of one of the melting cheeses I mention, you could grate a little fresh Parmesan over the pizza as soon as it comes out of the oven.

^{1}/2 recipe All-Purpose Pizza Dough (page 210)

6 medium red-skinned potatoes, scrubbed

salt

3 tablespoons olive oil

1 garlic clove, minced

semolina, for dusting the baking sheet

1 teaspoon chopped fresh rosemary or ^{1}/2 teaspoon dried

freshly ground pepper

^{1}/4 to ^{1}/2 pound grated fontina or sharp Cheddar cheese (optional)

Prepare the dough and let it rise until doubled in bulk. While the dough is rising, slice the potatoes about ^{1}/8 inch thick. Lay the pieces in a steamer and steam for about 8 minutes, just until tender. Transfer the slices to a baking sheet lined with plastic wrap and salt them lightly.

Gently warm the oil and garlic in a small skillet for about 1 minute; set aside. Preheat the oven to 475°.

When the dough has doubled, punch it down; if you have made a full recipe of dough, you can use the other half to make another kind of pizza, or you can freeze half, or you can double this recipe. To get a good crisp crust, you'll need to roll the dough thin, ideally about ^{1}/4 inch thick. If you have a large baking sheet—either 14 × 14 inches or 12 × 18 inches—you will need a little less than half of a full recipe of dough. In any case, divide the dough appropriately and knead each piece into a ball. Set the pieces aside on a lightly floured surface and let rest for 5 to 7 minutes. Very lightly oil the baking sheet and dust it with semolina.

On a lightly floured surface, roll the dough out as large as your pan. Lift the dough into the pan, tucking and stretching it right up to the edge. Brush the dough lightly with the garlic oil, then arrange the potatoes in rows over the dough. Brush the potatoes with the remaining garlic oil. Sprinkle the potatoes with rosemary, then add salt and pepper to taste. Top with the cheese if you are using it.

Let the pizza rest for 10 minutes, then bake for 25 minutes, adjusting the position midway through the baking so it browns evenly. Slide the pizza onto a flattened paper grocery bag, slice, and serve.

Kale, Fresh Tomato, and Provolone Pizza

MAKES 1 LARGE PIZZA (6–8 SERVINGS)

Most of my kids are just nuts about kale, so it makes sense that this would be one of their favorite pizzas, even though it has sliced fresh tomatoes on it; generally, they don't go for fresh cooked tomatoes in big pieces like this, but for some reason it doesn't seem to bother them here. They devour this. Adults love it, too. Whenever I teach a cooking class on healthy vegetarian pizzas, this is always the biggest hit.

1 recipe All-Purpose Pizza Dough (page 210)

1 large bunch (about 1¹/₂ pounds) kale

¹/₂ cup water

salt

flour, for dusting the dough

semolina, for dusting the baking sheets

3 tablespoons olive oil

2 garlic cloves, minced

1¹/₂ tablespoons balsamic vinegar

2 large ripe tomatoes, cored and sliced about ¹/₄ inch thick

freshly ground pepper

¹/₄ to ¹/₂ pound grated provolone cheese (optional)

1 teaspoon chopped fresh rosemary or ¹/₂ teaspoon crushed dried

*F*irst make the dough and set it aside to rise until doubled in bulk; you will need half of it to make this pizza. You can either freeze the rest of the dough (simply freeze unrisen dough in a sealed plastic bag), use the other half for another kind of pizza, or double this recipe.

Strip the kale leaves from their stems, discarding the stems. Put the leaves into a very large bowl and cover with plenty of cold water. Agitate the leaves to remove any sand and grit. Transfer the leaves to a large nonreactive cooking pot and add about 1/2 cup of water. Steam the kale over high heat for about 10 to 12 minutes, salting it lightly about halfway through. Drain the kale in a colander. When it is cool enough to handle, squeeze out much but not all of the liquid and chop it coarsely. Set aside. Preheat the oven to 475° when the pizza dough has almost doubled.

When the dough has doubled, punch it down, turn it out onto a lightly floured surface, and divide in half. Knead each half into a ball. Dust with flour and set aside on a floured surface for about 10 minutes, until the dough is quite relaxed. While you are waiting, very lightly oil 1 or 2 large baking sheets and sprinkle with semolina. On a lightly floured surface, roll the dough out large enough to fit the pan and lift the pizza dough into the pan, tucking it up against the sides. Brush the dough with about 1 tablespoon of the olive oil.

Heat the remaining olive oil in a very large nonreactive skillet. Quickly stir in the garlic and then, before the garlic has a chance to brown, stir in the kale. Heat the kale, stirring, for about 1 minute, then sprinkle on the balsamic vinegar. Heat for another minute, then remove from the heat.

Spread the kale evenly over the pizza, then cover the kale with the sliced tomatoes. Lightly salt and pepper the tomato slices and arrange them over the kale. Cover with the cheese if you are using it or simply brush the tomatoes with a little olive oil. Sprinkle the top with the rosemary.

Bake the pizza for 20 to 25 minutes, until the crust is golden brown. Cool the pizza on a rack for about 5 minutes, then slice and serve.

Swiss Chard and Monterey Jack Pizza

MAKES 2 LARGE PIZZAS, ABOUT 6 SERVINGS

At first glance, this might not sound like the sort of pizza your kids would go for. But you might be wrong. It is actually a favorite of my two older kids, Ben and Tess. I think kids like this one for a couple of reasons. Swiss chard is one of the milder-tasting greens, and it cooks up quite tender in short order; for a child who isn't used to greens, this can be a good introduction to green veggies. The other reason is that the Monterey Jack cheese is mild, too; in general, kids don't go for strong-tasting cheeses. At least, that's been my experience. You could also use a mild Cheddar, mozzarella, or any other cheese your family likes. Finally, the splash of balsamic vinegar adds a pleasant sweetness to the topping, which kids like also.

1 recipe All-Purpose Pizza Dough (page 210)

1 large bunch Swiss chard (about 1 1/2 pounds), well rinsed

3 tablespoons olive oil

2 medium onions, halved and sliced

2 garlic cloves, minced

2 large tomatoes, cored, seeded, and cut into big chunks

1 tablespoon balsamic vinegar

salt and freshly ground pepper

cornmeal, for dusting the baking sheets

8 ounces grated Monterey Jack cheese

chopped fresh basil or parsley, for garnish (optional)

Prepare the pizza dough and let it rise. Meanwhile, cut the central stems out of the chard and cut the leaves coarsely, discarding the stems. Heat the oil in a large nonreactive pot or Dutch oven. Add the onions and sauté over medium heat for 8 minutes, stirring occasionally. Stir in the garlic, cook for several more seconds, then add the Swiss chard. Salt it lightly, cover, and let the chard steam for about 3 or 4 minutes. Stir in the tomatoes, cover again, and cook for 5 minutes. Uncover the pot and cook, stirring occasionally, until the tomatoes are quite soft, maybe 5 minutes more. Stir in the balsamic vinegar, then season to taste with salt and pepper.

Preheat the oven to 450°. Punch down the dough, divide in half, and shape into rounds. Place the rounds onto lightly oiled and cornmeal-dusted baking sheets. Spoon half the filling and pan juices over each round, then cover them with the cheese. Bake for about 20 to 25 minutes, until the crust is golden brown. Cool the pizzas on a rack for 5 to 10 minutes; garnish with the herbs just before serving.

Summer Pizza with Tomatoes and Roasted Tomato-Garlic Sauce

MAKES 1 LARGE PIZZA, ABOUT 4 SERVINGS

Here's one pizza you can really make successfully only in the summer, when the primary ingredients—tomatoes and basil—are ripe and plentiful. First you'll have to roast some tomatoes and garlic; they can be roasted simultaneously, though in separate pans so the garlic doesn't over-roast and dry out. These are processed with a little basil to make a smooth, thickish sauce. That's spread over the pizza dough, covered with fresh tomato slices to help prevent the sauce from drying out, then sprinkled with cheese; if you're serving kids and suspect they won't go for the tomato layer, just leave it off or cover only a portion of the pizza. I like to serve this with a green salad with lots of additional torn basil leaves thrown in.

1/2 recipe All-Purpose Pizza Dough (page 210)

10 good-size plum tomatoes, cored and halved

2 whole heads Roasted Garlic (page 109)

olive oil

small handful of fresh basil leaves

salt and freshly ground pepper

semolina or cornmeal, for dusting the baking sheet

flour

2 large ripe tomatoes, cored and thinly sliced

6 to 8 ounces grated Monterey Jack, mozzarella, or provolone cheese

Let the pizza dough rise in a warm, draft-free spot while you roast the tomatoes. (If necessary, the dough can have a second rising if you need extra time while you prepare the sauce.) Preheat the oven to 425°.

Lightly oil a large shallow roasting pan or baking dish. Arrange the tomatoes in the pan, flat side up. Roast the tomatoes until they're soft and somewhat charred, 40 to 50 minutes. Reset the oven temperature to 450°.

Let the vegetables cool slightly, then put the tomatoes in the bowl of a food processor. Squeeze the garlic cloves out of their skins and into the bowl. Add 3 tablespoons olive oil and the basil leaves, then process to a smooth, slightly textured puree; add salt and pepper to taste. Set aside. Lightly oil a large baking sheet and dust it with semolina or fine cornmeal.

When the dough has doubled, punch it down and turn it out onto a lightly floured surface. Knead for 1 minute, then dust the counter with flour and place the dough on it. Dust the dough with flour and let it rest for 5 to 8 minutes, then roll or pat the dough into a large circle or oblong slightly less than $^1/_2$ inch thick.

Lift the dough onto the prepared sheet. Spread the sauce over the surface, then cover that with a single layer of the tomato slices; cover with the cheese. Let the pizza rest for 10 minutes, then bake for 20 to 22 minutes, until the bottom crust is golden brown and crisp. Slice and serve right away.

Tomato, Pesto, and Fontina Pizza

MAKES 2 LARGE PIZZAS

Once you've made the dough for the crust, this is a breeze if you use prepared pesto; you can purchase it in the fresh pasta section of your supermarket. Of course, if you have lots of fresh basil on hand you'll probably want to make your own (page 289). Some of my kids like the fresh tomatoes on here, some prefer just the pesto and cheese, so I often leave some without tomatoes.

1 recipe Wheat Germ Semolina Pizza Dough (page 212)

cornmeal or semolina, for dusting the baking sheets

1 7-ounce container pesto

6 medium ripe tomatoes, cored and thinly sliced

1 pound grated fontina cheese

freshly ground pepper

Prepare the dough and let it rise until doubled in bulk. Lightly oil 2 large baking sheets and dust them lightly with cornmeal or semolina. Preheat the oven to 450°.

When the dough has doubled in bulk, punch it down. Turn the dough onto a lightly floured surface and knead for 1 minute; divide in half and knead each half into a ball. Let the dough rest on a floured surface for 10 minutes.

On a floured surface, roll the dough into large circles or oblongs just big enough to fit onto your baking sheets. Lift them onto the sheets and spread them out evenly. Divide the pesto between the 2 crusts, spreading it evenly over the surface. Cover each one with sliced tomatoes, then cover with the grated cheese. Let the pizzas rest for 5 minutes. Pepper them to taste.

Bake the pizzas for 20 to 25 minutes, until bubbly hot and the bottoms are browned and crusty. Transfer the pizzas to a rack and cool for 5 minutes before slicing.

❧ *Food for Thought* ❧
A PIZZA MISCELLANY

As Wolfgang Puck proved so profitably, there's almost no end to what you can put on pizza. Here are some possibilities you can try your hand at:

—**Grilled Vegetable Pizza**—Summer is the time for grilling fresh vegetables, and making incredible grilled vegetable pizzas. All veggies should be cut large enough to not fall through the grill; you can always cut them smaller later. Brush with olive oil, wait till the fire burns down to red-hot embers, then use any of the following: sliced rounds of eggplant, half or quarter sections of bell peppers—green, red, or any other color, diagonal slices of summer squash or zucchini, halved plum tomatoes, parboiled asparagus spears, even sliced, parboiled red potatoes. Brush the crust with olive oil, cover with coarsely chopped grilled tomatoes, then add anything else you like; cheese is optional. Sprinkle on fresh minced herbs at the end.

—**Greens and Olive Oil Pizza**—You can cover cooked kale with tomato slices, but just about any cooked green makes a great pizza. Squeeze most of the liquid out of the greens, toss them with olive oil and a teaspoon of vinegar, and spread over the crust. Drizzle with more olive oil; salt and pepper to taste. Add cheese or not. Bake as usual. If the greens start to get too black, cover loosely with foil.

—**Balsamic Portobello Mushroom Pizza**—Sauté sliced portobello mushrooms in olive oil, adding a splash of balsamic vinegar at the end. Spread over the crust, drizzle with olive oil, dust with crushed rosemary. Add cheese or not. Bake as usual.

—**Olive Oil Pizza**—(This is a plain one the kids like.) Brush crust generously with olive oil; salt lightly and sprinkle on crushed or chopped rosemary. Bake as usual. Remove and immediately sprinkle with Parmesan cheese. Red pepper flakes are good too.

—**Mediterranean Pizza**—Spread Mediterranean Relish (page 194) over dough. Top with cheese only (for the kids) or cover with quartered, marinated artichoke hearts, sliced olives, and feta cheese.

Yeast Breads, Ugly Breads

Making yeast bread was my first love in the kitchen, and it still is the one thing I never get tired of doing. I seem to connect with yeast bread baking on a deep, organic level; those of us who love to bake bread are allowed to talk this way because we're trying to explain something we don't fully understand and to which words can't do justice.

I learned to make bread twenty-five years ago, when I joined the navy as a seventeen-year-old kid. One of my navy buddies was into health foods and I remember him taking me to a health food store. Back in those days, the early seventies, health food stores were almost always these little out-of-the-way places and everybody who worked there looked like either Jerry Garcia or Grace Slick, or both, which was really scary. Anyway, I was impressed by this amazing place where they had all kinds of grains in large bulk containers. I purchased some of each, went to the local bookstore in Biloxi, Mississippi, and bought *Beard on Bread,* the James Beard work that was one of the best books on the subject for many years. With Beard's help I learned how to make delicious yeast bread (really far-out stuff, in the parlance of the day). Perhaps it was easier for me than it was for others, because my buddies and I already were serious students of fermentation, which is to say we drank our fair share of beer.

My, how things have changed. Today, eating healthy is about as mainstream an idea as you'll ever find. And you don't have to go to little side street shops to buy your fixings. People still make bread, too; I know because I give many workshops on the subject. But I sometimes lament that the most common question I hear is, *Can you adapt that recipe to a bread machine?* I don't have anything against bread machines, sorta. I just question the sanity of buying a machine that essentially mimics factory bread in your own home.

The beauty of handmade bread is not only in the end product; the process itself is incredibly satisfying. I think a lot of people are turned off by bread baking because it takes time to learn. To me, however, one of the great things about it is the ongoing sense of discovery. There's nuance, subtlety, technique. These things capture one's interest in a way that wouldn't be possible if making bread were as simple as heating up a can of soup.

In this chapter you'll find a few good breads worth learning how to make. And unless you're already an experienced baker, a few is probably plenty. My advice to beginners is to stick with one or two breads at the start and then learn them well before moving on to others. Repetition is essential to master a bread, and if you concentrate on one or two, you won't get lost trying to figure out the subtleties of many. It is easier to take lessons you've learned well and apply them to other breads than it is to try to learn too many lessons at once.

And I'm very, very sorry, but if you try to make any of these breads in your bread machine, your house will blow up.

Ugly Breads

Although I call these Ugly Breads, I say that tongue-in-cheek because I think they're actually quite lovely in a free-form fashion. Observant bakers will note that these are quite similar to the Italian *ciabatta* loaves. You will need to start this crusty bread the day before by making the starter; allow 3 to 4 hours the next day for mixing, rising, shaping, and baking. Note that the dough is quite sticky and the preliminary kneading must be done in a heavy-duty electric mixer.

STARTER
1 1/2 cups lukewarm water
big pinch active dry yeast
1 1/2 cups unbleached all-purpose flour
1/2 cup whole wheat flour

FINISHED LOAVES
3/4 cup lukewarm milk

2 teaspoons active dry yeast

1 tablespoon olive oil

2 teaspoons salt

2³/₄ cups unbleached all-purpose flour, plus more for kneading

cornmeal, for dusting the baking sheets

*F*or the starter: Put water in a medium mixing bowl; sprinkle yeast over it and set aside for 5 minutes. Stir in flours and beat well with a wooden spoon for 2 minutes. Cover and leave at room temperature for 12 to 24 hours.

Stir down the starter; cover and refrigerate for 1 hour.

Pour the milk into a small bowl and sprinkle the yeast over it. Whisk to blend; set aside for 10 minutes. Scrape the starter into the bowl of a heavy-duty electric mixer. Stir in the dissolved yeast, oil, and salt. Add the unbleached flour and mix with the flat beater on low speed for 6 minutes. Let the dough rest in the bowl for 10 minutes; it will be quite sticky.

Scrape the dough out onto a well-floured surface. Using a dough scraper, fold the sides of the dough onto itself, then knead gently with floured hands for 2 minutes, using more flour as necessary to prevent sticking. Dough will feel very soft, satiny, and smooth. Place the dough in an oiled bowl. Cover bowl with plastic wrap and set aside in a warm, draft-free spot for 1 to 2 hours, until doubled in bulk.

Punch dough down and turn out onto a floured surface. Knead for 1 minute; divide dough in half. Let halves rest for 5 minutes on floured surface, then roll each portion up into a loose log. Flour the logs and let rest on a floured surface for 5 minutes. Very lightly oil 2 large baking sheets; dust with cornmeal.

Gently stretch each half into a rough rectangle about 6″ wide and 14″ long; periodically let dough rest for 3 to 4 minutes if it is too elastic. Dust the tops with flour, then place each one on a baking sheet. Cover loosely with lightly oiled plastic wrap and let rise in a warm, draft-free spot for 30 minutes.

Using your fingertips, "dimple" the dough by making deep indentations here and there on the surface with your fingertips; lightly dust again with flour and cover with plastic. Set aside for 20 minutes; preheat oven to 425°.

After 20 minutes, remove plastic and bake the loaves until golden and crusty, about 23 to 25 minutes. To brown evenly, switch the positions of the loaves midway through baking. Cool briefly on a rack, but serve as soon as possible. To serve, break off pieces; don't cut.

N O T E :   The breads may be reheated at 400°, directly on the racks, for 7 to 8 minutes.

100% Whole Wheat Bread

MAKES 1 LARGE LOAF

More and more, it is getting easier to find quality artisanal bread in this country. That's good on the one hand, but on the other it might discourage some of us from taking the time to make a good loaf of bread at home. And that would be too bad because there's really nothing like a loaf of homemade whole grain bread. Yes, the flavor and texture isn't the same as some of the sourdough breads you find in artisan bake shops. Not the same, but not inferior either. Just different. And—this has been repeated so often to the point that it has almost become trite—bread making really is an almost meditative exercise. Lately, I've been in the habit of getting up early and starting this, so we'll have a loaf of bread around for the day (it makes one large loaf, and, in fact, seldom lasts past noon). And at the risk of sounding like Mr. Zen, it nearly always has a calming—some might say centering—effect on me. I like that.

1 1/2 cups lukewarm water

2 tablespoons honey

1 teaspoon (1/2 packet) active dry yeast

approximately 4 cups whole wheat flour

2 teaspoons salt

2 tablespoons flavorless vegetable oil or olive oil

1/3 cup toasted sesame seeds

Pour the water into a large mixing bowl and stir in the honey. Sprinkle the yeast over the water and wait 2 minutes. Add 3 cups of flour, then stir vigorously with a wooden spoon for 50 strokes; this will get your heart pumping a little. Stir the salt into the dough, followed by the oil and 2 tablespoons of the sesame seeds. Stir another 50 strokes. Cover the bowl with plastic wrap and let the dough rest for 5 minutes.

Gradually start stirring the rest of the whole wheat flour into the dough; as it starts to cohere, I often switch to a large rubber scraper and start paddling the dough in the bowl to begin the kneading. When the dough is firm enough to start kneading, dust your counter with whole wheat flour and place the dough right on it. Flour your hands and start kneading, not too vigorously at first. Knead for 3 minutes, then cover the dough with plastic wrap and give it a 5-minute rest. Use more flour on your counter as necessary to keep the dough from sticking. Knead for 3 more minutes, followed by another 5-minute rest. Then repeat one more time. (During one of the rest periods, wash and dry the bowl; then put a teaspoon or so of oil in it and oil the bowl.)

Place the dough in the bowl, rotating it to oil the entire surface. Cover the bowl with plastic wrap and lay a tea towel over it to help trap the warmth. Let the dough rise at room temperature; this is a relatively slow riser, which helps develop good flavor. It may take 2 to 3 hours to double in bulk. While you are waiting, butter a large loaf pan (I use a $4^1/_2 \times 10$-inch ceramic pan).

Once the dough has doubled, punch it down and knead for 1 minute. Shape the dough into a loaf, then spread the remaining sesame seeds on the counter in a rectangle pattern roughly as long as the loaf and about 5 inches wide. Lightly brush as much of the loaf as you can with water, then roll the dough in the seeds; they'll stick. Coat as much of the loaf with seeds as you can.

Put the loaf in the pan, seam side down, and cover the pan with plastic wrap. Set the dough aside and let it rise at room temperature, until nearly doubled in bulk. Preheat the oven to 400° and set the rack in the lowest position. Using a serrated knife, make 3 diagonal slashes on top of the loaf about $^3/_4$ inch deep.

When the oven has preheated, bake the loaf for 45 minutes. When done, the bottom of the loaf will give a hollow retort when tapped with a finger; if it needs more time, put it back in the oven, out of the pan. Cool for 30 minutes— or at least try to!—before slicing.

Burger Buns

MAKES 10 BUNS

These are the buns I make when I make my own buns for veggie burgers (pages 87 and 88). They're good-sized, wheaty, soft but still sturdy, and you'll find many more uses for them than burgers. They make a good all-purpose sandwich bun, and they're excellent with soup and salad, too, though you may want to make them a little smaller if that's how you plan to serve them. If you like a seeded bun, use the egg-milk mixture and sprinkle with your choice of seeds; they taste wonderful either way. In fact, you might want to hide these until the burgers are served; if the rest of the family finds them beforehand, they'll be gone before dinner.

2 cups warm water

$^1/_4$ cup regular or instant rolled oats

2 tablespoons honey

1 $^1/_4$-ounce package (2 teaspoons) active dry yeast

$1^1/_2$ cups whole wheat flour

approximately 3¹/₂ cups unbleached all-purpose flour

2 teaspoons salt

2 tablespoons flavorless vegetable, sunflower, or olive oil

semolina or fine cornmeal, for dusting the baking sheet (optional)

1 egg, lightly beaten with 1 tablespoon milk

2 tablespoons poppy or sesame seeds

*P*ut the water, oats, and honey in a large mixing bowl and sprinkle the yeast over the top. Stir briefly, then set aside for 5 minutes. Stir the whole wheat flour and 1¹/₂ cups of the unbleached flour into the water. Mix vigorously for 100 strokes, then scrape down the sides and cover the bowl with plastic wrap. Let this sponge sit undisturbed for 15 minutes.

After 15 minutes, stir the salt and then the oil into the sponge. Stir in enough of the remaining unbleached flour, about ¹/₂ cup at a time, to make a soft, kneadable dough. Turn it out onto a lightly floured surface and knead for 8 to 10 minutes, using only enough additional flour to keep the dough from sticking. When the dough feels bouncy, place it in an oiled bowl, turning the dough to coat the entire surface with oil. Cover the bowl with plastic wrap and set it aside in a warmish, draft-free spot for about 1 hour, or until the dough is doubled in bulk.

While the dough is rising, lightly oil a large baking sheet and dust with semolina or fine cornmeal, if you have some.

When the dough has doubled, punch it down and turn it out onto a floured surface. Knead for 30 seconds, then divide the dough into 10 equal pieces, setting them aside on a lightly floured surface. Let the pieces rest for 3 to 4 minutes.

Working with one piece of dough at a time, shape each piece of dough into a ball; the best way I've found to do this is to bring up the sides and tuck them into the center of the dough as you rotate it. You're essentially pushing the dough ball inside of itself, but try not to rip the surface of the dough as you do this. Put the resulting balls of dough on the baking sheet, leaving about 3 inches between them. Wait 5 minutes, then lightly oil your fingertips and press gently on top of each piece of dough to flatten slightly; if you don't do this, the rolls tend to bake up too tall and not wide enough. Lightly oil 2 long pieces of plastic wrap and lay them over the buns, oiled side down. Place the buns in a warm, draft-free spot and let them rise until doubled in bulk, about 40 minutes; as they approach that point, preheat the oven to 375°.

If you are glazing the rolls, gently brush each one with the egg-milk mixture, using a pastry brush. Sprinkle with seeds, then bake the buns for 25 to 30 minutes, until golden brown. Transfer the buns to a rack to cool and wait at least 20 minutes before slicing them.

Cheddar, Onion, and Herb Crescents

~

MAKES 16 LARGE ROLLS

Make these in early summer, with fresh herbs, or with dried herbs for your Thanksgiving bread basket. Either way, they're wonderful: big flavor, nice bronze color, quite dramatic looking.

1 ¼-ounce package (2 teaspoons) active dry yeast

⅓ cup water

1 12-ounce bottle lukewarm beer or 1½ cups water

1 tablespoon sugar

1 teaspoon Dijon mustard

1 large egg at room temperature, lightly beaten

3 tablespoons butter, melted

2 tablespoons chopped fresh chives

2 teaspoons minced fresh thyme or 1 teaspoon dried

2 teaspoons minced fresh sage or 1 teaspoon crumbled dried

2 teaspoons salt

1 cup whole wheat flour

⅓ cup toasted wheat germ

approximately 4½ cups unbleached all-purpose flour

ONION FILLING AND ASSEMBLY
2 tablespoons unsalted butter

2 good-size onions, chopped

1½ cups grated extra-sharp Cheddar cheese

cornmeal or semolina, for dusting

1 egg, beaten with 1 tablespoon milk

Sprinkle the yeast over the water in a small bowl. Stir briskly to mix, then set aside for 5 minutes.

Whisk the beer or water, sugar, mustard, egg, and melted butter in a large mixing bowl. Stir in the herbs, salt, whole wheat flour, and wheat germ. Stir in 2½ cups of the unbleached flour and beat vigorously with a wooden spoon for 100 strokes. Cover the dough and let it rest for 10 minutes.

Stir in enough of the remaining unbleached flour, ¼ cup at a time, to make a soft but kneadable dough. Turn the dough out onto a floured surface and knead the dough, gently at first, for 8 to 10 minutes, using flour as necessary to keep the dough from sticking. When the dough is smooth and elastic, place it in an oiled bowl and rotate to coat the entire surface. Cover the bowl with plastic wrap and set aside in a warm, draft-free spot until doubled in bulk, 45 to 60 minutes.

While the dough is rising, melt the butter for the filling in a large skillet. Add the onions and sauté them over medium heat, stirring often, for about 10 to 12 minutes, until golden. Remove from the heat. Cool.

Once the dough has risen, sprinkle about one-third of the cheese over the top. Punch the dough down, add more cheese, and knead it in. Keep kneading as you add the rest of the cheese. Turn the dough out onto a floured surface and knead for 2 minutes. Divide the dough in half, knead each half into a ball, and set them on a lightly floured surface. Cover loosely with plastic wrap and let the dough rest for 10 minutes. Lightly butter 2 large baking sheets and dust them very lightly with cornmeal or semolina.

Working with 1 piece of dough at a time, roll the dough into a 13-inch circle on a lightly floured surface. Evenly spread half of the onions over the dough. Using a pizza cutter or sharp knife, cut the circle into 8 wedges as you would a pizza. Starting at the wide end, roll each wedge up snugly. Curl the ends down, into a crescent shape, and place on the baking sheet. Repeat for the remaining dough. Leave as much room as possible between the rolls. Cover very loosely with plastic wrap and set them aside in a warm, draft-free spot for about 30 to 40 minutes, until quite swollen. Preheat the oven to 375°.

When the rolls are swollen, brush lightly with the egg-milk mixture and bake them for 30 to 35 minutes, until golden brown. Cool briefly on a rack, then serve.

Thick Potato and Onion Focaccia

MAKES 3 THICK 10-INCH ROUND FOCACCE

Flatbreads have really taken off in the 90s, with Italian focaccia leading the way. Bistros and cafés are serving creative sandwiches on focaccia bread, big bread companies sell prepackaged versions, and I even know of one bakery in San Francisco where it is the only thing they sell. Still, there is nothing like your own homemade focaccia. Here is one version I'm simply mad about, made with a base of a single mashed potato and flavored with a bit of rosemary. The potato adds flavor and a touch of softness to the dough, which makes this wonderful for sandwiches or just plain, right from the oven. This is called "thick" because I bake the dough in 9- or 10-inch pie plates, so it rises more than it would on a baking sheet; the thicker breads are excellent for sandwiches, but if you won't be making sandwiches from it, you can just pat it out onto a baking sheet and bake it like that. This is sensational with soup or your favorite Italian dinners, and it is an easy, fun bread to make when you have a little extra time to play in the kitchen some weekend afternoon.

1 large all-purpose potato, peeled and diced

3 cups water

1 $1/4$-ounce package (2 teaspoons) active dry yeast

$1/2$ cup whole wheat flour

approximately 5 cups unbleached all-purpose flour

2 teaspoons salt

6 tablespoons olive oil

2 teaspoons crushed dried rosemary or 1 tablespoon chopped fresh

1 large onion, finely chopped

Put the potato into a medium saucepan with $2^1/2$ cups of the water. Bring to a boil, then gently boil the potato for about 10 minutes, until quite tender. Drain, reserving the potato water. Measure $1^1/2$ cups of the potato water into a large mixing bowl. Finely mash the potato and stir it into the potato water. Set aside to cool. While you are waiting, measure $1/2$ cup fresh lukewarm water into a small bowl and sprinkle the yeast over it. Set aside.

When the potato mixture has cooled down—it should feel warm to the touch—stir in the liquid with the dissolved yeast. Using a wooden spoon, briskly stir in the whole wheat flour and $2^1/2$ cups of the unbleached flour. Mix vigorously for 100 strokes, then cover the bowl with plastic wrap and set aside for 10 minutes.

After 10 minutes, stir the salt into the dough, followed by 1 tablespoon of the olive oil and the rosemary. Stir in enough of the remaining flour, about $1/2$ cup at a time, to make a soft, kneadable dough, stirring well after each addition. Turn the dough out onto a floured surface and knead, gently at first, for about 7 minutes. Place the dough in a lightly oiled bowl, cover the bowl with plastic wrap, and set aside in a warm, draft-free spot until doubled in bulk, about 1 hour or a bit more. Meanwhile, lightly oil 3 deep-dish pie pans or round casseroles, 9 or 10 inches in diameter. If you prefer, and you don't care about the thickness, lightly oil 1 or 2 large baking sheets to bake the dough on.

Once the dough has doubled, punch it down and turn it out onto a lightly floured surface. Divide the dough into equal thirds, briefly kneading each third. Let the pieces of dough rest for 5 minutes, then place one in each pan. Flatten each one with your fingers—don't try to make the dough fill the pan at this point; it will be too elastic—then brush each one with about 1 tablespoon of olive oil. Every few minutes, press on the dough again until the dough fills the pans. Set the pans aside in a warm spot—it isn't necessary to cover them— and preheat the oven to 450°.

While the oven preheats, heat the remaining 2 tablespoons of olive oil in a skillet. Add the onion and sauté over medium heat for about 10 minutes, until nicely browned, stirring often. Remove from the heat and set aside. When the onions have cooled down a bit, divide them among the 3 breads, spreading them evenly over the top.

Once the breads have rested for 25 to 30 minutes, place them in the oven and bake for 25 minutes; there's no reliable way to check them, but they'll be done and probably well browned. Also, the onions on top will be dark and crispy. Cool the breads in the pans for 3 to 4 minutes, then slide them out of their pans and transfer to a rack. You can slice them into wedges and serve immediately, or cool for about 15 to 20 minutes if you'll be making sandwiches with them right away.

❧ *Food for Thought* ❧

AND WHAT ABOUT THOSE CUTE DIMPLES?

Many recipes I see for focaccia require you to dimple the dough after it has risen. Dimpling, as I suppose it must be called, is a matter of fluttering your fingertips over the dough, leaving the surface with a whole bunch of little holes. Besides making you look like you really know what you're doing, dimpling leaves a place for olive oil to drizzle into and saturate the dough. Otherwise, if you drizzle extra oil onto the dough before you bake it, it may run off the top of the dough onto the sheet and smoke up your kitchen.

The reason I don't dimple my thick focaccia is to get a more uniform bread that's better for sandwich making. If you don't care about this, by all means dimple the dough—leaving impressions about $1/2$ inch deep (from Italian baking expert Carol Field)—and then let the dough rise for an additional 20 minutes before baking. With the dimples in place, you are free to drizzle extra olive oil over the dough before baking if you like.

Parmesan-Basil Fougasse

MAKES 2 BREADS

Fougasse is a traditional French bread made from the most basic of doughs; it is the shape and handling—the cutting and stretching of the dough into various shapes such as a ladder or spoked wheel—that distinguish them. This is the consummate break-and-serve bread. No knife is necessary; just tear off a spoke or rung. According to one account, French bakers would reach for a piece of fougasse if a customer bought a loaf of bread that fell short of an even weight. The hunk of fougasse would make up the difference. Your concern won't be short weight. It will be how to keep this from being prematurely devoured by your kids if you pull it out of the oven more than a few minutes before mealtime, so time things carefully. The dough is about as easy to mix as they come, so even someone with the most rudimentary bread-baking skills can master fougasse. Dip this in olive oil or serve it with soups and stews or Italian entrées. This will become a family favorite, guaranteed.

2 cups lukewarm water

1 1/4-ounce package (2 teaspoons) active dry yeast

pinch of sugar

approximately 4 1/2 cups unbleached all-purpose flour

1/4 cup whole wheat flour

2 teaspoons salt

1 tablespoon olive oil, plus a little extra for brushing on the dough

1 tablespoon dried basil

1/2 cup freshly grated Parmesan cheese

semolina, for dusting the baking sheets (optional)

Pour the water into a large mixing bowl and sprinkle the yeast over it. Stir in the pinch of sugar. Let the yeast dissolve for a minute or so, then stir 3 cups of the unbleached flour and the whole wheat flour into the water to form a thin dough. Beat this dough rapidly for 100 strokes, then cover the bowl with plastic wrap and set it aside in a warmish, draft-free spot for 15 minutes.

Once the dough has rested, stir the salt, oil, basil, and cheese into the dough. Stir in the remaining unbleached flour, about 1/4 cup at a time, beating well after each addition. When the dough is firm enough to knead, turn it out onto a lightly floured surface and knead it for about 7 minutes, using only enough of the remaining flour to keep the dough from sticking to the surface. When the dough is soft and supple, place it in an oiled bowl, turning to coat the entire dough. Cover the bowl with plastic wrap and set the dough aside in a warm, draft-free spot until doubled in bulk, about 1 hour. While the dough rises, lightly oil 2 large baking sheets and dust them with semolina if you have some on hand.

When the dough has doubled, punch it down and turn the dough out onto a floured surface. Divide the dough in half, kneading each half into a ball. Dust the balls with flour and let them rest on a lightly floured surface for 10 minutes.

Pat each piece of dough into a circle or oblong (for a ladder) about $3/4$ inch thick. Transfer the pieces to the baking sheets and lightly brush them with olive oil. To make a ladder fougasse, make 3 evenly spaced slits in the dough with a razor blade; the cuts should be made on a slight diagonal. Don't cut all the way across the dough; begin and end the cuts with an approximate $1^1/2$-inch border of dough on each side. As soon as you make the cuts, carefully lift/stretch the sections of the dough to enlarge the bread slightly and accentuate the spacing between the cuts. Be careful, however, not to stretch the dough too thin.

To make a spoked wheel, make 6 evenly spaced radial slits in the dough; again, do not cut through the perimeter of the dough and leave an uncut circle of dough in the center about $1^1/2$ inches in diameter. Lift/stretch the dough as above. Cover the breads loosely with plastic wrap and set them aside for 30 minutes. Preheat the oven to 450°.

Bake the breads for 20 to 25 minutes, until golden brown; shift their positions about halfway through the baking so they brown evenly. Cool the breads on a rack for 5 minutes before serving.

Quick Breads

Quick breads, by definition, are those that can be assembled and baked quickly. They differ from yeast breads in that the primary leavenings are baking powder and baking soda. Also, unlike yeast breads, quick breads aren't kneaded; you just mix the wet ingredients with the dry ingredients and scoop the batter into the appropriate pan (or cut the biscuit dough, as the case may be).

Quick breads have another defining characteristic: They should be eaten without much delay. With few exceptions, a quick bread is at its prime while it is still slightly warm, or it has just reached room temperature. The leavenings are largely responsible for the fact that quick breads dry out before long. That's why it is so difficult to buy good quick breads at the supermarket or bakery; unless you're there at the right time, they just don't taste fresh. The other reason is the quality of ingredients: Your own are almost certain to be of higher quality than most commercial operations'.

If you have kids, I probably don't have to tell you how much they love muffins. My kids certainly do. Muffins have really soared in popularity these last few years, in large part, I think, because most cooks have learned that there are alternatives to the overly sweetened, overly fatty muffins many of us have known. Today, good muffins are made with whole wheat flour and wheat germ, sweetened with fruit juice and natural sweeteners, and good enough to eat without gobs of butter. Instead of butter, my kids often spoon plain yogurt and applesauce on their muffins, which gets quite sloppy but tastes extraordinary. Muffins are a great after school snack, and good for school lunches too.

Here's a tip I've been passing on for years, one that many busy people have found useful. You can do this with almost any quick bread. If your mornings are hectic—and whose aren't?—you can do much of the advance work for quick breads the night before. (This is a project your kids might even be willing to take on.) If you're making muffins, for instance, you can mix the dry ingredients (flour, leavening, spices and stuff) in a bowl. Cover and leave it on the counter. You can also blend the liquid ingredients (though it is best not to add the melted butter or it won't mix in thoroughly once it has congealed). Cover and refrigerate overnight. First one who rolls out of bed turns on the oven. Then, it's just a simple matter of mixing the wet and dry ingredients and getting them into the pan (which can be buttered the night before too).

Me and Mani's Ginger-Maple Crumb Muffins

MAKES 12 MUFFINS

This is a muffin with a great story. You know who "me" is, but the Mani in this recipe is Mani Niall, a really swell friend and baker. If you're from California, you probably know him as L.A.'s "baker to the stars." Mani has four bakeries in southern California and I understand that lots of movie stars—dashing between sets or personal trainers or whatever movie stars dash between—stop by his bakeries for one of his healthy scones, muffins, or pastries. Anyway, Mani and I were asked by the good folks at Kretschmer wheat germ to collaborate on a muffin recipe that he would sell in his bakery for several weeks, the proceeds of which would then be donated to Share Our Strength, the nation's leading anti-hunger organization. So we tossed the idea around, added our special signatures, and came up with this. It was a real hit at his bakery, and I think you're going to love it, too. It's a great, wholesome muffin. Oh, yeah, one other really cool thing about Mani: He used to be the personal chef for Michael Jackson!

CRUMB TOPPING
1/2 cup all-purpose flour

1/3 cup toasted unsweetened wheat germ

1/3 cup quick or old-fashioned rolled oats

1/3 cup packed light brown sugar

1/4 cup (1/2 stick) cold unsalted butter, cut into pieces

MUFFIN BATTER

1 cup buttermilk

$^1/_3$ cup quick or old-fashioned rolled oats

1 large egg

$^2/_3$ cup maple syrup

$^1/_2$ cup unsalted butter, melted, or $^1/_2$ cup flavorless vegetable or
sunflower oil

1$^3/_4$ cups unbleached all-purpose flour

$^1/_3$ cup toasted unsweetened wheat germ

1 teaspoon baking soda

$^1/_2$ teaspoon salt

2$^1/_2$ teaspoons ground ginger

1 teaspoon each ground cinnamon and ground allspice

$^1/_2$ teaspoon ground cardamom

*P*reheat the oven to 400°. Butter 12 muffin cups and set aside.
Prepare the topping. Mix the flour, wheat germ, oats, and brown
sugar in a medium bowl. Add the butter, then rub the butter and dry
ingredients together with your fingertips, forming coarse crumbs; set aside.

Make the muffins. Combine the buttermilk and oats in a medium bowl; let
stand for 5 minutes. Add the egg, maple syrup, and butter; whisk well. Add the
buttermilk mixture all at once to the remaining dry ingredients, stirring just
until the batter is uniformly mixed. Divide the batter evenly among the muffin
cups. Spread a generous amount of topping over each muffin, patting gently.

Bake the muffins for 10 minutes. Reduce the heat to 350° and bake 15 minutes more, until the topping is golden brown. Cool 5 minutes in the pan on a
rack. Transfer the muffins to a rack to finish cooling.

Alison's Banana-Ginger Muffins

MAKES 11 MUFFINS

All of our kids love to make muffins, not to mention eat them, this being one of
Ali's favorites. She and Karen came up with this recipe, which includes two of
Ali's signatures, the fresh ginger and the wheat germ. When I asked her why
she decided to put the wheat germ in, she reminded me that one time I put it in
a muffin recipe and it was her favorite; so much for kids not liking what's good

for them. Karen's trick was to make this work without using any dairy products, which she did with characteristic finesse; you simply can't tell there're no eggs or milk in these. A little bit of warm honey or a spoonful of raspberry preserves goes nicely on these. Alison says to watch your knuckles when you grate the ginger.

$^2/_3$ cup (about 2 small) mashed ripe banana

$^2/_3$ cup orange juice

$^1/_3$ cup maple syrup or warmed honey

$^1/_3$ cup flavorless vegetable oil

2 teaspoons freshly grated ginger

1 teaspoon grated lemon zest

2 cups whole wheat pastry flour

1 cup sweetened or unsweetened toasted wheat germ

1 teaspoon baking soda

1 teaspoon baking powder

$^1/_2$ teaspoon salt

*P*reheat the oven to 375°. Lightly oil 11 muffin cups, dusting them with flour. In the bowl of a food processor or blender, puree the banana, orange juice, maple syrup, oil, ginger, and lemon zest. Mix the dry ingredients, using only $^3/_4$ cup of the wheat germ, in a separate bowl. Make a well in the center and blend in the liquid, stirring just until mixed. Spoon the batter into the muffin cups and sprinkle a little of the remaining wheat germ over each muffin. Bake the muffins for 25 minutes. Cool the muffins in the pan on a rack for 3 to 5 minutes, then remove from the pan and serve soon. Leftovers may be frozen or bagged up and served the next day.

Morning Glory Oat Bran Muffins

MAKES 11 MUFFINS

It seems that a lot of bakeries and cafés these days sell something called morning glory muffins. I'm not sure where the original name comes from, but I like it; it's uplifting, like a sunny weather forecast, and can't we all use a little lifting up in the morning? Generally speaking, morning glory muffins appear to be modeled after carrot cake, and along with grated carrots, they have raisins, nuts, sometimes sunflower seeds, spices, and molasses. I've included all of those here in this version, opting for walnuts instead of seeds. Instead of slathering these with butter, try a dab of plain yogurt. When my kids were younger they regularly made muffin sandwiches, with yogurt and applesauce for the filling. Sloppy, but good!

$^3/_4$ cup oat bran, plus a little extra for dusting the muffin cups

$^3/_4$ cup unbleached all-purpose flour

$^3/_4$ cup whole wheat flour

2 teaspoons baking powder

$^1/_2$ teaspoon baking soda

$^1/_2$ teaspoon salt

2 teaspoons minced fresh ginger or $^1/_2$ teaspoon ground

$^1/_2$ teaspoon cinnamon

1 large egg

1 cup plus 2 tablespoons milk

$^1/_4$ cup blackstrap or unsulphured molasses

$^1/_4$ cup flavorless vegetable or sunflower oil

$^1/_4$ cup packed light brown sugar

finely grated zest of 1 orange

1 cup grated carrot

$^1/_2$ cup finely chopped walnuts

$^1/_2$ cup raisins

Preheat the oven to 400° and lightly oil 11 muffin cups. Sprinkle a little oat bran in each one and tilt the pan this way and that to coat the sides of the cups.

Combine all of the dry ingredients—the oat bran up to the cinnamon—in a large mixing bowl and mix well. In another bowl, whisk the egg, then whisk in the remaining liquids, brown sugar, and orange zest. Make a well in the dry mixture, add the liquid, and stir the batter until uniformly blended. Fold in the grated carrot, walnuts, and raisins.

Divide the batter evenly between the 11 cups. Bake for 20 to 22 minutes. Press the top of a muffin with your finger; if the muffins are done, they should not seem soft or squishy underneath. Transfer the pan to a rack and cool for 5 minutes, then remove the muffins from the cups. Serve at any temperature. Store thoroughly cooled leftovers on a plate, covered with plastic wrap. Or wrap and freeze, 1 or 2 at a time, in foil. Reheat them in a hot oven right in the foil.

Lemon-Poppy Seed Fruit Juice Muffins

MAKES 12 MUFFINS

If you prefer not to use milk in your diet, you can still make healthy, delicious muffins by replacing the milk with fruit juice, as we have here. No one will notice, and your kids may tell you this is one of the best muffins you've ever made; my kids have made such comments. These are built around one of my favorite flavor combinations, lemon and poppy seeds; I use both lemon extract and lemon zest for a big hit. Most of the flour is whole wheat pastry, so you get a very tender, delicate muffin with as much fiber as flavor.

2 cups whole wheat pastry flour

$1/2$ cup unbleached all-purpose flour

2 teaspoons baking powder

$1/2$ teaspoon baking soda

$1/2$ teaspoon salt

$1/4$ cup poppy seeds

1 large egg

$1^{1}/4$ cups unfiltered apple or pear juice

$1/3$ cup honey, warmed slightly

$1/4$ cup flavorless vegetable or sunflower oil

1 teaspoon lemon extract

finely grated zest of 1 lemon

TOPPING (OPTIONAL)
3 tablespoons toasted wheat germ

3 tablespoons packed light brown sugar

Preheat the oven to 400° and lightly oil or butter 12 muffin cups. Dust the cups with flour or wheat germ, tapping out the excess.

Into a large mixing bowl, sift the flours, baking powder, baking soda, and salt. Stir in the poppy seeds. In a separate bowl, whisk the egg lightly, then whisk in the juice, honey, oil, lemon extract, and lemon zest. Make a well in the dry mixture, add the liquid, and stir briefly, just until the batter is uniformly blended. Give the batter a few moments to rest and while you're doing so, mix the wheat germ and brown sugar together with your fingers if you want to use this topping.

Divide the batter evenly between the muffin cups. Sprinkle each one with a little of the topping and bake the muffins for 20 minutes. Cool the muffin pan on a rack for 5 minutes, then remove the muffins from the pan. Eat warm or cool the muffins on a rack. Store thoroughly cooled leftovers on a plate, covered with plastic wrap. The muffins can also be frozen, 1 or 2 together, wrapped in foil packets. Reheat in a hot oven in the foil for about 10 minutes.

Stina's Blueberry-Cornmeal Muffins

MAKES 12 MUFFINS

We used to have a sweet old mutt, Stina, who had the most unusual habit of eating blueberries—right off our blueberry bushes. She went about it so deliberately and delicately—sort of peck-pecking at only the ripest ones like it was the most natural thing a dog could do—that it was hard to be angry with her. As it is, the bushes have never been wildly productive, so there were some years where she'd enjoy the lion's share, leaving us with a few paltry half-blues to put in pancakes. Good for us that our neighbor, Elzey, has always let us pick from his bushes. His do a lot better than ours and he pretty much lets us snag as many as we want, with the tacit understanding that we'll return some of the bounty in baked goods. Here's one way we've done just that, in this muffin Elzey has enjoyed; we think you will, too. They're good with or without a streusel topping, but we always like them better with.

1¹/₂ large very ripe bananas

1 large egg

¹/₂ cup packed light brown sugar

¹/₄ cup flavorless vegetable oil

1 teaspoon vanilla extract

1³/₄ cups unbleached all-purpose flour

¹/₂ cup yellow cornmeal, preferably stone-ground

1¹/₂ teaspoons baking powder

¹/₂ teaspoon baking soda

¹/₄ teaspoon salt

2 tablespoons poppy seeds (optional)

1 cup fresh blueberries

Pretty-Good-for-You Butterless Streusel (page 285), sweetened wheat germ, or any other streusel-like topping (optional)

*B*utter or lightly oil 12 muffin cups and dust them with flour. Preheat the oven to 400°. Put the banana, egg, and brown sugar in the bowl of a food processor and process to a smooth puree. Blend in the oil and vanilla.

In a separate bowl, sift the flour, cornmeal, baking powder, baking soda, and salt. Stir in the poppy seeds if you're using them. Make a well in the dry mixture, add the liquid, and stir until the batter is uniformly mixed, folding in the blueberries at the end.

Divide the batter evenly between the muffin cups and sprinkle each one with a little of the topping if you're using it. Bake the muffins for 22 to 25 minutes, until done; the tops will be resistant to gentle finger pressure. Cool the muffins in the cups for 3 to 4 minutes, then remove them and transfer to a cooling rack. Serve at any temperature.

Magnificent Muffins (Dairyless Blueberry-Pumpkin Muffins)

MAKES 12 TO 14 MUFFINS

Kids are a great source for spontaneous recipe titles (though the closer they get to adolescence, the less printable the titles tend to be). This title is straight from the horse's mouth, the horse in question being my son Ben. Karen served these up one morning, and when she asked how everyone liked them Ben managed to come up for air somewhere between his fifth and sixth muffin just long enough to offer that "these are *magnificent* muffins!" The name stuck like Super Glue. It's really true; they *are* magnificent. We've had a number of adult friends tell us that these were the best muffins they'd ever eaten. It's always a pleasure to be able to follow up a comment like that with: Can you believe they're dairyless? Not only is the flavor wonderful, but I love the pumpkin-orange background against the dark blue of the berries. You can make these without the topping, but I don't recommend it since that's one of the best parts. This makes enough for 12 really full muffin cups; if you have 2 little ramekins, you might want to just make up a couple of extra muffins. You'll have to make up the topping ahead if you don't have any in the freezer.

1 scant cup canned cold pack pumpkin

1 cup orange juice

$^{1}/_{2}$ cup maple syrup or mild-tasting honey, such as clover or orange blossom

$^{1}/_{2}$ cup flavorless vegetable or sunflower oil

1 teaspoon vanilla extract

2 cups whole wheat pastry flour

1 cup whole wheat flour

1 cup walnuts, processed to a fine meal in the food processor

$1^{1}/_{2}$ teaspoons baking powder

1 teaspoon baking soda

$^{3}/_{4}$ teaspoon salt

$1^{1}/_{2}$ teaspoons cinnamon

$^{1}/_{4}$ teaspoon grated nutmeg

$^{1}/_{4}$ teaspoon allspice

1 cup fresh blueberries, preferably the small, low-bush variety

about $^{3}/_{4}$ cup Pretty-Good-for-You Butterless Streusel (page 285)

*P*reheat the oven to 350° and lightly oil 12 to 14 muffin cups; see headnote. Either flour them lightly, tapping out the excess, or dust them with toasted wheat germ. Karen sometimes uses extra streusel topping to coat the cups; that's the best.

Puree the pumpkin, orange juice, maple syrup, oil, and vanilla in a food processor. Set aside. In a large bowl, mix the flours, walnuts, baking powder, baking soda, salt, and spices. Make a well in the dry ingredients and add the liquid, stirring just until smooth. Fold in the blueberries. Divide the batter evenly among the muffin cups. Top each one with a scant tablespoon of the streusel. Bake the muffins for 35 minutes.

Cool the muffins in the pan on a rack for 10 minutes. After 10 minutes, run a butter knife down one side of each muffin, giving it a little lift onto its side so the muffins sit at a 45° angle in the pan. Let them cool for 10 more minutes, then transfer them to a rack to finish cooling. Serve warm or at room temperature. Store leftovers on a plate covered with plastic wrap.

VARIATION: Magnificent Cranberry Muffins. Process 1 cup fresh or frozen cranberries to a semicoarse consistency in the food processor. Fold them into the batter in place of the blueberries.

Maple Walnut Soda Bread

MAKES 2 MEDIUM LOAVES

Soda breads are just the thing if you want to serve a nice loaf of bread for dinner or any other meal but there's just no time to make a yeast bread. The most famous soda bread, of course, is Irish soda bread, but there are many other variations I've made up over the years; this is one of my favorites. It is made with lots of whole wheat flour, a bit of cornmeal, and some unbleached flour for a bit of loft. I sweeten it with good old New Hampshire maple syrup—you could use honey—and add chopped walnuts for good measure.

3 cups whole wheat flour

$^1/_2$ cup unbleached all-purpose flour

$^1/_2$ cup yellow cornmeal, preferably stone-ground

$1^1/_2$ teaspoons baking powder

1 teaspoon baking soda

$1^1/_2$ teaspoons salt

$^1/_2$ teaspoon cinnamon

$1^1/_2$ cups yogurt

$^1/_2$ cup milk

$^1/_3$ cup maple syrup

2 tablespoons flavorless vegetable or sunflower oil

$^3/_4$ cup chopped walnuts

Preheat the oven to 400° and lightly butter or oil a large baking sheet. Sprinkle the sheet with cornmeal and set aside. Put the flours, cornmeal, baking powder, baking soda, salt, and cinnamon in a large mixing bowl and mix thoroughly with your hands. In a separate bowl, whisk together the yogurt, milk, maple syrup, and oil. Make a well in the dry ingredients, add the liquid and walnuts, then stir briskly with a wooden spoon until the dough is uniformly mixed. Let the dough rest, uncovered, for 2 minutes. Meanwhile, heavily dust your work counter with unbleached flour, then flour your hands.

Scrape half of the dough onto the counter. Fold it over on itself, then knead the dough for 2 minutes; keep the surface well floured. Shape the dough into a stumpy-looking football and place it on the baking sheet. Repeat for the other loaf. Using a serrated knife, make 3 diagonal slashes about $^3/_4$ inch deep on top of each loaf.

Bake the loaves for 20 minutes, then lower the heat to 375° and bake an additional 20 minutes. When done, they'll sound hollow when you tap the bottoms with a finger. Cool on a rack for about 30 minutes before slicing; sooner than that and they're liable to seem a bit underdone.

Whole Wheat Corn Bread

MAKES 8 SERVINGS

This is a fairly traditional family corn bread, with a dry, coarse interior. It is excellent with just about any stew or soup, and the leftovers, if there are any, can be butter-fried the next morning (or toasted dry, in a toaster oven) and drizzled with honey. But there's nothing like it just plain fresh from the oven. If you like a slightly sweet corn bread, add 1 or 2 tablespoons sugar or honey to the liquid; otherwise just omit it. Note that melting the butter in the pan before adding the batter is optional; you can also just lightly oil the hot pan and proceed from there.

1 cup yellow cornmeal

$^2/_3$ cup whole wheat pastry flour

$^1/_2$ cup whole wheat flour

$1^1/_2$ teaspoons baking powder

$1^1/_2$ teaspoons baking soda

$^1/_2$ teaspoon salt

1 large egg

$1^1/_2$ cups buttermilk

3 tablespoons flavorless vegetable or safflower oil

1 to 2 tablespoons sugar or honey, to taste

1 tablespoon unsalted butter or 1 teaspoon oil, for the pan

Preheat the oven to 400° and get out a 10-inch ovenproof cast-iron skillet. In one bowl, mix the cornmeal, flours, baking powder, baking soda, and salt. In another, beat the egg lightly, then whisk in the buttermilk, oil, and sweetening.

Put the butter in the skillet and heat until melted. If you aren't using the butter, rub the oil in the skillet with a paper towel and heat the skillet until hot. Either way, make a well in the dry ingredients and stir in the liquid just until the batter is evenly blended. Scrape the batter into the pan and even the top with a rubber spatula or spoon. Bake the corn bread for 25 minutes; when done, the center of the corn bread will feel slightly bouncy to the touch, not squishy underneath. Cool in the pan for 5 to 10 minutes before slicing.

Desserts and Other Finishing Touches

I have four kids, so I know something about having a big family. But I came from an even bigger one: There were seven of us Haedrich kids and God only knows how my mom kept enough food on the table, and how my Dad didn't go broke putting it there. My mom was not a fancy, gourmet type cook. She did, however, feed us three squares a day and it wasn't unusual for us to have two desserts at dinner. (Mom loved to go to the local bakeries, so one dessert was usually a bakery item.)

So that's where my sweet tooth came from.

Here is a pretty big chapter devoted to sweet stuff, for those of you with a sweet tooth—cookies, cakes, frozen treats, and fruit preparations for just about any occasion from after school snacks to party desserts. I have written a dessert cookbook, *Simple Desserts*, and while most of the recipes were indeed simple enough, many of them were not overly concerned with butter, sugar, eggs, and other dairy products—items that many people these days would like to use less of.

Those ingredients aren't without representation in this section. There are, however, a number of recipes that use reduced quantities of them, or eliminate them altogether. In particular, I should draw your attention to the cookies. My partner, Karen, makes a lot of the sweets for our kids. She's a vegan, and she has developed several dairyless cookie (and cake) recipes that she can feel good about serving on a regular basis, and that taste every bit as good as traditional cookies. It is hard to single out one favorite, but if I had to it would probably be the Chocolate Chip-Walnut Cookies on page 252. Karen doesn't use refined sugar, so many of her recipes call for maple syrup instead. If you're lucky to live in one of the maple producing regions of the country, you can find maple syrup for a reasonable price, especially if you buy one of the darker cooking grades.

Speaking of alternative sweeteners, there's a pie in this chapter made with maple syrup and cider, reduced to a lovely syrup. This is a wonderful pie, based on an old Shaker recipe.

If you're planning a menu, my feeling is that almost everyone is willing to eat a little less, a little lighter, if there's going to be a tempting sweet at the end of the meal. This is pretty obvious, but I'll mention it anyway (in part because I have to be reminded myself): If you're serving a big meal, serve a modest dessert—fruit, or a little scoop of sorbet. If the meal is modest, serve a killer, take-no-prisoners dessert. Everyone should leave feeling satisfied, but not stuffed.

And remember: Dessert is good strategy. It raises the level of excitement and anticipation among your guests, and provides tremendous leverage with guests and kids alike. Dessert? Oh sure—*as soon as the dishes are done!*

Maple-Peanut Butter Cookies

MAKES ABOUT 20 COOKIES

Peanut butter is the perfect ingredient for a dairyless cookie, rich in flavor, creamy, and butterlike. Of all the cookies in this section, this is the "butteriest" without the butter. Like many of our cookies, we usually sweeten this one with maple syrup; I've made it with a blend of honey and maple syrup and just plain honey, and both are good, but none as good as the plain maple syrup. We use Teddie brand peanut butter, an all-natural brand available in the northeast; I'm not sure what their secret is, but it has a great flavor and it's always fresh tasting. I even prefer it to the freshly ground peanut butter you buy at health food stores. (But do use that if it is your best option.) These are big soft cookies that stay fresh for at least 2 days in an airtight container.

1 cup natural, unsweetened, unsalted chunky or smooth peanut butter

1 cup maple syrup, honey, or a combination (see Note)

2 tablespoons flavorless vegetable oil

1 1/2 teaspoons vanilla extract

2 1/2 cups whole wheat pastry flour

1 teaspoon baking powder

1 teaspoon baking soda

$^1/_2$ teaspoon salt

*P*reheat the oven to 350° and butter or lightly oil and dust with flour 2 large cookie sheets. Or you can simply line the sheets with parchment paper.

In a mixing bowl, whisk the peanut butter, maple syrup, oil, and vanilla until smooth. In a separate bowl, mix the flour, baking powder, baking soda, and salt. Make a well in the dry mixture and blend in the liquid, stirring just until blended. Using your hands, shape the dough into $1^1/_2$-inch balls and place them on the sheets, leaving about $2^1/_2$ inches between them. With a cup of water nearby, dip a fork into the water and press down on the balls in several places, flattening them to about $^1/_2$ inch thick; make a crisscross pattern if you like. Bake the cookies for 10 to 12 minutes; when done, the surface will be lightly crusted over but the cookies still soft. Cool on the sheets for 2 minutes, then transfer to a rack and cool completely before storing.

N O T E : If you are using honey, or a blend of honey and maple syrup, gently heat the honey to about body temperature in a small saucepan before proceeding.

Carob Drop Cookies

MAKES ABOUT 18 COOKIES

This is a great cookie, one we've enjoyed for as long as I can remember. If you don't have carob on hand you can always use unsweetened cocoa powder; both are fine. The steps are quite simple, so this is a good one for kids who like to tackle recipes alone.

$^3/_4$ cup maple syrup

$^1/_4$ cup molasses

$^1/_2$ cup flavorless vegetable or sunflower oil

$1^1/_2$ teaspoons vanilla extract

2 cups whole wheat flour

2 tablespoons carob powder or unsweetened cocoa powder

1 teaspoon baking powder

$^1/_2$ teaspoon salt

1 cup unsweetened shredded coconut or flaked sweetened coconut

1 cup coarsely chopped walnuts

$^1/_2$ cup raisins

*P*reheat the oven to 350° and lightly oil 2 large baking sheets. In one bowl, whisk together the maple syrup, molasses, oil, and vanilla. In a separate large bowl, sift the flour with the carob or cocoa, baking powder, and salt. Make a well in the dry ingredients and stir in the liquid until the batter is almost smooth, then fold in the coconut, walnuts, and raisins.

Drop mounded tablespoons of dough onto the sheets, leaving about 2$^1/_2$ inches between each mound. Bake the cookies for 12 to 15 minutes; when they're done they'll be resistant to gentle finger pressure. Cool the cookies on the sheet for 2 or 3 minutes, then transfer the cookies to a rack to finish cooling.

Oatmeal Raisin-Walnut Cookies

MAKES ABOUT 24 COOKIES

Buttery cookies are wonderful, but when you find a recipe that's butter- and egg-free and still wonderful, like this one, that's something really special. These are a dairyless version of a favorite oatmeal cookie I included in my previous book, *Simple Desserts* (Bantam, 1995). I wasn't sure how the flavor of this cookie would measure up without the richness of butter, but Karen tinkered with the original formula until she got it to the point where we didn't miss it at all; the oats, maple syrup, and walnuts provide all the flavor you'd hope for without the butter. These can bake up either flattish or slightly rounded, depending on how long you wait to bake the cookies. If you bake them right away before the liquid has had a chance to soak into the oats, they come out rather flat; if you wait several hours or overnight, they're higher and rounder. You can approximate the latter look by adding an additional $^1/_4$ cup of whole wheat pastry flour to the dough and baking them right away. Either way they taste wonderful. For a special touch, you can add regular chocolate chips to the dough or chop a small bar of dairyless chocolate (available at health food stores) into coarse chunks and stir them into the dough.

1 cup maple syrup

$^1/_2$ cup flavorless vegetable oil

$^1/_2$ teaspoon vanilla extract

1³/₄ to 2 cups (see headnote) whole wheat pastry flour

1 teaspoon baking powder

¹/₂ teaspoon baking soda

¹/₂ teaspoon salt

1 teaspoon ground cinnamon

1¹/₂ cups noninstant rolled oats

³/₄ cup walnuts, processed to a fine meal

³/₄ cup raisins

¹/₂ cup chocolate chips or chunks, optional (see headnote)

*P*reheat the oven to 350°. Combine the maple syrup, oil, and vanilla in a mixing bowl. In a separate bowl, mix the whole wheat pastry flour, baking powder, baking soda, salt, and cinnamon. Make a well in the dry ingredients, whisk the liquids to blend them, and pour them into the well. Mix the dough until smooth, then stir in the oats, walnut meal, raisins, and chocolate. Cover the dough and refrigerate for at least 20 minutes or as long as overnight; see the headnote.

When you're ready to bake, butter 2 large cookie sheets; if you prefer, lightly oil them instead, dusting the sheets with flour. Or simply line the sheets with parchment paper. Handling the dough loosely with floured hands, roll the dough into 1¹/₂-inch balls and place them on the sheets, leaving about 2¹/₂ inches between them. Bake for approximately 20 minutes, until golden brown. Cool the cookies on the sheet for a minute or two, then transfer them to a rack to cool.

Almond-Orange Crumb Cookies

MAKES ABOUT 20 COOKIES

This is a hybrid, a cross between two of our all-time favorite cookies; both of them had butter and eggs, however, and this one has neither. What it *does* have is lots of crunchy-good almond flavor with a pleasant tang of citrus-orange. The combination really works well. The dough is damp and crumbly, so there's only one good way that I know of to shape the cookies: packing the dough into a tablespoon, then sliding the shaped mound onto your cookie sheet. Since there's no leavening, the cookies don't really rise or spread; perhaps they relax a tad and bake up to a chewy-soft texture. They're really excellent, and they will travel well because they're compact and durable. And

they're a really special holiday gift cookie for someone who is watching his in-
take of dairy products.

1 cup almonds

$^1/_3$ cup packed light brown sugar

finely grated zest of 1 large orange

$^1/_3$ cup flavorless vegetable, sunflower, or canola oil

$^1/_2$ teaspoon almond extract

1 cup whole wheat pastry flour

2 to 3 tablespoons water

Preheat the oven to 350°. Spread the almonds on a baking sheet and
toast in the preheated oven for 10 minutes. Slide them off the sheet
and cool thoroughly. Lightly oil a large cookie sheet. Put the almonds and brown sugar in the bowl of a food processor and process 10 to 20
seconds, long enough to make a fairly fine, uniform meal. In a small bowl,
blend the oil and almond extract. Remove the lid of the processor and pour the
oil over the ground nuts. Cover again, then pulse the machine half a dozen
times or so to mix everything evenly. Take the lid off, stir the mixture up with a
fork, and add the flour. Pulse as before, until uniformly mixed.

Transfer the dough—it will be crumbly—to a bowl and sprinkle 2 tablespoons of the water over it. Using your fingers, mix the dough in a fluttering
fashion so everything is dampened evenly; don't add any more water yet.

Using a tablespoon measure, preferably one that's deeper than it is wide
and flattish, pack a little of the dough into the spoon, leveling the top. Pushing
gently on one side, force-slide the cookie out of the mold and gently place it on
the cookie sheet. At this point, if the dough seems too crumbly to pack well,
work another teaspoon of water into the dough (or perhaps a bit more) until it
packs nicely. Use restraint, because when the dough gets too damp it is tricky
to pack.

Place the cookies about 1 inch apart on the sheet, then bake for 20 minutes.
When done, the surface will feel crusty and slightly resistant to gentle finger
pressure. Cool the cookies on the sheet for several minutes, then transfer them
to a rack to cool.

Pecan Cookies

֍

MAKES ABOUT 15 COOKIES

This recipe began as a quest to make a dairyless version of a popular variety of cookies known as pecan sandies. Pecan sandies are sweet and buttery, with a crumbly texture like shortbread. After a few tries it became apparent that despite our intentions this cookie had a mind of its own; it just wanted to be a deliciously plain pecan cookie, not some clone of something we had envisioned. So here you have it: a wonderful pecan cookie without butter, eggs, or other dairy products. Because they have their own flavorful oils, nut cookies are at a natural advantage when you leave out the butter. You discover that even if the butter adds flavor, it really isn't necessary to make a great-tasting cookie. Try these with a cup of Mom's Hot Soy Milk (page 13); they're excellent that way. The dough is pretty stable so the kids can help roll them. And if 15 cookies just isn't enough, the recipe can easily be doubled.

1 cup coarsely chopped pecans, plus 15 or so small pecan halves for decoration

1/2 cup packed light brown sugar

1 cup whole wheat pastry flour

1/4 teaspoon salt

1/4 cup flavorless vegetable oil

1/4 cup soy milk

1 teaspoon vanilla extract

Preheat the oven to 375° and very lightly oil a large cookie sheet. Put the pecans in the bowl of a food processor and process to a fine meal. In a mixing bowl, mix the pecan meal, brown sugar, whole wheat flour, and salt. Whisk the oil, soy milk, and vanilla in another bowl. Make a well in the dry ingredients, add the liquid, and stir to blend evenly. Let the dough rest for 5 minutes.

Using your hands, shape the dough into balls roughly 1 1/4 inches in diameter. Place them on the sheet, leaving about 1 1/2 inches between them; use your fingertips to flatten them slightly. Gently press a pecan half into the top of each cookie. Bake for 15 minutes. Place the sheet on a cooling rack for a couple of minutes, then transfer the cookies to the rack and cool.

Chocolate Chip-Walnut Cookies

MAKES ABOUT 24 COOKIES

A delicious, *healthy* chocolate chip cookie? This is probably about as close as you'll ever come to that ideal. It uses no refined sugars, has all whole wheat flour, and contains no dairy products; if you are adamant about this latter point, you can find nondairy chocolate bars or chips at your local health food store. Otherwise you can use any chip or chunk you like. Karen started tinkering with the idea of the ultimate chocolate chip cookie when we returned from a trip to Mexico, where someone had given us a pound of incredible Mexican chocolate, made with cinnamon and finely ground almonds, unlike any we'd ever eaten. She quickly came up with the magic formula, which includes Cafix or an equivalent amount of powdered coffee substitute and a generous dose of chopped walnuts. As usual, we just don't miss the butter; the cookie is everything a good cookie should be without the extra calories and fat. These are best eaten the same day they're baked; that should be *no* problem!

1 cup maple syrup

$1/3$ cup flavorless vegetable, sunflower, or safflower oil

2 tablespoons Cafix or other instant powdered coffee substitute

2 teaspoons vanilla extract

2 cups whole wheat pastry flour

$1/4$ cup whole wheat flour

$1^1/2$ teaspoons baking powder

$1/2$ teaspoon cinnamon

$1/4$ teaspoon salt

1 cup coarsely chopped walnuts

$3/4$ cup chocolate chips or chopped chocolate chunks

Whisk the maple syrup, oil, Cafix, and vanilla in a mixing bowl. Sift the flours, baking powder, cinnamon, and salt in a separate bowl. Make a well in the dry ingredients, add the liquid, and stir until uniformly blended. Fold in the walnuts and chocolate chips. Cover the dough with plastic wrap and refrigerate for 15 minutes while you preheat the oven to 375°. Lightly oil 1 or 2 large cookie sheets.

Using a heaping tablespoon, spoon mounds of dough onto the cookie sheet, leaving about 2 inches between each mound; you should be able to get 12 mounds on each large sheet. Bake the cookies for 13 to 15 minutes; to check for doneness, press gently on the doughy part of the cookie. It should offer a little resistance. Try not to overbake them. Cool the cookies on the sheet for 1 minute, then transfer them to a rack to finish cooling. Use caution if your kids are clamoring for these as soon as they're done, as I'm certain they will; the chocolate chips can stay quite hot for several minutes.

Walnut and Orange Biscotti

MAKES ABOUT 30 COOKIES

If you're looking for a good, crisp, butter-free cookie, then here they are. These are twice baked: the first time as logs, then as slices, which dries them out and gives them their customary crunch. That crunch makes them just right for dunking in your favorite hot drink. If you're looking for an alternative to coffee, I suggest Mom's Hot Soy Milk (page 13).

$1^1/2$ cups walnuts

$2^3/4$ cups unbleached all-purpose flour

$3/4$ teaspoon baking powder

$1/2$ teaspoon salt

$1/2$ teaspoon crushed fennel seed or $1/2$ teaspoon cinnamon

3 large eggs, at room temperature

1 cup sugar

1 teaspoon vanilla extract

finely grated zest of 1 large orange

1 egg, beaten with 1 tablespoon milk

Preheat the oven to 325°. Spread the walnuts on a baking sheet and toast them in the oven for 12 minutes. Slide the nuts onto a counter to cool. Chop coarsely and set aside. Butter and lightly flour a large baking sheet.

In a small bowl, mix the flour, baking powder, salt, and fennel seed. Set aside. Using an electric mixer, beat the eggs and sugar on high speed for 5 minutes, until quite thick and pale in color. Blend in the vanilla and orange zest. Stir in the dry ingredients, about half at a time, then stir in the nuts. Let the dough sit for 5 minutes.

Turn the dough out onto a floured surface and divide in half. Using floured hands, gently roll each half into a 10-inch-long log. Place the logs on the prepared sheet, leaving plenty of room between them. Brush lightly with the egg-milk mixture, then bake for 40 minutes, until golden. Remove from the oven and leave the logs on the sheet for 10 minutes. Reduce the heat to 275°.

Using a large spatula, slide the logs onto a cutting board. With a serrated knife, slice them on the diagonal into $1/2$-inch-wide pieces. Place the biscotti, cut sides up, on 2 baking sheets. Bake 20 to 25 minutes longer, to dry out the cookies. Cool on a rack before storing in an airtight container.

Honey Hermits

MAKES ABOUT 18 COOKIES

Here's a soft, chewy, spicy cookie you'll want to share with extended family and friends. The dough is very moist because of the honey and molasses, and it would be tricky to handle without giving it the specified 2-hour rest. Note that the surface will feel soft, though not squishy-soft, when the cookies are done. If you overbake you'll lose that chewy texture, so watch them.

$2/3$ cup mild honey, at room temperature

$1/3$ cup unsulphured molasses

$1/4$ cup unsalted butter, melted

$1/4$ cup flavorless vegetable or sunflower oil

$2^1/3$ cups whole wheat pastry flour

$1/3$ cup whole wheat flour

1 teaspoon ground ginger

1 teaspoon cinnamon

$1/2$ teaspoon grated nutmeg

1 teaspoon baking powder

1 teaspoon baking soda

$1/2$ teaspoon salt

$1/2$ cup chopped golden raisins

$1/2$ cup finely chopped walnuts

Whisk the honey, molasses, melted butter, and oil in a bowl until blended. Mix the remaining ingredients in a separate large bowl. Make a well in the dry ingredients and stir in the liquid until the dough is uniformly blended; it will be damp and somewhat sticky. Cover and refrigerate for at least 2 hours. Preheat the oven to 350°.

Lightly butter 2 large cookie sheets. Using generous spoonfuls of dough, roll into 1³/₄-inch balls; use floured hands if the dough feels sticky. Place the balls about 3 inches apart on the sheets and bake for about 15 minutes. When done, the cookies will have spread and have small cracks over most of the surface. They'll feel soft but not squishy to the touch. Cool on the sheets for 1 minute, then transfer to a rack to finish cooling.

Spiced Pumpkin Indian Pudding Pie

MAKES 8 TO 10 SERVINGS

I'm a fan of anything with cornmeal, especially soft-cooked mixtures like polenta and cornmeal mush. Indian pudding is another in that category, and here I blend it with pumpkin to make a firm-textured pie filling that my family loves. It has classic New England written all over it, but do try it, no matter where you live. It is great with whipped cream or vanilla ice cream. The pie will need to cool at least an hour before you slice it. It is also excellent cold.

1 recipe pie pastry (page 278), chilled

FILLING AND ASSEMBLY
1¹/₂ cups milk
¹/₂ cup fine yellow cornmeal, such as Quaker brand
¹/₄ teaspoon salt
1 tablespoon unsalted butter
²/₃ cup packed light brown sugar
¹/₃ cup maple syrup
1 cup canned pumpkin
3 large eggs
1 teaspoon vanilla extract
¹/₂ teaspoon cinnamon
¹/₂ teaspoon ground ginger
¹/₄ teaspoon grated nutmeg
¹/₄ teaspoon ground cloves

On a sheet of lightly floured wax paper, roll the pastry into a 12-inch circle. Invert the pastry over a 9-inch pie pan and peel off the paper. Gently press the pastry into the pan, then curl the overhanging edge under, sculpting it into an upstanding ridge. Cover the shell with plastic wrap and freeze for 30 minutes.

Preheat the oven to 400°. Line the pastry with foil and weight it down with beans or rice. Bake the pastry for 20 minutes, then remove the foil, beans and all. Prick the bottom of the pastry 3 or 4 times, then bake another 10 minutes. Cool on a rack. Reduce the oven temperature to 375°.

Prepare the filling. Combine the milk, cornmeal, and salt in a small saucepan. Gradually bring to a boil, whisking, until the mixture thickens. Switch to a wooden spoon and stir the mixture over low heat for 2 minutes. Remove from the heat and whisk in the remaining ingredients one at a time; the spices can all go in at once.

Pour the filling into the pie shell and bake the pie for 45 to 50 minutes. When the pie is done, the surface will have risen and it will seem firm if shaken. Cool on a rack.

Shaker Cider Pie

MAKES 8 SERVINGS

This is one of my favorite pies of all time and my idea of the quintessential New England dessert. Two of the primary ingredients—cider jelly and maple syrup—have deep roots here in this part of the country; I think of them as the original natural sweeteners. The Shakers, whose Canterbury village is located just south of my home in New Hampshire, made and used both extensively in their own cooking. For a time, it was much more economical for them to use these native sweeteners than it was to use refined sugar. As for the pie, I can best describe it as similar to a maple-apple custard. The egg whites are whipped into the batter at the end, leaving a sort of very thin meringue topping; in general I don't like meringue pies, but this is very different, very low-key and pleasant. To make the pie you'll first need to reduce fresh cider to somewhere between a thick syrup and jelly consistency, or you can order organic cider jelly from my friends Mike and Nancy Phillips; see *Food for Thought* below for details. The pie is best served chilled, so make it early in the day to serve for dinner. A dab of plain yogurt is good with this. The pie is pretty sweet and the tartness of the yogurt is a good balance.

1 9-inch pie unbaked pie shell; I like the Semolina Pastry (page 279)

FILLING
³/₄ cup reduced cider (see *Food for Thought*)
³/₄ cup maple syrup
1 tablespoon unsalted butter

pinch of salt

3 large eggs, separated

nutmeg, for garnish

*M*ake the reduced cider if you haven't already. In a small saucepan, combine the reduced cider, maple syrup, and butter over low heat, whisking to blend. When the butter melts, pour the mixture into a mixing bowl and set aside to cool slightly. Whisk in the salt. Preheat the oven to 425°.

Whip the egg whites just until they hold soft peaks. Whisk the yolks in a small bowl, adding a little of the warm syrup mixture. Stir the yolks back into the syrup mixture, then add the whites and whisk vigorously for about 10 seconds; the egg white froth won't disappear, but it will be reduced. That's fine. Slowly pour the batter into the pie shell. Bake on the center rack for 15 minutes, then reduce the oven temperature to 350° and bake for 25 to 30 minutes more. When done, the center of the pie will still be a little wobbly, but the surface of the pie should not move in waves.

Cool the pie on a rack, then transfer to the refrigerator uncovered. If you don't plan to eat the pie within about 3 hours, cover it with a foil tent after the initial chilling so you don't disturb the fragile topping. Eat within 36 hours.

❧ *Food for Thought* ❧
HOW TO BOIL CIDER

My friend Mike Phillips, the only source I know of organic cider jelly in the country, boils down his cider in a maple syrup evaporator. Since you probably don't have one of those hanging around, here's how you can do it at home. It's quite easy.

First you will need a source of good fresh preservative-free cider. Measure out 8 cups into a medium nonreactive pot or large saucepan. Note how high the cider sits in the pan. Say, for instance, that it comes about 2 inches up the pan; when the cider is reduced to the proper density, to almost one-eighth of its original volume, it will only come up the sides by about 1/4 inch. Note that the exact density isn't critical, but it should be close. You can in fact easily turn off the pan and pour what you have into a glass measuring cup to check. Get as close to 1 cup as possible, but as much as 1 1/4 cups is okay too.

And if this seems like too much trouble, simply write to Mike and Nancy Phillips for a current price list: Lost Nation Cider Mill, RFD 2, Box 105, Lancaster, NH 03584.

Sweet Corn Custard Pie

ᘓ

MAKES 8 SERVINGS

This is an unusual and delectable pie, kernels of sweet corn set in a sort of polenta custard. It reminds me of something the Shakers might have made. For a
custard pie, it is not particularly rich. The trick is in the cornmeal-thickened
custard, which bakes up to a semisolid, custardlike consistency without the
need for gobs of eggs or cream; you'll notice that there's only 2 eggs and milk,
not cream (for an even leaner version, see the variation below). The pie is
sweetened with brown sugar, the hint of molasses (in the sugar) giving it a
New England orientation. This is excellent alone or with a spoonful of vanilla
ice cream or applesauce on the side.

1 9-inch pie shell, partially baked (page 278) and cooled

FILLING

2 large ears of corn, kernels scraped off

1^1/2 cups cold skim or regular milk

^{1}/3 cup yellow cornmeal

^{1}/2 cup packed light brown sugar

1 tablespoon unsalted butter, cut into several small pieces

^{1}/2 teaspoon vanilla extract

^{1}/4 teaspoon salt

finely grated zest of 1 lemon

2 large eggs, lightly beaten

*I*f you haven't already, prepare and cool the crust. Set the oven at 375°.
Put the corn in a skillet and cover with lightly salted water. Bring to a
boil, then boil for about 5 minutes, until the water has evaporated. Set
the pan aside.

Whisk the milk and cornmeal in a small saucepan. Place over medium heat
and cook, whisking often, until the mixture thickens, about 5 minutes. Remove
from the heat and scrape the cornmeal mush into a medium mixing bowl. Whisk
in the remaining ingredients in the order listed, then fold in the cooked corn.

Scrape the filling into the crust and bake the pie for about 45 minutes, until
set in the center; even if it seems a touch loose in the center, it will finish cooking as it cools. Cool the pie on a rack and serve at room temperature. (Or, my
preference, cool, then refrigerate for an hour or so before serving. Cover and
refrigerate any leftovers.)

VARIATION: To make a leaner version of this same pie, omit the tablespoon
of butter. Use 1 egg instead of 2 and increase the cornmeal by 2 teaspoons.

Low-Fat Cornmeal Sponge Cake

MAKES 6 TO 8 SERVINGS

This is light, soft, cornmeal-crunchy cake you can serve with just about any-thing, from fruit compote to ice cream, or with fresh sliced fruit or berries in their own juice. It is made without any butter and you really don't miss it. In-stead, I use a little olive oil. It adds just the right amount of body and flavor to the cake without loading it up with calories and fat. My kids will gladly devour this without any adornments. However, the spongelike texture really invites something juicy to go with it. May I suggest the cranberry and pear compote on page 266? Or how about fresh sliced peaches, tossed with a little sugar and lemon juice? Allow the fruit to sit and exude juice for about 15 minutes, then spoon it over individual slices of cake.

3 large eggs, at room temperature

$^1/_3$ cup plus 1 tablespoon sugar

finely grated zest of 1 lemon

$^1/_3$ cup fine yellow cornmeal, such as Quaker brand (stone-ground cornmeal doesn't work as well here)

$^1/_3$ cup unbleached all-purpose flour

$^1/_8$ teaspoon salt

3 tablespoons olive oil (it should not be a very dark or deeply flavored variety)

1 teaspoon lemon extract

$^1/_2$ teaspoon vanilla extract

*P*reheat the oven to 350°. Butter a 7-inch round cake or springform pan. Line the bottom with a circle of wax paper and butter it, too.

Put the eggs in a bowl of hot water for 1 minute to warm. Crack 2 of the eggs and 1 egg white into a mixing bowl. (Reserve the leftover yolk for another use.) Begin beating the eggs on medium-high speed, gradually adding the sugar with the mixer going. Beat the eggs and sugar for 4 to 5 min-utes, until the mixture is thick enough to fall from the beaters in a thick ribbon. Blend in the lemon zest.

Put the cornmeal in a small bowl, then sift the flour and salt over it; mix with your hands to combine. Sprinkle the dry mixture over the batter about one-third at a time, gently folding it in with a large rubber spatula after each addi-tion. Measure the olive oil and extracts into a cup, then quickly but gently fold the liquids into the batter. When the batter is uniform and free of dry streaks, scrape it into the prepared pan and bake for 25 to 30 minutes, until the top is springy and a tester inserted in the center of the cake comes out clean.

Cool the cake in the pan on a rack for 5 minutes. Run a knife around the edge of the pan to loosen the cake. Invert it onto a wire rack or remove the sides of the pan, peel off the wax paper, and cool completely. The texture is improved by wrapping the cooled cake in plastic wrap and letting it sit at room temperature for several hours. This will keep 3 days at room temperature, covered, in a coolish spot.

Dairyless Pineapple Upside-Down Cake

MAKES 7 TO 10 SERVINGS

Not only is this cake healthy, but it is thrifty and ingenious to boot since the juice from the can of pineapple is used in the batter. We use Dole canned pineapple slices; there are ten slices to the twenty-ounce can. Seven of the slices go in the pan and the remaining three are pureed and added to the batter also. I like that there's no waste and you don't have to figure out what to do with the leftover slices. This tastes great and it is *very* popular around here. I can remember a time when we took this cake to a friend's house who had invited us over for dinner. After I had sliced and served the cake the center piece was left. The kids were pretty much horrified when I announced we'd be leaving the remaining piece for our guests, and thus began the usual litany of whispered comments like, *Are you sure they're really going to eat it? Can't I just pick at the corner? Pull off the pineapple?* We've gone through stretches where it was the birthday cake of choice for many consecutive birthday celebrations. Because there are six of us, we polish off the six huge outer pieces and the seventh piece in the center goes to the birthday kid the next day. If you're on a dairy-free diet, this is great with one of the rice-based ice creams.

TOPPING

1 20-ounce can Dole pineapple slices in clarified pineapple juice

2 tablespoons flavorless vegetable oil

1/4 cup maple syrup

2 tablespoons packed light brown sugar

CAKE

1/2 cup canned pumpkin or squash

3/4 cup pineapple juice (from the can)

$^{1}/_{2}$ cup unsulphured molasses

$^{1}/_{3}$ cup maple syrup

$^{1}/_{3}$ cup flavorless vegetable oil

1 tablespoon finely chopped fresh ginger

$2^{1}/_{2}$ cups whole wheat pastry flour

1 teaspoon baking powder

1 teaspoon baking soda

2 teaspoons ground ginger

1 teaspoon cinnamon

$^{1}/_{4}$ teaspoon ground cloves

$^{1}/_{4}$ teaspoon grated nutmeg

$^{1}/_{4}$ teaspoon salt

pinch of cayenne

Preheat the oven to 350° and get out a 10-inch cast-iron pan. Drain the pineapple slices, reserving $^{3}/_{4}$ cup of the juice in a measuring cup; if it comes up a little short, add water. Heat the oil, maple syrup, and brown sugar in the skillet over medium heat, stirring, until the mixture boils across the entire surface. Turn the heat off and arrange 6 pineapple slices around the perimeter and 1 in the center. Set the pan aside.

Make the cake. Put the pumpkin and 3 remaining pineapple slices in the bowl of a food processor and process to a smooth puree, gradually adding the reserved pineapple juice. Add the molasses, maple syrup, oil, and ginger and process again, until smooth.

Sift the remaining (dry) ingredients into a large mixing bowl. Make a well in the center and add the liquid. Stir just until the batter is smooth and uniform, then slowly pour the batter over the pineapple slices. Smooth the top, then bake for 40 to 45 minutes, until a tester inserted in the center of the cake comes out clean. Run a knife around the side of the cake to loosen it completely, then immediately invert the cake onto a cake platter. Let the cake cool for at least 30 minutes before slicing.

Applesauce-Pecan Streusel Cake

MAKES 9 TO 12 SERVINGS

My family and I are totally in love with this cake; it is every bit as good as any other traditional rich coffee cake you may have eaten and then some, the difference being this one has no dairy products in it whatsoever. The texture is soft and moist—again, due to the wonderful baking qualities of whole wheat pastry flour. There's a thick layer of nut streusel in the center of the cake and more on top; we make a double recipe of the Pretty-Good-for-You Butterless Streusel and use much of it, though you could get by with just a single recipe of it. If you'd rather use walnuts in the streusel—pecans are pretty expensive—that's fine. I'll be very surprised if this doesn't become a regular with your family. Karen says this is good for breakfast or lunches and it travels well, wrapped in plastic.

1 cup natural unfiltered apple juice

1 cup unsweetened applesauce

2/3 cup maple syrup

1/3 cup flavorless vegetable, safflower, or canola oil

2 teaspoons vanilla extract

3 cups whole wheat pastry flour

1 1/2 teaspoons baking powder

1 teaspoon baking soda

1 teaspoon cinnamon

1/2 teaspoon salt

1 or 2 batches (see headnote) Pretty-Good-for-You Butterless Streusel
    (page 285), pecan variation

Preheat the oven to 350° and lightly oil and flour a 9 × 9-inch or 10-inch cake pan; a springform pan is fine. Put the apple juice, applesauce, maple syrup, oil, and vanilla in a blender or food processor and process to a fine puree. Set aside.

In a large bowl, sift the whole wheat pastry flour with the baking powder, baking soda, cinnamon, and salt. Make a well in the dry ingredients, add the liquid, and stir until uniformly blended. Scrape half of the batter into the prepared pan and level it with a spoon. Sprinkle a generous layer of the streusel over the batter, keeping it back slightly from the edges. Slowly pour the remaining batter over the streusel and level it with a spoon. Top with another generous layer of the streusel.

Bake the cake for 35 to 40 minutes, until a tester inserted in the center of the cake comes out clean; the cake should also feel resistant to gentle finger pressure at the center. Cool the cake in the pan on a rack. It can be sliced while it is still slightly warm or at room temperature. Store leftovers right in the pan, tightly covered. This will keep for 48 hours, or individual slices may be wrapped in foil and frozen for several weeks.

Fall Fruit Crisp with a Whole Wheat Topping

MAKES 6 SERVINGS

I love baking with fall fruit. Cranberries, apples, pears—these three seasonal stars are featured here in this soft fruit crisp topped with a whole wheat streusel; the earthiness of the whole grains seems just right against this sweet-tart harvest. This makes an excellent dessert or breakfast. For the latter, I'd serve with cold plain yogurt. For dessert, I'd go with a dab of vanilla ice cream. Hint: Cranberries freeze beautifully. When they go on sale, buy a truckload and stash them in your freezer. Then you'll have them for baking year-round.

4 pears, peeled, cored, and sliced

3 baking apples, peeled, cored, and sliced

1 cup fresh cranberries

1/3 cup maple syrup, honey, or sugar

2 tablespoons unbleached all-purpose flour

1/4 teaspoon grated nutmeg

juice of 1 lemon

TOPPING
1 cup whole wheat flour

1/2 cup packed light brown sugar

1/2 teaspoon cinnamon

1/4 teaspoon salt

6 tablespoons cold unsalted butter, cut into small pieces

Preheat the oven to 375°. Butter a medium shallow casserole and set aside. Mix the fruit and maple syrup in a large bowl. Sprinkle the flour, nutmeg, and lemon juice over the fruit and toss to coat. Spread the fruit in the casserole and place it in the oven.

Make the topping. Put the whole wheat flour in a large mixing bowl. Add the brown sugar, cinnamon, and salt and rub with your hands to mix. Add the butter and rub it with the flour until the butter is rubbed into small flakes and the mixture resembles a coarse meal. Remove the casserole from the oven and spread the topping evenly over the fruit. Bake about 30 minutes longer (total baking time should be about 35 minutes), until the topping has darkened a shade or two and the fruit is bubbly-hot throughout.

Peach-Blueberry Crisp with Mixed Grain Topping

MAKES 6 SERVINGS

I love whole grains and I do a lot of baking, so I'm often left with odds and ends of grains to use up. I made this excellent crisp on one such occasion. Much as I love buttery toppings, in this case I was looking for something that needed only a minimum of butter and where oil could be substituted with good results. This grainy, crunchy topping satisfies that requirement, in part I think because whole grains are so inherently satisfying on their own. You could, of course, use this topping on other fruit crisps; I just happen to like the combination of these two end-of-summer fruits, peaches and blueberries. I've sweetened them judiciously, adding just a bit of lemon juice; if the fruit is good, that's all it will need. Serve for dessert or breakfast.

FRUIT
4 cups peeled and sliced ripe peaches

1 cup blueberries

1/3 cup sugar

juice and finely grated zest of 1 lemon

1 tablespoon unbleached all-purpose flour

MIXED GRAIN TOPPING
1/2 cup toasted wheat germ

1/3 cup unbleached all-purpose flour

1/3 cup finely chopped walnuts, almonds, or pecans

1/3 cup noninstant rolled oats

1/4 cup yellow cornmeal

$^{1}/_{4}$ cup fine, dry bread crumbs

$^{1}/_{2}$ teaspoon cinnamon

$^{1}/_{4}$ teaspoon grated nutmeg

$^{1}/_{4}$ teaspoon salt

$^{1}/_{2}$ cup maple syrup or mild honey, such as clover or orange blossom

3 tablespoons unsalted butter, canola oil, or flavorless vegetable oil

1 teaspoon vanilla extract

*G*et out a large gratin dish or ceramic pie plate and butter or oil it thoroughly. Preheat the oven to 375°. Mix all of the fruit filling ingredients in a bowl and distribute the mixture evenly in the baking dish. Place it in the oven while you make the topping.

To make the topping, mix the dry ingredients up to and including the salt in a large bowl. In a small saucepan, gently heat the maple syrup or honey and butter or oil. When the butter melts and the mixture is warm, remove it from the heat and stir in the vanilla. Cool briefly, then stir the liquid into the dry ingredients and let it sit for 5 minutes; it will be damp and clumpy. Work the mixture with your fingers or a fork to combine everything thoroughly and break up the mixture into crumbs.

Remove the baking dish from the oven and spread the topping over it. Bake for about 30 minutes more; total baking time should be about 35 to 40 minutes. When it is done you'll probably be able to see the fruit bubbling thickly at the edges. Cool the crisp on a rack for about 10 to 15 minutes before serving.

Cinnamon Applesauce Crepes

MAKES 4 SERVINGS

Dessert crepes don't have to be complicated and rich; these are neither, but you'd still have to look hard to find a tastier crepe. We love them for dessert or breakfast. The crepes are brushed with a little warm raspberry or apple jelly, dusted with cinnamon sugar, then folded into quarters and browned in the tiniest bit of butter. I serve two per person, with store-bought applesauce in the center. I mean, you could almost make these in your sleep. Consider serving a dollop of plain yogurt next to the applesauce for a tart balance.

8 crepes (page 285)

$^{1}/_{2}$ cup currant jelly or raspberry preserves

2 tablespoons sugar

$^1/_2$ teaspoon cinnamon

1 tablespoon unsalted butter

$1^1/_2$ to 2 cups favorite applesauce

1 cup plain yogurt (optional)

coarsely chopped walnuts, for garnish (optional)

*W*orking with 1 crepe at a time, brush the surface with about 1 table-spoon of currant jelly or preserves; if you heat the jelly first, it will spread easier without tearing the crepe. Mix the sugar and cinnamon in a small bowl and sprinkle a little over the crepe. Fold the crepe in half, then in half again, leaving you with a quarter wedge. Repeat for the remaining crepes.

Heat a sliver of the butter in a nonstick skillet. Add 2 crepes at a time (or 4 if they'll fit without crowding) and brown the crepes over medium heat, about $1^1/_2$ minutes per side. Serve 2 crepes per person, with a little of the applesauce and yogurt, if you're using it, to one side. Garnish with walnuts if you like.

Cranberry and Pear Compote with Star Anise

MAKES 6 SERVINGS

Simple, delicious, refreshing—this is all that and more. The surprise here is the star anise: It gives an exotic fragrance to the fruit and a lovely flavor. The deep cranberry-red color is spectacular also, and it only deepens as it cools. This is great alone, for breakfast or dessert.

$1^1/_2$ cups water

$1^1/_2$ cups fresh cranberries

scant $^1/_2$ cup sugar

2 pieces of star anise

several long strips of orange zest

2 large pears, ripe but still firm, peeled, cored, and quartered

*P*ut the water, cranberries, sugar, star anise, and orange zest in a medium nonreactive saucepan. Gradually bring the mixture to a boil, then lower to a simmer. Simmer—it should just barely boil—for

5 minutes, then add the pears. Continue to simmer the mixture for about 20 minutes, until the pears are tender.

Remove the compote from the heat, then transfer the fruit and poaching liquid to a large ceramic bowl. Cool to room temperature, then cover and refrigerate until serving. It can be served cold or at room temperature. However, the flavor improves and the color becomes deeper if it has had several hours to sit. Serve the fruit with plenty of its own juice. If you're going to be using the compote with cake, it would be best to spoon out the fruit with a slotted spoon. Pour the liquid into a nonreactive saucepan and boil until reduced and syrupy. Top the cake with the fruit and some of the sauce.

Cranberry and Apricot Baked Apples

MAKES 6 SERVINGS

I hope baked apples never go out of style. I must admit, I do like them all fancied up with nuts, raisins, preserves, and all that, because I find them a bit boring otherwise. I like these best cold, but they're good warm, too, for breakfast or dessert. Serve with cold light cream. Golden Delicious apples will hold their shape pretty nicely during baking; many others will not. That's why I like them here.

6 Golden Delicious apples

$1/2$ cup fresh cranberries or $1/4$ cup dried

$1/3$ cup walnuts or pecans

$1/4$ cup raisins

$1/4$ cup packed light brown sugar

$1/2$ teaspoon cinnamon

$1/4$ teaspoon ground cloves

2 tablespoons cold unsalted butter

6 tablespoons thick apricot preserves

a little cider, cranberry juice, or water, for baking the apples in

Preheat the oven to 400° and get out a large shallow casserole. Prepare the apples by taking a thin slice off the bottom so they'll stand upright. Core the apples all the way through, then make an $1/8$-inch-deep score around the apples about a third of the way down. Peel this upper section, at the same time cutting the upper section of the hollow into a wide crater; this will help hold the filling and preserves.

Put the cranberries, nuts, raisins, brown sugar, and spices in the bowl of a food processor; process until finely chopped. Working right in the casserole, divide the filling evenly between the apples, pushing it down into the cores. Put a small pat of butter on top of each one, then spoon about 1 tablespoon preserves over each. Pour enough water or cider in the pan to just cover the bottom.

Cover with foil and bake for 20 minutes. Reduce the heat to 375° and bake another 30 to 40 minutes, uncovered, until the apples are tender, basting with the pan juice about every 10 minutes during the final 30 minutes. Serve at any temperature.

Ginger-Honey Spiced Applesauce

MAKES 4 TO 6 SERVINGS

There are dozens of different ways to make applesauce, and over the years I think I've probably tried and adored all of them. I've made it with cranberries, maple syrup, pears, and with all three in the same batch even. This one relies on honey for a sweetener, though you could use maple syrup or sugar if you prefer, and is cooked with finely chopped candied ginger. The mixture is pureed in the food processor, seasoned with cinnamon, and served cold. We especially love our applesauce in the fall, served with freshly baked squash.

5 large apples, peeled, cored, and cut into chunks
juice of 3 navel oranges
juice of 1 lemon
$^1/_4$ cup honey, maple syrup, or sugar
1 tablespoon minced candied ginger
$^1/_3$ cup water
cinnamon

Put the apples into a medium nonreactive saucepan and add the juices, honey, ginger, and water. Bring to a boil, then reduce the heat to an active simmer and cook the apples, covered, for 15 minutes, until tender. Remove from the heat and let sit at room temperature, covered, for 30 minutes.

Transfer the apples and any juice to the bowl of a food processor and puree to a slightly textured consistency. Add the cinnamon to taste. Taste, adding more sweetener or lemon juice if needed. Transfer the applesauce to a bowl, cover, and refrigerate until serving.

Monkeys on the Rocks

MAKES 5 TO 6 SERVINGS

I mean, don't you just love the name? It came from our friend Theo Kalikow, who had been making a simple apple and raisin compote like this for years, previously known as Apple Delight. One day she was reading Patrick O'Brian's Aubry-Maturin series of novels set in the nineteenth-century British navy, musing, as she puts it, "on Stephen Maturin's adventures on the Rock of Gibraltar. Inveterate naturalist that he was, he'd been observing the flora and fauna, including the apes who inhabit the Rock, to the neglect of his duties—his usual pattern, as readers of the series will know. So there I was, reading at dinner and chuckling over Stephen when . . . I looked into my dessert bowl, and there it was . . . Monkeys on the Rocks."

We've taken a few liberties with Theo's recipe—mainly just adding some additional poaching liquid—but it still very much looks like monkeys on the rocks. And you won't find a better-tasting apple compote around. Serve with yogurt cheese, plain yogurt, sour cream, or just as is.

5 large Golden Delicious, Winesap, or other firm cooking apples

1 cup dark raisins

4 or 5 thickish slices of fresh ginger

1 cinnamon stick

2 cups apple-apricot juice

juice of 1 lemon

Peel, quarter, and core the apples. Cut the quarter sections into large, bite-size chunks and put them in a large nonreactive saucepan with the raisins, ginger, cinnamon stick, and juice. Gradually bring the mixture to a simmer, then simmer for about 5 minutes, until the apple chunks are just barely tender; don't overcook or they'll turn to mush. [Theo's original instructions to me read: "Cook a few minutes, until soft (will depend on the type of apple and how mooshy you like it.)"] Remove the mixture from the heat and pour it into a heatproof bowl. Stir in the lemon juice and let the fruit cool. You can eat this warm, or cover and refrigerate until serving.

Blueberries, Melon, and Basil

❧

MAKES 6 SERVINGS

When summer comes, I generally adopt a "less is more" attitude about dessert; this one embodies that thinking quite nicely. Cool and colorful, refreshing and light, it's a great finish to any summer meal. If the fruit is perfectly ripe, you don't even need to add the small amount of honey I've included; but since I often end up with less-than-perfect melon, the honey returns some of its promise. You can make this in a jiffy.

1 cantaloupe
1 pint blueberries, rinsed
juice of $^1/_2$ lemon or lime
$1^1/_2$ tablespoons honey
small handful of fresh basil leaves, finely chopped

Halve the cantaloupe and scoop out the seeds. Halve each half, then cut each quarter into 3 or 4 more wedges. Make several crosswise cuts through the flesh almost to the rind, then cut the chunks out and let them fall into a bowl. Add the remaining ingredients and toss well. Cover and refrigerate, if possible, for 30 minutes before serving.

Blueberries with Frosted Peach Foam

❧

MAKES 5 TO 6 SERVINGS

If you're wondering what frosted peach foam is, it is a thickish, pourable cream—like partially whipped cream—made from pureed fruit and nonfat yogurt; there's no actual cream in it, and in fact it can be made without any dairy products whatsoever (see the vegan variation below). This frosted cream is flavored with ginger, sweetened with a hint of sugar, honey, or maple syrup, and poured over fresh blueberries. Pureeing the cream in the blender leaves it with a foamy consistency, thus the name. If you grow lemon thyme or mint, a sprig of either is a pretty garnish. To keep the foam foamy, chill your bowls about an hour before serving. Use only fresh juicy peaches. This is good summer eating in a snap.

5 small ripe peaches, peeled and sliced

2 tablespoons sugar, honey, or maple syrup

$3/4$ cup plain nonfat yogurt

2 tablespoons frozen peach or white grape juice concentrate

1 teaspoon freshly grated ginger

1 pint fresh blueberries, rinsed

lemon thyme or mint, for garnish (optional)

About $1^1/2$ hours before serving, arrange the sliced peaches in a shallow casserole and toss them with the sugar, honey, or maple syrup. Place them in the freezer. One hour before serving, put the yogurt in a bowl and place it in the freezer; chill the dessert bowls also. When you are ready to serve, put the peaches, yogurt, juice concentrate, and ginger in a blender and process to a smooth, foamy puree; taste and see if it could benefit from a bit more sweetener or a squeeze of lemon juice. Arrange a crowded layer of blueberries in the bowls and pour some of the peach cream over each portion. Garnish and serve right away.

VARIATIONS: Karen makes a vegan rendition of this by substituting vanilla-flavored soy milk for the yogurt. You can also substitute nectarines or apricots for the peaches.

Mocha-Carob Slush

MAKES 6 SERVINGS

This isn't quite an ice cream, perhaps closer to a sorbet, though I really like the name *slush;* it is much more descriptive of the loose, slushy texture this has after it comes out of the food processor. Here's how it works: First you make a sort of sweetened hot carob drink, flavored with coffee substitute for that mocha touch (and by the way, hot from the saucepan it makes a great winter drink). The mixture is poured into a shallow casserole, cooled, then frozen overnight. Next day, you buzz the frozen mixture in the food processor until smooth. I think I've said elsewhere that, in general, I have only lukewarm feelings about carob, but I take that back for the time being; this is really an excellent warm weather dessert. Be absolutely certain to chill the serving dishes lest this immediately revert to liquid.

$^{1}/_{3}$ cup packed light brown sugar

$^{1}/_{4}$ cup carob powder

2 tablespoons Cafix or other instant coffee substitute

big pinch of cinnamon

$^{1}/_{4}$ cup water

2 cups milk or soy milk

1 teaspoon vanilla extract

a few additional tablespoons milk or soy milk for the processing

*P*ut the brown sugar, carob, Cafix, cinnamon, and water in a small nonreactive saucepan, whisking to blend. Gradually bring the mixture to a boil, whisking, then let it boil gently for 1 minute. Remove from the heat and stir in the milk and vanilla. Set aside.

Very lightly oil a medium shallow ceramic casserole or gratin dish. Pour the liquid into the casserole and cool to room temperature. Place the casserole in the freezer and let the mixture freeze solid, at least 3 hours or overnight. You will notice, if you stir this while it's in the freezer (and sneak a few sips), that it will be somewhat separated, the carob settling to the bottom; that's fine.

About 15 minutes before you plan to serve this, chill the serving glasses (small ramekins are good) and put about $^{1}/_{4}$ cup milk in the freezer in a glass. Chill the processor blade also. Break the mixture up—I cut into it with a dough scraper—and transfer it to the bowl of the food processor. Process until smooth, adding as much of the milk as needed to make a smooth texture; you may have to scrape down the sides of the bowl several times. Serve at once.

Winter Citrus Fruit with Instant Raspberry Sorbet

MAKES 4 SERVINGS

This easy dessert grew out of my habit of spreading raspberry preserves over my grapefruit, which I especially love when the fruit is so big and juicy in the winter months. All I do is take juicy grapefruit and oranges and section them into individual chilled dessert bowls. The sorbet it is served with isn't a genuine sorbet but a quick version I make with frozen raspberries, tangerine juice, and a bit of sugar and lemon juice. Just throw everything in the food processor and it whips up to a semifirm—which is to say somewhat soft—instant "sorbet." It is immediately spooned over the sectioned fruit and eaten at once, a refreshing, light finish to any filling winter meal.

2 big juicy ruby red grapefruits

2 large navel oranges

2 cups packaged frozen raspberries

strained juice from 2 tangerines

2 to 3 tablespoons sugar

juice of $1/2$ lemon

About 30 minutes ahead, chill medium dessert bowls. Halve, seed, and section the grapefruits and oranges into a mixing bowl; refrigerate. Put the remaining ingredients in the bowl of a food processor and process to a smooth, sorbetlike consistency, scraping down the sides of the bowl if necessary. If it seems to need it, add a bit more fruit juice or water to loosen the texture. Divide the fruit evenly between the dessert bowls and top with some of the sorbet. Serve at once.

Strawberry Sherbet

MAKES 6 SERVINGS

I had never made sherbet this way before, but it came out just great. Raw ripe strawberries—and they must be ripe; don't even bother making this with out-of-season berries—are combined with cooked ones and pureed in the food processor, then mixed with plain yogurt. The mixture is still-frozen (you don't, in other words, use a machine, though you could), then processed again briefly just before serving to give it a smooth texture. It's intensely red and fresh-strawberry-tasting, and should be served in small chilled bowls, garnished with mint leaves.

1 quart ripe strawberries, rinsed and hulled

$1/2$ cup sugar

juice of 1 lemon

1 cup regular or low-fat plain yogurt

a few tablespoons milk or fruit juice

fresh mint leaves, for garnish

*H*alve about half of the berries and combine them in a medium non-reactive saucepan with the sugar. Bring to a simmer over low heat, stirring occasionally. When the sugar has melted, transfer the mixture to a food processor and add the remaining berries. Process the berries to a smooth puree, then transfer to a shallow bowl and whisk in the lemon juice and yogurt. Place the bowl in the freezer and let it freeze solid, taking the bowl out and stirring about every 30 minutes. When the mixture is solid—it will probably take 4 to 6 hours—transfer the strawberry ice to the food processor and process in 5- to 8-second bursts, adding a little of the milk as you do so to make the sherbet smooth. (If you'd rather not use the milk, you can use a little fruit juice instead.) Serve at once in chilled bowls, garnished with the mint leaves.

Creamy Dairyless Maple Pudding

MAKES 4 TO 6 SERVINGS

Anyone serious about a vegan diet will want this delicious tofu-based pudding in their dessert repertoire. It is indeed creamy and there are several tricks to keeping it that way. The first is to use soft tofu rather than firm; soft tofu blends up more easily so any graininess is minimized. The other secret is the tahini, which really smooths out the texture yet firms it at the same time. You may need more or less tahini, depending on the texture of the pudding. The texture is right when it is soft, fluffy, stable but not runny. It will firm up nicely as it chills. Make it at least 3 hours before you plan to serve it.

1/2 cup maple syrup

1/2 cup plain or vanilla-flavored soy milk

1/2 teaspoon vanilla extract

2 teaspoons Cafix or other instant coffee substitute

big pinch of cinnamon

1 pound soft tofu

2 to 3 tablespoons tahini

1 1/2 tablespoons lemon juice

banana slices and/or chopped walnuts, for garnish (optional)

*P*our the maple syrup, soy milk, and vanilla into a blender. Add the Cafix and cinnamon. Lay the tofu on one of its narrow sides and slice in half so you have 2 thin slabs. Put them on a double layer of paper toweling and press hard with more paper towels to blot up some of the water in them.

Crumble the tofu and add it to the blender. Blend to a smooth puree, scraping down the sides if necessary. Blend in 2 tablespoons of the tahini and the lemon juice. Check the consistency; if it seems to need more tahini to thicken it up, add 1 more tablespoon.

Divide the pudding between small serving dishes or ramekins. Cover with plastic wrap and refrigerate for at least 3 hours before serving. Garnish with the banana slices and walnuts, if you're using them, and serve.

Creamy Peanut Butter and Banana Pudding

~

MAKES 4 SERVINGS

When you puree tofu with the right ingredients, you get a smooth, creamy dessert very much like a regular dairy-based pudding. But unlike those puddings, this one is not cooked: You just buzz everything right in the blender, pour into custard cups, chill, and serve. It's that easy. It tastes wonderful plain or dusted with finely chopped peanuts and flaked coconut. The pudding can also be made without the banana if someone in your family prefers a plain peanut butter pudding. This mixture can be pretty sluggish in the blender, so expect to scrape down the sides. I usually keep the top off and scrape the sides down with a rubber spatula as it purees, though this isn't a particularly smart or safe idea. You will only add 2 tablespoons of the soy milk to start; add the rest gradually as you need it.

1/3 cup maple syrup

4 tablespoons plain soy milk

1/2 medium ripe banana

1 teaspoon lemon juice

1/2 teaspoon vanilla extract

1/2 pound firm or extrafirm tofu

1/3 cup smooth natural salted peanut butter

Put the first 5 ingredients in a blender in the order listed, using only 2 tablespoons of the soy milk to start. Cut the tofu into 3 pieces, then, working with 1 piece at a time, squeeze out most of the liquid from each piece in your cupped hands. Crumble all of the tofu and drop it into the blender also. Add the peanut butter. Start processing the mixture to make a smooth puree. Gradually add as much of the remaining soy milk as needed to make the pudding smooth, scraping down the sides. Scrape the pudding into ramekins or custard cups. Cover and refrigerate for at least 2 hours before serving.

Pantry

Pantries hold all sorts of surprises and odds and ends. This one is no different. Here are the recipes that don't fit logically elsewhere—a pesto, yogurt cheese, a couple of pie pastries, and a few others.

While we're on the subject of what we commonly think of as pantry foods, perhaps a few words are in order.

Olive Oil—Much has been written about olive oil, a lot more than I ever care to know about it. If you like to experiment and can afford the luxury, there are many wonderful varieties and labels on the market. For my purposes—cooking for a family—I like the common supermarket brands; Berio is the brand I buy. It has a nice flavor, works great in salad dressings, the kids like it, and—in a pinch—you can even use it for a massage. At least I have.

Other Oils—For the sake of simplicity, I have one basic cooking oil, pure Wesson sunflower oil. It has the right amount of flavor for cooking, which is to say very little. I have used unrefined oils from health food stores, but generally speaking I find that most of them impart too much of their own flavor. And they're expensive. Unrefined canola oil is supposed to be one of the healthiest oils for you, but again I don't care for the flavor. Bottom line is: Keep experimenting until you find one you like. If you don't go through oil quickly, store it in a cool spot when you're not using it.

Vinegar—Again, there are a ton of them out there; many are excellent, but for the most part we mainly use plain old Progresso red wine vinegar. I do buy one balsamic vinegar at the grocery, called Roland, and that suits us: It has a little body, a pleasant sweetness, good flavor. From what I gather, I'm not buying the really genuine balsamic vinegar they sell in Italy. And at the price it commands, I gather I never will. Occasionally a friend will give us some homemade, flavored vinegars, and they're great to have around and experiment with. But nowadays, for day-in and day-out cooking, I stay pretty basic; I've had a bottle of champagne vinegar in my fridge for almost a year now and it is still nearly full.

Herbs and Spices—By all means, buy dried herbs and spices in bulk at a health food store and keep them in jars on your shelves; you'll pay an arm and a leg for herbs and spices in the supermarket. Buy quantities commensurate with your use, because they'll lose their flavor in storage. We have larger jars for basil, oregano, cinnamon, cumin, and coriander; smaller jars for most of the others.

Nuts and Dried Fruits—Keep them on hand at all times, for spontaneous baking. Nuts should be kept in a cool spot, or refrigerated, in an airtight container. The same goes for dried fruit, though you should keep some at room temperature for snacking purposes.

Traditional Pastry

MAKES ONE 9-INCH PIE OR TART SHELL

If you're looking for one good standard pastry, try this one. It has the typical amount of butter for a pastry of this size, tastes great, and is easily thrown together in the food processor. It is one of the most popular recipes from my cooking classes.

1 1/2 cups unbleached all-purpose flour

2 tablespoons sugar (omit if you're making a savory tart)

1/4 teaspoon salt

1/2 cup (1 stick) very cold unsalted butter, cut into 1/4-inch pieces

1 egg yolk

2 to 3 tablespoons water

Put the flour, sugar (if you are using it), and salt in the bowl of a food processor and give it several short bursts to mix. Take the cover off the processor bowl and scatter the butter pieces over the dry ingredients. Process for about 8 seconds, until the butter is broken into very small pieces.

Stir the yolk and 2 tablespoons of the cold water in a small bowl. Take the lid off the machine again and sprinkle this egg-water mixture over the flour. Turn the machine on for 4 seconds, then stop it. Take the lid off, fluff the ingredients with a fork, then re-cover and process for about 4 more seconds, until the pastry just starts to gather into a mass.

Dump the pastry out onto your work counter and try packing it into a ball. If it doesn't pack easily, sprinkle a teaspoon of the remaining water over the dry areas and quickly work it in with your fingertips. Use even a bit more water if necessary to pack the dough into a ball. Knead several times, then place the dough on a sheet of lightly floured wax paper. Flatten the dough into a disk about ³/₄ inch thick and refrigerate for 45 to 60 minutes. It shouldn't get rock hard.

When the dough is firm, roll it into a 12-inch circle on a sheet of lightly floured wax paper. Invert the pastry over a 9-inch pie pan and peel off the paper. Tuck the pastry into the pan and turn the edge under, shaping an upstanding edge. Freeze the shell for 20 minutes before using.

To bake the shell, preheat the oven to 400°. Line the shell with foil and weight it down with dried beans or rice. Bake for 15 minutes, remove the foil with the weights still in it, and bake for another 7 minutes (for a partially baked shell) or about 12 minutes for a fully baked shell. (Save the weights for future shells.) If the shell starts to puff during the second part of the baking, pierce it once with a fork to let the steam escape. Cool the shell on a rack.

Semolina Pastry

MAKES ENOUGH PASTRY FOR ONE 9-INCH PIE OR
12-INCH FREE-FORM TART

Here is a reduced butter pastry crust made with fine semolina flour. For the fat I use a combination of olive oil and butter and it bakes up beautifully, with a slightly dry, crumbly, and gritty texture, the semolina providing the bit of grit. This is a good choice for most any savory pie, though it works well as a sweet crust, too; just add 2 teaspoons of sugar to the dry mixture. I like it as the foundation for the Caramelized Onion Tart (page 206).

1¹/₄ cups unbleached all-purpose flour

¹/₃ cup fine semolina

¹/₄ teaspoon salt

1^1/$_2$ tablespoons olive oil

4 tablespoons cold unsalted butter, cut into ^{1}/$_4$-inch pieces

4 to 4^1/$_2$ tablespoons cold water

$\mathcal{C}$ombine the flour, semolina, and salt in the bowl of a food processor. With the machine running, gradually add the olive oil in a thin stream. Remove the lid and scatter the butter over the flour. Pulse the machine 5 or 6 times in 1- to 2-second bursts, breaking the butter into small bits. Sprinkle 3^1/$_2$ tablespoons of cold water over the pastry and pulse the machine as before 4 or 5 times. At this point, check the consistency of the pastry, pressing it together between your fingers. Add as much of the remaining water as seems appropriate and pulse again until the pastry starts to get clumpy; it should not ball together in the machine.

Turn the pastry out onto the work surface and pack it together like a snowball. Knead the pastry 2 or 3 times to redistribute the butter and place it on a large piece of plastic wrap. Flatten the pastry into a disk about ^{3}/$_4$ inch thick. Wrap the pastry and refrigerate for 45 to 60 minutes.

Roll the chilled dough onto a piece of wax paper. For a standard 9-inch pie, roll the dough into a 12-inch circle. Invert the pastry over the pan and peel off the paper. Carefully tuck the pastry into the pan without stretching it. Turn the upper edge back and under, pinching it into an upstanding ridge. Cover the pastry with plastic wrap and freeze for 30 minutes before using.

Wheat Germ Cream Cheese Pastry

MAKES ENOUGH PASTRY FOR ONE 9- OR 10-INCH
PIE OR TART, OR 6 TURNOVERS

I've used this recipe in cooking presentations as an example of how, even when you're making a fairly traditional-style pastry, you can do little things to upgrade the nutritional profile of a recipe. In this case, it's the wheat germ that gives the pastry a nutritional boost, but that's not all. It also adds a pleasant nutty flavor and a nubby surface texture that I find appealing. (Be sure to buy the unsweetened kind, not the sweetened; that's used more as a topping on sweet foods.)

1^1/$_2$ cups unbleached all-purpose flour

^{1}/$_4$ cup toasted unsweetened wheat germ

¹/₄ teaspoon salt

pinch of sugar

¹/₂ cup (1 stick) cold unsalted butter, cut into 10 to 12 pieces

4 ounces cold cream cheese, cut into 6 pieces

1 tablespoon cold water

*P*ut the flour, wheat germ, salt, and sugar in the bowl of a food processor. Pulse 3 or 4 times to mix. Add the butter and cream cheese to the bowl; pulse in 3- to 4-second bursts about 10 times. Add the water and pulse in 3- to 4-second bursts until the dough starts to pull together in large clumps (it should not, however, form a large ball).

Turn the dough out of the machine and pack it together. On a lightly floured surface, knead the dough 2 or 3 times. Shape the dough into a ball.

To prepare the dough for a quiche or other large savory pie, place the pastry on a piece of plastic wrap and flatten into a ³/₄-inch-thick disk. Cover tightly with the plastic wrap and refrigerate for at least 1, preferably 2 hours before rolling on a sheet of flour-dusted wax paper.

Note that because of the cream cheese, this dough tends to get soft if it is overworked or stays at room temperature for any length of time. If this should happen, don't worry: Simply slide the pastry (and wax paper you're rolling it on) onto a small baking sheet and refrigerate for 5 to 10 minutes to firm. Then proceed.

Whole Wheat Press-In Oil Pastry

MAKES ENOUGH PASTRY FOR ONE 10-INCH PIE SHELL

There was a time when I wouldn't even give an oil pastry a second glance, perhaps because I had tried several over the years and experienced such miserable results. *And* because I'm very partial to a good butter crust. But Karen, who eats almost no butter, was determined to make an oil pastry that not only worked but tasted great besides. I'm happy to say that she did, and now I'm quite fond of this alternative to a butter pastry. The whole grains are important here because they give the crust its delicious nutty taste; I can't imagine you'd get anything even remotely resembling this if you used white flour instead. The balance of grains is fine tuned. There's whole wheat pastry flour for tenderness, a little regular whole wheat flour for strength (it helps hold the crust together), and wheat germ for flavor and texture. The unrefined corn oil—

which, like the grains, adds a nutty taste—is important to the flavor of the crust. The flavor can be assertive, so we use part vegetable oil as well. Be aware that when it is mixed, this crust will not feel quite as dry as a butter pastry; it feels dampish, which is necessary in order to press it into the pan and to prevent it from drying out when you prebake it. That's another big discovery we made: You can easily dry out an oil crust like this if you over-prebake it without the filling; 7 to 8 minutes seems to be just right. Though it has many uses, don't miss our Squash Shepherd's Pie (page 176) with this pastry, it is really good! I describe two methods for making this; Karen's hand method, using a pastry blender, and the food processor method.

1 cup whole wheat pastry flour

$^1/_2$ cup whole wheat flour

$^1/_2$ cup toasted wheat germ

$^1/_2$ teaspoon salt

3 tablespoons flavorless vegetable oil or olive oil

3 tablespoons unrefined corn oil

4 tablespoons cold water

Preheat the oven to 400°. To make the pastry by hand, mix the dry ingredients in a large bowl. Mix the oils and water in a measuring cup. With a pastry blender in one hand and your measuring cup in the other, pour the liquids over the dry ingredients in a slow gradual stream, mixing dry and wet together with the pastry blender. Continue in this fashion until all of the liquid is mixed in and the pastry dough is uniformly damp; it will be loose and crumbly overall. Squeeze some of it between your fingers; it should hold together easily, and not feel dry. If it does, sprinkle as much as an additional tablespoon of water over the dough, working it in with your fingertips.

To make the pastry using the food processor, put the dry ingredients in the bowl and pulse several times to mix. Combine the liquids in a measuring cup. With the machine running, add the liquid ingredients in a gradual 7- to 8- second stream. Once all the liquid is added, pulse the machine in a series of 3- to 4- second bursts, until the mixture is uniformly dampened; it will be loose and crumbly overall. Dump the pastry into a bowl and check the consistency: If it seems a bit on the dry side, sprinkle as much as an additional tablespoon of water over the dough, working it in with your fingertips.

Dump the crumbs into the bottom of a 10-inch pie plate. Press the crumbs into the sides of the pan first, in a heavy $^1/_8$-inch-thick layer. Then press the crumbs into the bottom of the pan. Bake the crust for 7 minutes, then cool on a rack before proceeding with your recipe.

VARIATIONS: If you are using this pastry to make a sweet pie, as opposed to a savory one, you can add ¹/₂ teaspoon of cinnamon to the dry ingredients if you like. Also, if you're out of wheat germ or you would rather, you can replace the wheat germ with an equal amount of yellow stone-ground cornmeal.

❧ *Food for Thought* ❧
BUT HOW DOES IT SLICE?

The pastry, that is. Well, I'd be lying if I told you this grainy pastry holds up under the knife quite the same as a butter-and-white-flour pastry does; that's not the case. All the coarse particles of grain make this slightly more brittle, almost like a shortbread. So your slices won't have the same clean edges. And there's a *slim* chance that a chunk of crust will break off your slice of pie, hopefully not in mid-flight to someone else's plate. Is this a problem? All depends, I suppose, on your priorities and whom you're serving. We all have meals where we have better things to worry about than the possibility of flying whole wheat pastry shrapnel . . . say, for instance, when your in-laws—who are already suspicious of your diet—are coming for dinner. On the other hand, if you're serving your family, your immediate circle of friends, or anyone else who you know would appreciate the healthy gesture, then go for it. Chances are the crust will be fine anyway.

Whole Wheat and Corn Tortillas

MAKES 10 LARGE TORTILLAS

It is almost impossible not to use prepared tortillas when you're cooking for a busy family. I use them even though they leave something to be desired. For one, they never taste very fresh. And the texture is too firm for my taste, sometimes bordering on rubbery. If you want to experience what a really good homemade tortilla tastes like, try these. They're made with whole wheat flour and fine cornmeal and the dough is very, very dense, something like a yeast dough where you forgot the yeast. The dough is divided, the pieces are left to rest, then rolled so thin that you can practically see through them. They make incredibly tender, great-tasting wrappers. It might take several tries to get the rolling under control. Just be patient and go slowly.

1¹/2 cups whole wheat flour

¹/2 cup unbleached all-purpose flour

1 tablespoon yellow cornmeal

¹/2 teaspoon salt

2 teaspoons flavorless vegetable oil

¹/2 cup plus about 2 tablespoons water

In a large bowl, mix the flours, cornmeal, and salt. Drizzle the oil over the dry mixture. Using your fingers, rub the oil into the dry ingredients for about 1 minute, until there are no traces or streaks of oil. Make a well in the dry ingredients and add ¹/2 cup of the water. Stir well. Add enough of the remaining water, a teaspoon or so at a time, to make a very firm but cohesive dough. Knead the dough in the bowl for a minute, then turn it out onto a work surface and knead for 5 minutes; do not use any additional flour unless absolutely necessary. Cover the dough and let it rest for 10 minutes.

Roll the dough into a log 10 inches long. Cut the dough into 10 equal-size pieces and shape them into balls. Flatten the balls into thick disks and let them rest on a lightly floured surface, covered with plastic wrap, for about 10 minutes.

Working with 1 piece of dough at a time, roll the ball into an approximate 10-inch circle on a lightly floured surface; a narrow, tapered rolling pin is better here than a big thick one. Dust the surface of the tortilla, if necessary, to keep the pin from sticking. When rolling, use short strokes and push directly away from you, turning the tortilla as you roll. Place each tortilla aside on a floured surface as you do the others; don't stack them.

To cook the tortillas, heat a large (12-inch) cast-iron skillet over medium-high heat. When the skillet is preheated, lay 1 tortilla flat on it and cook just until it blisters, about 30 to 40 seconds. Flip and cook on the second side for about half the time you cooked the first side. Remove from the skillet and cool on a rack. Continue to cook in this manner until all the tortillas are done.

Pretty-Good-for-You Butterless Streusel

MAKES ABOUT 1 1/2 CUPS

I don't know anybody who doesn't love the crunchy brown sugar topping—streusel—that goes on top of muffins, pies, and other baked goods. Traditional versions are loaded with butter, so I was hoping to come up with one that wasn't and still tasted like something special. This is what I came up with. I don't miss the butter because I think using walnuts gives the topping a buttery flavor. Brown sugar and cinnamon help to make this taste like the original and there's a touch of oil to dampen the mixture. An excellent, all-purpose topper, stash this in the freezer and pull it out when you need it. If you bake often you might want to double the recipe.

1/3 cup packed light brown sugar

1/4 cup instant or noninstant rolled oats

1 teaspoon cinnamon

pinch of salt

1 1/2 cups walnuts

1 1/2 tablespoons flavorless vegetable oil or canola oil

Put the brown sugar, oats, cinnamon, and salt in the bowl of a food processor and process for about 10 seconds to chop up the oats. Add the walnuts and process for 5 to 10 seconds, until finely chopped but not clumpy. Finally, pulse the machine several times as you drizzle in the oil; don't overmix. Transfer the mixture to a plastic bag and freeze until needed.

VARIATION: Use pecans instead of the walnuts. This is excellent on muffins, in sticky buns, and on pies.

Basic Crepes

MAKES ABOUT 1 DOZEN CREPES

Crepes, someone told me recently, are back in, which took me totally by surprise since I never even knew that they had fallen out in the first place. That's the way it is, I suppose, when you live in the hinterlands of New Hampshire. How, I had to wonder, could anything so versatile as crepes ever lose favor? For vegetarians, crepes hold numerous possibilities. When necessary, they possess the twin virtues of elegance and acceptability, sufficiently mainstream to serve visiting guests who might otherwise cast a wary eye on vegetarian cuisine. You can use crepes to wrap around all kinds of vegetable or cheese fillings. And for dessert, they're a perfect companion with fresh fruit or jam. I think most people worry that crepes are high in fat, and in fact they are often teamed up with some pretty rich foods. But that doesn't have to be the case. One of my favorite desserts is a crepe filled with nothing more than cinnamon sugar, then browned in a speck of butter and served with applesauce. It couldn't be simpler and it's not at all fattening. Note that these can be made with oil instead of butter if you wish.

Here is a good reliable recipe for both sweet and savory crepes. The only difference for sweet crepes is a bit of sugar added to the batter. Remember that crepes are delicate and they need to be handled carefully; see *Food for Thought* for my foolproof way of turning crepes without tearing them. (Incidentally, if they are tearing, there's a good chance your batter is a bit too thin. If that appears to be the case, add about 1 1/2 tablespoons flour to the batter and rebuzz in the blender.) As they come out of the skillet, stack the crepes between pieces of wax paper. They can be refrigerated for a couple of days or frozen for later.

3 large eggs

1 1/4 cups milk

1 cup unbleached all-purpose flour

2 teaspoons sugar (optional; omit for savory crepes)

1/4 teaspoon salt

1 tablespoon butter, melted, or mild-tasting olive oil, plus a little extra for the pan

*P*ut all of the ingredients except the butter or oil in a blender and puree until smooth. Add the butter and puree briefly again. Pour the batter into a large measuring cup or pitcher and let it sit at room temperature for 30 minutes, or overnight in the refrigerator, covered.

When you're ready to cook the crepes, heat an 8- or 9-inch nonstick skillet over medium heat. Rub a little butter or oil in the pan with paper towels.

Ladle a scoop of batter into the pan, then immediately tilt and twirl the pan to spread the batter evenly. Pour off the excess; from the time the batter hits the pan until the time you pour off the excess is no more than 3 to 5 seconds. Cook the crepe on the first side for 30 to 45 seconds, then flip the crepe (*see Food for Thought*) and cook on the other side for 20 to 30 seconds more.

Slide or invert the crepe out of the pan onto a baking sheet lined with wax paper. Continue to cook the crepes in this manner, brushing the pan with butter between every other crepe. Place a piece of wax paper between the crepes.

The crepes can be used right away or you can let the stack cool, then cover with plastic wrap and refrigerate for several days. They can also be frozen for several weeks, well wrapped in plastic, then thawed at room temperature.

❧ *Food for Thought* ❧
FLIPPING CREPES: A CHILLING SUGGESTION

Crepes are one of my favorite foods to demonstrate at cooking demonstrations and classes. Without fail, people are surprised at just how easy they are to make. But what really brings the house down is my technique for flipping them, daffy as it may seem at first glance. First, understand that crepes are very delicate, like lace. And where many run into problems is turning them; try using a conventional spatula to turn your crepes and you often end up with something that looks like it went through a document shredder.

The solution is to flip them by hand and the secret is chilling your fingertips in a bowl of ice water just before you do so. It works like this: When you pour the excess batter out of the pan it leaves a pancake "tail" up the side of the pan; that tail is where you grasp the crepe. Just before you turn the crepe, stick your fingers in a bowl of ice water placed nearby. Keep your fingers there for 5 seconds, quickly dry them with a towel, then loosen the top of the tail with a knife.

Now, gently peel the crepe out of the pan like you would a sticker. Occasionally, when I have someone at one of my cooking demonstrations come up and try this, they'll yank up on the crepe like they're taking out twenty years of frustration on their spouse; the thing just *rips* in half. So peel gently, then flip it onto side two. Once it has cooked on side two, get the crepe out by inverting the pan. If it sticks, gently rap the pan on the counter and let the crepe fall onto your waiting piece of wax paper.

If you do it this way—chilling your fingers before every flip—you should never even feel the heat from the pan or crepe.

The Easiest Garlic-Parmesan Toasts

MAKES 4 TO 5 SERVINGS

No Italian meal seems complete without hot garlic bread on the side, and the kids are absolutely fanatical about it. I mean, we'll go to an Italian restaurant, order a small fortune in exotic pasta dishes, salads, and pizza, and by the time all of it arrives the kids are so stuffed on cheesy garlic bread that they can't eat a thing. Except dessert, of course. ("How can you even *think* about eating dessert when you didn't touch half the food on your plate?" "I've got a separate stomach for dessert.") The thing about this easy treatment is it does wonders for even lousy bread; it's almost as dramatic as one of those makeovers you see in the magazines where they take some average-looking gal and turn her into a willowy clone of Martha Stewart. Nonetheless, you should use the best Italian or French bread you can get your hands on. The kids can make this themselves: All you do is toast the bread in the oven, rub it with garlic, and top with olive oil and cheese. It goes back into the oven for a minute or so while you're putting the finishing touches on your meal. The rosemary adds a fragrant touch, but you can skip that if you like. Figure on at least 2 slices of bread per person.

1 or 2 loaves of French or Italian bread

3 to 4 large garlic cloves

olive oil

approximately 1 cup freshly grated Parmesan cheese

1 to 2 teaspoons dried crushed rosemary

freshly ground pepper to taste

Preheat the oven to 425° and get out a large baking sheet. Cut the bread into slices about 1 inch thick and lay them on the sheet. Place the bread in the oven until it is golden brown on each side, about 5 to 10 minutes depending on the kind of bread; dense sourdough bread will take longer to brown than lighter white bread.

Cut the cloves of garlic in half lengthwise, then scrape the flat cut part of the garlic over the top of each piece; you should be able to do 2 or 3 slices of bread with each piece of garlic. Lightly brush the garlicked area with olive oil, then sprinkle lightly with Parmesan cheese, rosemary, and pepper. Drizzle each piece with a little more olive oil, then put the toasts back in the oven for a minute or two, until the cheese browns. Serve hot.

❧ *Food for Thought* ❧

Maybe you've made garlic bread before, but have you ever made it with real garlic? A lot of people—and a lot of restaurants, unfortunately— use garlic powder or garlic salt on their garlic bread; that's a little like putting grapes on your peanut butter sandwich instead of grape jelly, or comparing orange-flavored Kool Aid to fresh squeezed orange juice. It just isn't the same. Garlic powder has a bitter flavor. Fresh garlic tastes fresh, not bitter. You can see for yourself if you help make this recipe. Rub the flat part of the cut garlic over the toasted bread; the rough crusty part of the bread acts like sandpaper. It catches the garlic oil and little bits of garlic. And that's what makes really good garlic bread.

Basic Pesto

MAKES ABOUT 1 CUP

There are many ways to make pesto, but I stick with this basic version I've been using for years. The food processor makes short work of it. All you need now is a big basil patch or a friend with one. My son Ben eats this by the spoonful. That, along with the fact that there's so much you can do with it, makes it hard to keep around. Luckily, the recipe multiplies beautifully.

2$^{1}/_{2}$ cups packed fresh basil leaves

2 to 3 garlic cloves, peeled

$^{2}/_{3}$ cup good-quality olive oil

$^{1}/_{4}$ cup (about 1 ounce) walnuts or pine nuts

$^{1}/_{8}$ teaspoon salt

$^{3}/_{4}$ cup freshly grated Parmesan cheese

In the bowl of a food processor, process the basil, garlic, olive oil, nuts, and salt until smooth, stopping occasionally to scrape down the sides. Scrape the mixture into a small bowl and stir in the Parmesan cheese. Cover and refrigerate until needed. If you don't plan to use it within 4 or 5 days, freeze it.

Oven-Dried Oil-Packed Tomatoes

I don't know enough about it to tell you whether all of the so-called sun-dried tomatoes we buy in this country are actually dried by the sun. Something tells me not; I may be wrong, but I have a hard time picturing the hungry wheels of American commerce waiting around for Mother Nature to do her thing on racks of tomatoes; that just isn't like us. My guess is that ovens come into the picture, and I can't knock it because that's the way I do mine and with wonderful results. The method I give is my self-taught technique; it works, and the tomatoes are wonderful, but this is not to say that you won't make refinements in the process once you've tried it.

There are two kinds of sun-dried tomatoes: oil-packed and, well, *not* oil-packed. The latter come in plastic bags, are tough as shoe leather, and need to be rehydrated before using. They're a far cry from the more expensive and much more versatile oil-packed tomatoes, like these, that you can use right out of the jar. Doing it yourself is cheaper and quite easy, so I rarely buy them anymore. Because drying intensifies the flavor, I even use this method in the colder months on mediocre tomatoes, with good results.

Select as many ripe plum tomatoes as you like, keeping in mind that they shrink considerably in the oven, to (it seems) about one-third of their original volume. I never dry less than about 3 pounds at a time; to do any less would not take full advantage of my oven's size and the energy it uses in the process.

Core the tomatoes and slice them in half lengthwise. Place the halves, flat side up, on cooling racks, leaving at least 1½ inches between them. Lightly brush the exposed flat surfaces with olive oil, then salt them sparingly. Place in a 150° oven overnight, or until they've lost most of their moisture and taken on a soft, leathery feel. Check them after several hours to determine if the temperature seems right. If they seem to be getting crispy in spots, turn the oven down. You can do this too quickly, but not too slowly. Cool thoroughly.

To pack the tomatoes, you will need widemouthed jars; I use several smaller ones, which gives me the impression that I might give some away if I like, though I never really do. Wash and dry the jars well, then squeeze half a lemon into each one. Pour in a few tablespoons of olive oil, then swirl to mix it with the lemon juice. Then just start packing in the tomatoes, one right on top of the next; you don't have to pack them tight as sardines, but keep them snug; add olive oil to cover every few tomatoes. And if you're occasionally frugal, as I am, cheat a little and use some flavorless vegetable oil along with the olive oil. Top with oil to cover by about ½ inch and a squeeze of lemon juice. Cover and refrigerate.

Frankly, I'm not sure how long these will last. I've never kept them around for more than about a month, and they were still in perfect condition. If you're concerned, check for signs of mold; if you keep the jars topped off with oil every time you use some tomatoes, mold shouldn't be a problem.

Yogurt Cheese

MAKES ABOUT 1 1/2 CUPS

Yogurt cheese is yogurt minus its liquid element, the whey. If you've never tasted it before, you should: It's rich and creamy tasting, a little softer than cream cheese, more like mascarpone. It has all sorts of wonderful uses in the vegetarian diet. You can mix it with herbs and use it as a spread on sandwiches. You can sweeten it and spread it on crackers, bagels, and the like. Add a dollop to fresh sliced fruit or berries. Or swirl it into black bean chili. Mixed with other cheeses and a few fresh herbs, it makes a great omelet filling. And it can be used in place of butter on pancakes or waffles.

To make about 1 1/2 cups of yogurt cheese, use 1 quart of plain yogurt. Line a colander with several thicknesses of cheesecloth. Place the colander in a large bowl. Stir the yogurt and pour it into the colander. Place a piece of plastic wrap over the yogurt and refrigerate overnight. Scrape the yogurt cheese into a widemouthed jar, discarding the whey. Cover and refrigerate until needed.

❧ *Food for Thought* ❧
MINDFUL EATING, SMILING GRACE

When I was growing up, we said grace every evening: one grace, the same grace, before dinner. The intention was good and proper, but I think the point was often lost on myself and siblings by the mechanical repetition of the same words. I believe that's one of the reasons many families don't say grace anymore.

Kids, I think, need a less routine way to say grace to make it matter. Almost as long as I can remember, we've said grace with our children—not because we're religious, but simply as a way to slow down, check in with one another, and express our gratitude for the gift of food on our plates. We keep it pretty loose, but in general we try to focus on what the beautiful Vietnamese Buddhist monk and poet Thich Nhat Hanh calls the "interbeing" of us and our food. To "inter be" with something is to be aware of our relationship and connectedness with it. Thus, when we look at our food, we say we're grateful for the sun and the rain and the soil. We might send thanks for the workers who picked the crops, the truck driver who brought it to our market, and the stock clerk who put it on the shelves. We're grateful to the cook and the person who did such a nice job setting the table. We just say it the way it comes out, working our way around the table, with no pressure to be pious with the delivery.

One of our favorite graces is what we call a smiling grace, another idea we borrowed from Thich Nhat Hanh. What I love about a smiling grace is the way it diffuses any of the premeal tensions that can arise in a crowded kitchen. It is a good family grace for our times. To do a smiling grace we all join hands. Then we just put on our biggest smiles (it's okay to force it at first), and go around the table smiling at everyone there. We take a few seconds to make a nice connection, then on to the next person. Generally, everyone ends up giggling and feeling good inside, which gives you a great peaceful place to start dinner. You should try it and see.

Occasionally we like to recite this grace together:
We're thankful for our happy hearts,
For rain and sunny weather,
We're thankful for the foods we eat,
And that we are together.
Amen, peace.

Index

About the Author

KEN HAEDRICH, a winner of the Julia Child Cookbook Award, is the author of *Country Baking, Home for the Holidays, Country Breakfasts,* and *Simple Desserts.* He is also a contributor to *Bon Appetit* and *Parenting.* He lives in rural New Hampshire with his wife, Karen, and their four children, Sam, Alison, Tess, and Ben.